Our Fathers' Wells

Our Fathers' Wells

❀

*A Personal Encounter
with the Myths of Genesis*

PETER PITZELE

HarperSanFrancisco
A Division of HarperCollins*Publishers*

Grateful acknowledgment is made to the following for permission to reprint the following
material:

Reprinted from *Memories, Dreams, Reflections* by C. G. Jung, edited by Aniela Jaffe, translated
by R & C Winston. Translation © 1961, 1962, 1963, 1989, 1990, 1991 by Random
House, Inc. Used by permission of Pantheon Books, a division of Random House, Inc.

Reprinted from *Collected Poetry of Charles Olson*, translated and edited by George Buttermilk
© 1987 Estate of Charles Olson. © 1987 University of Connecticut. Used by permission
of the University of California Press.

Excerpt from *The Twins* by James Stephens. Used by permission of The Society of Authors
on behalf of the copyright owner, Mrs. Iris Wise.

FIRST EDITION
Book design by Ralph Fowler
Set in Perpetua

Library of Congress Cataloging-in-Publication Data
Pitzele, Peter.
Our fathers' wells : a personal encounter with the myths of genesis / Peter Pitzele.—1st ed.
    p.   cm.
Includes bibliographical references and index.
ISBN 0–06–250617–X (cloth : alk. paper).
ISBN 0–06–251240–4 (pbk. : alk. paper).
    1. Bible. O.T. Genesis—Miscellanea.   2. Patriarchy—Religious aspects.
3. Men—Religious life.   4. Psychodrama.   5. Men's movement.   6. Pitzele, Peter.
I. Title.
    BS1235.5P58 1994
    222'.1106—dc20   94–27892
                                                                              CIP

95 96 97 ❖ RRD(H) 10 9 8 7 6 5 4 3 2 1

This edition is printed on acid-free paper that meets the American National
Standards Institute Z39.48 Standard.

To Susan

*"I have choices now
and voices I never had before . . ."*

And Isaac dug anew the wells of water his father had dug and that the Philistines had stopped up after Abraham's death. And Isaac gave them the same names his father had called them. (Genesis 26:18)

O sages standing in God's holy fire
As in the gold mosaic of a wall,
Come from the holy fire, perne in a gyre,
And be the singing-masters of my soul.

William Butler Yeats, "Sailing to Byzantium"

CONTENTS

The search for a credible spirituality began for me as a solitary quest. It began in response to a few scattered moments of transcendent, almost hallucinatory, insight that had moved and troubled me as a young man. Those moments set in motion a lifelong interest in spirituality and led me toward a variety of religious institutions, some Christian, some non-Western. I often sampled and studied these but found I could not stay. I seemed unable or unwilling to conform my ideas about God and the meaning of life to any existing tradition or school of thought. I composed my own private theology—an eclectic system of ideas, Eastern and Western, shamanic and poetic, classic and romantic. But at a certain point in my midforties, my quest curved back toward my own birthright and its oldest and deepest sources. In the past ten years I have been exploring the old myths of Judaism and the Judeo-Christian tradition, in particular those found in the Book of Genesis. I have been—to use a metaphor from that tradition—redigging "the fathers' wells," and this work is the issue of that labor.

Such wells are not those of my biological father. Nor of my mother, for that matter. Both of my parents were Jewish, and therefore I was born a Jew. But neither of my parents had anything to do with Judaism, except in their rather Jewish antipathy to being thought of as Jews. My mother, though the daughter of a woman who came to America as an Orthodox Jew from Russia in 1907, broke away from her mother's house and her mother's ways and never looked back. My father grew up in a midwestern family whose reform Judaism appeared, to his jaundiced eye, empty. Orphaned by sixteen, my father set out to become his own person, and like many of his generation he became engaged with the atheistic philosophies of Marxism and radical progressive politics. Even when he outgrew these persuasions, he retained his scorn of all spiritual opiates and panaceas, of religion in general, and of Judaism in particular. I grew up in a godless house; I was never bar mitzvah'd; I never set foot inside a synagogue.

My own spiritual history began in my early adolescence with an experience of epiphany. I had a sudden, utterly unexpected, and soul-altering revelation; it came as a *knowing* that contained an essential and, what seemed to me then, absolute apprehension of God. This knowledge exerted a deep pull on me throughout my adolescence. I was drawn toward something for which I had no name and no clear idea, toward poetry, though I did not believe I was a poet; toward churches and mystics, though I had no religious affiliation; and—somewhat precociously for the times—toward the East.

In my teens I read the Upanishads and later studied Vedanta; in my twenties I concentrated on Western mystical and romantic poetry; in my thirties I found a guru and studied bhakti yoga; in my early forties I read Jung and Campbell and Hillman, seeing archetypes everywhere. I was also drawn to the shamanic traditions: I sat in medicine circles; I did a lot of drumming and ingested various sacraments. During these years I put together my own patchwork of a spiritual life, eclectic and antiorthodox; it had no clear or consistent practice or set of observances; it asked little of me. It had no core or coherence but reflected and gave shape to those cardinal spiritual experiences I had had in my life and with which I wished to keep faith. I knew that all religious traditions were diverse languages attempting to articulate the same ultimate reality I had glimpsed in my adolescence. I felt at home in all of them and grounded in, committed to, none.

In the past decade my spiritual course has turned in a new direction. In all my questings and eclectic appropriations there was one tradition I ignored, the tradition that had been mine as a birthright. As I found myself taking an interest in Judaism, I realized I was not only starting from nothing but was working against the deeply ingrained legacy of my father's aversion to all things Jewish and my mother's spiritual indifference. Through their eyes what little I had seen of Judaism seemed vulgar and glitzy. Through my own I had seen a Judaism that appeared alien and dangerous. The glimpses I had of the holocaust in the newsreels of my childhood transmogrified the Jewish world into a nightmare. Its languages and accents seemed harsh, its customs strange. And its observance could get you killed. When I was called a "kike" in summer camp as a kid, I was angry, but more than that I was confused. I wasn't a Jew; such identifications—racial, regional, ethnic, religious—didn't say anything about who I really was. Moreover, such incidents were rare. I grew up in circles where anti-Semitism did not reach me. When I set out to fashion a spiritual identity, I joined a classless movement of chameleon-pilgrims who were looking for God everywhere but in our own backyards. We were all transients, migrants, explorers. We were hooked on the spiritually exotic; we were all bent on leaving home.

But in my midforties something changed. Call it a midlife crisis or the creeping conservatism of middle age; I think of it as something more providential than that. But for whatever reason, I began a cautious, crablike approach to something I never belonged to. Oddly, that approach felt like a return. I returned to Judaism from my various odysseys in alternative faiths with an inexplicable appetite for what had been right there under my nose. I found I was now interested in and willing to engage with the tradition I had overlooked on my way to Esoterica.

This return coincided with and was fueled by my reading of the Book of Genesis. I was immediately seized by its tales. What began as a perusal turned into a concentrated study that lasted for years and still continues. Of this study—the reasons for it and how it evolved—I shall have more to say later, but this book is the fruit of that endeavor; its subtext is the story of my return. Paradoxically, this book is the essay of an outsider who is an insider, of a Gentile who is a Jew, of a hesitant convert to his own religion. It is a commentary on a sacred text undertaken by a layman who still honors other sacred texts and often feels more comfortable in other traditions. I have written an orphan's account of my family of origin.

Looking back now, I see that as a student and transient in Christian, Eastern, and Native traditions, it was easy for me to romanticize their lore and practices. After all, I had not been indoctrinated as a boy by their strictures. Their gods and rites were not bound up with the craziness of my own family or with the hypocrisies of my immediate society. I did not have to deal with Hindu priests who merely went through the motions, or with Buddhist monks who habitually broke their vows. I could overlook the bloody history of indigenous peoples while savoring their communion with the earth. I could pay homage to the Mother Goddess without having to face her cruelties. I could celebrate the psychological richness of Greek polytheism without having to experience it as a living faith.

My relation to these spiritual traditions was fruitful and fertile in part because they were distant. They were at some comfortable remove from the twists and scars in my own psyche. I could learn wisdom from a foreign teacher because his very foreignness lent him an aura of mystery. Take the same wisdom and put it in the mouth of a priest or rabbi, and it seemed not only less exotic but also less pure.

Though no student of religion, I knew something of the history of priesthoods in my culture. I avoided any affiliation with the Judaism that came with my birth certificate; I only sampled the environing Christianity to which I was exposed during my education. The sullied "sacred" history of the West—a history of enforced conversions, bigotry, crusade, and crucifixion, of the terrible bloodlettings of the pious, to say nothing of the sexual and gender persecutions the privileged sanctified with their words and power—appalled me. And when, in recent decades, that history was labeled *patriarchy* (complete with skull and crossbones on the bottle), I did whatever I could to distance myself from that tradition. Whether that meant reading the feminists or following my breath, I disguised my affiliation with patriarchy. I denied it.

Yet when I began in my middle age to return to my "fathers' wells" and to consider the inheritance that was my birthright, I was compelled to confront that very patriarchy. One of the results of that confrontation is this book.

My struggle with patriarchy has required me to wrestle with the legacy of the fathers. I have contended with both my own father, who has profoundly influenced my sense of what it means to be a man, and with the Father whose immense and immemorial form lies embedded in our culture. That Father spoke through my father and, in ways obvious and subtle, lent my father his authority. That Father—constructed of hundreds of generations of fathers who form a tradition of fathers, a patriarchal tradition—is the mythic source of a body of laws, modes of perception, ideas about the world, and all manner of habits and values. Our culture's first envisioning of that Father was articulated perhaps as long ago as four thousand years in a skein of myth and lore that came in time to be called the Book of Genesis. Genesis is one of the sourcebooks of patriarchy. My own book, a very personal commentary on Genesis and on the ways it constructs patriarchy, represents my intimate quarrel with my tradition.

My book is an extension of patriarchy and a challenge to it, for what I have wrestled with I love. Like Jacob, the wrestler in Genesis whose story forms one of the crucial episodes in the myths of patriarchy, I have been changed by my encounter.

INTRODUCTION

In My Beginning Is My End

These Days

*whatever you have to say, leave
the roots on, let them
dangle*

And the dirt

> *Just to make clear
> where they come from*

Charles Olson[1]

The field of encounter I enter with this book on Genesis and patriarchy is sown thick with contentions. For more than a generation, feminists, literary critics, seminarians, congregants, priests, ministers, and rabbis have been reading the Bible in new ways. Challenging the gender-based theology of the Bible's stories, these women and men have sought to include new voices and perspectives. In this endeavor they confront inveterate institutions, deeply conditioned habits of thought, and a growing religious fundamentalism. Often at odds with one another as well as with common adversaries, these writers, thinkers, and teachers insist that no approach to the Bible can be merely academic; methodology itself is a statement, however veiled, of a position, of a set of beliefs. As a man seeking to reclaim an ancient body of biblical myth and theology and to explore his own connection to the patriarchal inheritance, I bring to this field my own passion, protest, poetry, and deep commitment to engage with the legends and legacies of the Judeo-Christian tradition.

Furthermore, I realize that to speak of patriarchy in anything but critical terms opens me to the charge of defending a cultural category that is almost universally decried. Patriarchy is, according to a critique now widely adopted on all sides, the pernicious gender history of the West from time immemorial. That history is written in the dynastic succession of sons to the estates of their fathers and in the blood feuds of the brothers for their share in those estates. Patriarchy, without a face and without a name, seeks to marginalize women and to separate them from their own powers and mysteries. Patriarchy, like some colossal demon fueled by misogyny and paranoia, has made wars, colonized the innocent, brainwashed the generations, and created the very forms of thought and discourse that ensure its continuing hold on our souls. Patriarchy is father power in its most ruthless form, a twisted paternalism whose roots are sunk deep in our myths and whose branches spread through many of our social and cultural traditions. Seen from this current perspective, patriarchy merits no further discussion.

For most of my adult life I have listened to this polemic against patriarchy. The feminist agenda has worked to open my eyes to the blatant and latent patterns of male (and white) privilege in our culture. Schooled by its analysis, I began to think about things I had taken for granted. I came to new conclusions, and I am permanently impressed with the very real, though I think partial, truths of the feminist critique of patriarchy.

My reassessment of patriarchy began during the late 1980s. In part as a result of the men's movement, I began to question the wholesale feminist onslaught against patriarchy and to wonder what I, as a man, might celebrate about manhood. I listened to men such as Robert Bly, Sam Keen, Michael Meade, John Lee, James Hillman, et al., who in various ways were attempting to reclaim and redefine the masculine for men. Though feared by some feminists as a form of backlash, this movement seemed to me by and large a bold attempt to provide us with new images of manhood and to develop a safe haven where men could ask their own questions and find support in a new fraternity.

Using literature and myth for image and inspiration, the leaders of the men's movement steered clear of cultures too deeply associated with patriarchy. The folktale was favored over traditional myths from the Greco-Roman or Judeo-Christian traditions; the lore of indigenous peoples was valued over the colonizing stories of the settlers. In other quarters men were encouraged to write their own myths, unaware perhaps that the personal myth often rests on unexamined paradigms.

For reasons having nothing to do with feminism and the men's movement, I had begun to study the Book of Genesis some years earlier. At first in an almost casual way, and then with growing interest and concentration, I had begun to make that book my own, to read it, to write about it, and to use it as a text in my work as a teacher and therapist. As I traveled the byways of the men's movement, I became increasingly aware that in all the talk of fathers and sons there was hardly a reference to Abraham and Isaac or to Jacob, later called Israel, and his clan. In all the talk of brotherhood no one mentioned Cain. In the so-called movement, these rich and troubling tales of men seemed beneath or beyond consideration. Men seemed in flight from this lore and from the book that contained it.

In time my interest in this body of myth was compounded by the gender debates that the men's movement had restimulated. The mythopoetical focus of the men's movement had its own yeasty effect on my imagination, and I wanted to add Genesis to the bubbling melange of texts and tales that men and women were stewing over. It seemed to me that having accepted the general blackballing of patriarchy in any and all of its forms, we were in danger of submitting too much to the feminist perspective and of losing something precious in the bequest of the patriarchal imagination. As the men's movement faded from cultural center stage, I was left wrestling with a number of questions—and for a while I was alone with them.

I wondered, through my reading of Genesis, what this thing called patriarchy is, not in its modern usage as a shibboleth, not as a polemical straw man, but as myth-theology, as a part of my own intellectual and spiritual inheritance. What is to become of the legacy of two hundred generations? Granted, it is a legacy largely the province of educated white males. But as one such male, am I to abandon this past? Disown it? Could or should anything be salvaged from that inheritance? Where are men like me to find roots? And are those roots as dead or as lethal as many claim? What in patriarchy and in ourselves do we need to face because if unconfronted it will live on in the shadow of our denial? If patriarchy is the whole historical shooting match, and if it needs to be discarded, then is there for me, as a man and an inheritor of the Judeo-Christian tradition, no usable past? And why, I asked myself, why am I so fascinated with the Book of Genesis? These are some of the questions that accompanied me through my return to those sources of patriarchy found in Genesis.

Surely Genesis is an odd subject, my friends said to me (when they were being kind)—a cultural non sequitur, an anachronism, this old patriarchal document that belongs to a world thousands of years in the past. All the more strange, they said (fearful they were witnessing some conversion), it being the first book of the Bible and underpinning the moribund forms of the old-time religions, forms that almost every self-respecting intellectual long ago abandoned. At best it is a somewhat forbidding compendium of old myths, this Genesis; at its worst, the repository of reactionary beliefs. If I were going to refurbish a text for the times, then why not the *Odyssey,* or *King Lear,* or *The Prelude,* or *Ulysses?* Why Genesis?

At first defensive before this question—why anything? why Thai food? why sailing? why Susan?—I later found it crucial and useful. It forced me to admit that my interest in Genesis went deep. Looking inside myself, I found a welter of answers, each one coming from some different aspect of myself and addressing a differing concern. Like answers to the koan "Who are you?" my answers all seemed valid, yet all were incomplete as well.

Why Genesis? Because I am searching, and have been for some time, for what it means to me to be a Jew. With not an iota of Jewish education, I went to schools in which there were Protestant religious services: chapel, vespers, hymns, prayers. I didn't set foot in a synagogue until I was in my middle forties. It was as if the Jew in me had been sealed away by my father's anti-Semitism, and in part too by the shadow of the holocaust. It was not safe for me to identify myself as a Jew; my father could disown me, and the dominant culture could destroy me. Reading Genesis was, at least at the beginning, a safe way for me to explore my Jewish roots. As a man with a literary education, I could disguise my work with Genesis—from my father and from myself—as an intellectual investigation. But in some left-handed way I was searching out the ancestral origins of what was in time to become Judaism. In grappling with the text, I was unlocking the hidden possibility of the Jew in myself.

Why Genesis? Because I know what it is like to have a strong father. I know how much of my identity has been shaped by his dreams and desires for me; I know how hard I have struggled against him. Though he was no Abraham and I am no Isaac, I found in that biblical pair a powerful image for my dad and me. Through them I understand what it means to be a son entangled by his father's agenda. Indeed, in Genesis I discovered a supreme set of tales about fathers and sons that addresses these entanglements in generation after generation. Through its tales I have asked myself what I have received from my father and what I am passing on to my son and to my daughter.

Why Genesis? Because I am a wanderer in a culture of wanderers. The sense of being unmoored from the past, a stranger in a strange land, has haunted me since my childhood in the madness and aftermath of World War II. My family moved every few years; when I was seven, my parents divorced. My

sense of coming from a broken home was both a personal fact and a 'social reality in the world of refugees and exiles that I was growing up in. I felt I was,
to use Paul Cowan's indelible phrase, "an orphan in history."[2]

In Genesis I found figures—men and women—who are also migrants
and wanderers. They have the strangest relationship to the past, at once sundered from it and connected to it, making a new life, yet by their repetitions
and returns creating a tradition. They struggle to make sense of experience
while being alone in a universe that neither reason nor imagination can entirely comprehend. Yet they persist. They are highly susceptible to some call of
the spirit while wondering whether it is divinity, the diabolical, or madness
that calls. And they find a vocation that costs them everything.

Like them, incontestable spiritual experiences have marked my life.
From these it has followed that I require that my chosen myths contain
episodes of epiphany and revelation. Why Genesis? Because there I found
mythic ancestors in the very act of constructing meanings out of their odd and
radical spiritual experiences. Furthermore, these ancestors preexist Judaism
and Christianity, whose creeds were yet to be written. The dire and destructive history of canonized texts and rigid orthodoxies does not condition the
world of the patriarchs; their stories do not demand the dogmas of subsequent
interpreters.

So I can say all this and more, and in all of it there is truth, but the sum
of these answers does not quite add up to the whole. There is something that
eludes the question, something I cannot pin down. I think it has to do with the
primitive, with my need to be in touch with the irrational, the wild, even the
savage in my soul. If religion is something that binds people into some shared
community of faith, then I was searching for a faith community that reads
Genesis as I read it—as a primitive Scripture whose raw pre-theologized intensity shakes one from any dogmatic certainty and sends one out again and
again into the immense speculative vistas of what we call *patriarchy*.

My perspective on patriarchy, then, is not that of the feminists. For me,
patriarchy, as I find it conceived in Genesis, is a supreme myth-theology of
the Western (perhaps the masculinized) imagination. This myth-theology is
built upon the sober and even tragic perception of the limited and lonely nature of the human being–in-the-world, of our separation from the direct life-
giving creativity of nature, and our search for some causality, some necessity
that might anchor our wandering souls to a world of creative purpose.
Though men may have composed and canonized these tales, they seem to me
to speak at times beyond gender; they grope to establish a common psychology of the soul. In place of the instinctual life of nature, human beings have

. . . what? Only our imagination. Imagination is our God. The myth-theology of patriarchy presents us with a body of legends in which men and women, gifted and burdened by an immense freedom of imagination, search for some way to express their desire to create. These men and women are entangled in a relationship with a creative God. This God is the limitless and the liminal, within and beyond the personal imagination. With this "God," men and women forge a bond with the cosmos and out of that bond find a way of being in the world that confers a sense of purpose, dignity, and meaning.

I see the patriarchal myths as an unsystematic attempt on the part of our most distant ancestors to compose a world-story within which women and men might understand themselves and share a community of spirit. At the same time, this world-story, if it is to be congruent with the actualities of human life, must reflect the complex and warring forces that seem hardwired into our souls. The myths of patriarchy are powerful constructions of a spiritual psychology, perhaps a fuller and more fertile one than the scientific psychologies we work out of today.[3] That psychology is concerned with our madness, dreams, visions, and revelations, with the demonic and the redemptive, with the sacrificial and the murderous impulses in our hearts. The skein of tales that make up Genesis tell a story of men and women not only as violent and repressive perpetrators but as creatures of clay and spirit seeking to understand how to live in some true, loving relationship to life. And Genesis tells how precariously we achieve that relationship, if we achieve it at all.

As well as having a deep concern with life, the patriarchal imagination is also obsessed with death. Death provides the human soul with its edge of necessity; and from our engagement with death we wrest our highest callings. There is a side of patriarchy bound up with darkness. The God that patriarchy imagines does not require a devil; He has His own demonic, inscrutable side. If He is just, His justice does not always square with our human need for fairness and morality. The knowledge that comes to the women and the men of Genesis in their spiritual initiations is a knowledge of good and evil and of a God beyond their control. Through them we learn that we are two-natured creatures perpetually struggling between polarities in ourselves. With an imagination all compact of light and dark, we are free to choose and in part to create our realities. Genesis tells this story in its enigmatic myths.

In the end, the question "Why Genesis?"—and why my interest in patriarchy for that matter—must be answered by this present book, whole and entire. One must read the myths of Genesis afresh and enter their mazes. There one meets the spectral energies of the patriarchal imagination. The meetings with these energies are acts of encounter that evoke and correspond to something in the soul.

❀ ❀ ❀

I am keenly aware that my approach to Genesis is unusual. In daring to approach it at all I run the risk of the amateur who not only makes certain mistakes the professional scholar would avoid but also thinks he may be breaking ground that those same scholars would find commonplace. I take Wallace Stevens to heart when he says, "It is necessary to any originality to have the courage to be an amateur."[4]

But what is most unusual in my approach is that I come to Genesis as a psychodramatist. Psychodrama is a clinical modality that involves a group of people in the spontaneous enactment of personal stories, dreams, and fantasies under the leadership of a trained director. Under its more common name of *role-playing*, its purpose is to free a person for a more spontaneous and creative way of life. Group members may be enrolled to play significant others, figures in a distant past or an imagined future, or lost or disenfranchised parts of the self. There is no script. As group-work, psychodrama is a collaborative therapeusis, and the "drama" that is produced can be neither refined nor repeated. It blooms once, touches those who are present at its unfolding, and can never be re-created.[5]

For more than a decade I have been in clinical practice at Four Winds Hospital, a private psychiatric facility north of New York City. Early in my tenure there I found a friend and mentor in Sam Klagsbrun, M.D., the facility's owner and guiding light. Among his diverse activities, Sam was a teacher at the Jewish Theological Seminary in New York. He once asked me to cover some classes for him, and falling back on what I knew, I applied the techniques of psychodrama to the stories of Genesis. The results were exciting to me and to those who participated.

Gradually a new facet of my career began to open up. I found more and more people who were interested in reenacting biblical stories. In various settings—congregational, educational, and therapeutic—I led groups of men and women *into* the myths. We found and expressed surprising things. The words of the written text were like doors; we flung them open and explored what lurked behind them—the humor, the horror, the outrage, and the power. I began to see that Scripture was a kind of script, the details of the old stories providing the bare bones for an improvisational hermeneutics. Biblical material that had for many seemed remote, lifeless, and encrusted by dogma and commentary, broke free from its frieze. In action we possessed the texts as our own, found our voices within the characters, discovered the links between their dramas and our own. Patriarchy was personalized, and we often found its personae in our own inner world. We began to understand how patriarchy lived in us. Here were ancient metaphors and images through which the contemporary imagination could still find meaning. Our enactments had at times the feel of old rites and rituals, dream dramas; at other times they were festive; and sometimes they had the power of group therapy. I felt I had stumbled onto a vocation.

This psychodramatic work had the virtue of helping me to get past some of the limitations of my own personality by "reading" the myths in community. Myths are complex mirrors, the reading of which will always contain the distortions of one's own character and one's unconscious mind. To stand before a myth is in part to see what one looks for, in part to be blind to what one is not prepared to see. But here in active interchange I heard others embodying the myths. Through this varying, pluralistic community of reader-actors I was able to look at the texts from many perspectives—ethnic, gender-specific, psychological, and intimately spiritual—without sacrificing a respect for the actual words, their meaning and history. Genesis and the myth-theology of patriarchy came alive in astonishing ways.

This work made a deep impression on me. Acts of psychodramatic reading attain the status of lived experience. By virtue of physically enacting the stories, one takes into oneself the subtext of their emotional and physical dimensions. I was *in* these stories beyond the usual imaginative projections or identifications that come with close reading. As Adam I have kissed Eve. As Cain I have killed my brother. I have been drunken Noah naked in his tent and the wide-eyed Ham who found him there. I have heard God call to me as Abraham, and as Isaac I have seen my father raise his knife above my head; I have seen it glint in the sun, and I have seen my father's eyes. I have been banished with Ishmael and wept with my brother in the cave of Machpelah. I have played the women, too; Eve, Sarah, Lot's wife, Rebecca, Rachel, Leah, and Dinah. I have even spoken as certain inhuman things: the serpent in the garden and the garden itself; the ass that bears wood for the sacrifice of Isaac and the ram substituted for him. I have been Jacob and the nameless, dark adversary with whom he wrestled. There is much I have yet to be.

These acts of playing live in me in the same way the experiences of my life live in me. They are memories with the same body and potency as the memories of my life outside Genesis. For that reason my experience of this text has the nuance of actuality. My acts of playing are partly the work of the conscious player, partly the spontaneous creation of an unconscious force, even, it seemed at times, a transpersonal one. More vivid than a dream, my experiences of Genesis are like fragments of past lives revived in some communal trance, supported by others engaging in the same strong fiction.

The residue of my experiences as a reader and psychodramatist informs my wrestling with Genesis and gives this commentary its composite design. Though I cannot recover the material of the many psychodramatic sessions verbatim, I have re-created many moments from them here. Snatches of a scene; an encounter; a fragment of a soliloquy; a story told after a session showing the connection between the old myths and the living person—these are the sinews of this extended essay. But since I was a participant in many of these sessions as well as a facilitator, my book contains my own authorial psychodramas. In these pages I have enjoyed the pleasure of an old pastime; I have given voice to various biblical characters, as I have done in so many sessions, and I have spoken from there.

This work of freshly imagining the figures in Genesis, though unusual in its form, actually belongs to a recognized tradition; it is the tradition of *midrash*. Midrash in Hebrew means exploration or investigation. Midrashim (plural) took many forms, from analysis of biblical texts to the creation of fables and stories meant to amplify and extend biblical narrative. Midrash served to illuminate the text, to explain it, moralize upon it, contemporize its codes of conduct and proscriptions for observance, resolve textual questions and contradictions, and clarify points of meaning or law. Volumes of written midrash exist, while countless instances of the midrashic imagination have been heard—and still can be—in the home, the synagogue, and the house of study as part of oral, folk, and rabbinic traditions.

My psychodramatic art, harnessed to biblical myth, continues this tradition of midrash. As a form of poetic license, midrash liberates the spirit encased in the words. Underwriting my various approaches to the myths of Genesis is my desire to free them for our revel and revelation. In a sense I am returning a body of myth to its oral roots and beyond, to its sources in play, rite, ritual, and enactment. If, according to the mythographer J. G. Frazier, "ritual may be the parent of myth, but can never be its child," [6] then the psychodrama of biblical material may be closer to the original than all forms of a more literary commentary.

❦ ❦ ❦

This book is divided into three parts. Genesis lacks any such partitioning, but in my own reading I have identified three major sections. Part 1 I have called "Tales of a Lonely God"; part 2, "Tales of the Ancestral Family"; and part 3, "Tales of the Sibling Clan."

The myths of part 1 are fragments of what are in all likelihood the oldest shards of the most ancient traditions, dating back long before a written culture codified the tales into texts, and much later the texts into canon. Once a part of a nomadic culture's extensive oral myth-theology, these "Tales of a Lonely God," as I call them, tell of the solitary masculine deity, His mode of creation, His forming of human beings, their freedom and early fate, and His interventions in their world. Here patriarchy constructs its cosmos and hints of the great patterns of universal order and mystery that adumbrate all human endeavors. Dwarfed in an immense cosmos, the soul remembers and imagines its God. Single and solitary as the presiding Genius and Mystery of creation, He is beyond space and time—remote, inscrutable, wrathful, and frightening. He has yet to establish an intimate relationship with His creation.

The myths of part 2 begin with the story of Abram, later called Abraham. Abram is the first figure in Genesis to learn another aspect to this God; He is Presence, experienced as the Heavenly Father. He calls Abram forth from his life to serve in an arduous spiritual collaboration. As husband and father, Abram shares the burden of his mission with those he loves and who love him; the ordeals of their generation form the "Tales of the Ancestral Family" of part 2.

In the third phase God, as Mystery and Presence, gradually withdraws from the scene until, in the story of Joseph, He never once intervenes. This third part of the book—which I call the "Tales of the Sibling Clan"—asks what it is like for men and women to establish a covenant with one another, to work out among themselves and without divine intervention their issues of power, and to find a way to live together in community. In part 3 the question Genesis asks at its beginning, "Am I my brother's keeper?" finds its answer. The spirituality of siblings requires the supreme ability to live with differences in forgiveness and trust.

It is difficult not to read these three mythic zones as stages in a developmental paradigm, but it seems to me they are not progressive or evolutionary. We live, I believe, in these three zones simultaneously: We are alone with a lonely God; we are entangled in the inheritances and dreams of our family and ancestors; and we wrestle for atonement and recognition in a sibling community that forms our surrounding world. The three dimensions marked out in Genesis are permanently marked in the imagination of the West; each is mirrored in our lives; and each is a facet of our souls.

PART I

❀

Tales of a Lonely God

One is one and all alone
and evermore shall be so.

"Green Grow the Rushes O!"

1

Imagining God

Before I open the Book of Genesis to its beginning, I want to tell two stories about my own beginnings. Each story represents an aspect of my life I can neither explain nor forget; and the two stories seem permanently, even cosmically, at odds with each other. I tell them because they are the magnetic poles around which my enterprise of interpretation must turn, as if in a restless attempt to make sense of the deepest riddles of my own life.

The first story, a mere fragment, takes me back to the middle of the second grade; I was seven. It was 1948. It was the year my father moved out of our home, and in order to see him I had to walk eight wintry blocks alone to his small studio apartment. Gradually I realized that my mother and father were breaking apart. Sometime in that year I began to have a recurrent waking dream.

In it I am "asleep" in my bed when the crashing of a door startles me awake. I realize the front door of my house is being broken open. I hear my mother cry out. In my mind's eye I see that storm troopers have come into our house; they are the SS. They wear those tight-fitting helmets that curve down over the ears. There are swastikas like black spiders on their sleeves. Each one carries a machine gun. The next thing I know they are standing my mother and father up against the wall, and the leader is pointing his machine gun at them; he turns to me. "Which one do I kill?!" he screams at me. "Which one do I shoot? Decide!" I know that I have to answer; I see each of them, my father and my mother, with their backs to the wall, staring silently at me. There is no way out. At this moment I wake from the trance or the dream, but the memory has never left me.

Years later I came to understand that I was the storm trooper *and* the little boy. They were two sides of my rage at my parents, two sides of my loss.

Whom would I live with? Whom would I love? Whom would I blame? Whose fault was it? I had to make up my mind. My childhood wheeled in the double bind of this nightmare. My lifelong sense of being split and divided comes from that time, as does my sense of wandering between two worlds.

But I also found that this condition was not mine alone. In 1948 the world was a broken home. Nuclear physics was a terrible reality, and nuclear families like my own were in fission everywhere. This breaking apart was on view in newsreels, where I saw the mushroom cloud and pictures of the liberated concentration camps, the massive piles of bones and shoes, the stick figures, the staring, empty eyes.

In many ways my questions, which lived surrealistically in my unconscious, were alive in the world at large. These forces—evil and innocence, power and helplessness, rage and loss, death and survival—were the ideograms of the mid-twentieth century. Everyone in my generation heard the screams of history in World War II as the background noise to childhood.

This legacy of the twentieth century, writ small in my life, writ large in my culture, has been the legacy of refugees, of the murdered and the tortured. It contains cruelty on an inconceivable scale; it tells of divorce, division, brokenness, and the failure of any means—aesthetic or institutional—to resolve these tensions. In my time it seemed the storm troopers were at every door. I grew up knowing the reality of evil.

Fast forward through the next nine years to 1956, past the time when an only child shuttled unhappily across town between his parents. Skip the story of how his father remarried and how his mother never did. No need to dwell on the year she moved to California, abandoning him, at twelve, to the loving grip of his controlling father. This is not the place to speak of how a father's second marriage did not make a home for him, nor of the two stepbrothers and the blended family that never worked.

In 1955 my father placed me in boarding school. Though that placement fit in with my father's grand designs for me—that I receive the best education money could buy and thereby "maximize my options"—it also served to remove me from a family in which I was, increasingly, trouble.

I floundered my first year in a world of boys and rules, but gradually I found my footing in the soothing Berkshire hills of western Connecticut. In time I began to tolerate school, even, in small ways, to succeed. Then early in my second year an event occurred that was then and is now incomparable.

I was sitting in Mr. Wittemore's French 2A class. Outside it was mid-October in New England, the elixir season of morning mists and soccer afternoons. Mr. Wittemore was finishing up the lesson, his perfectly knotted bow tie bobbing above his Adam's apple as he spoke a French I was beginning to understand. From my seat next to the window, with a mere half turn to my left, I could look out over the trees and hills of that Indian summer morning.

Mr. Wittemore droned on and I began to slide into an unfocused reverie. I would have slid all the way into a doze had my attention not been caught by a buzzing sound at the windowsill.

A fly was lying on its back, its tiny legs in the air. I watched as it righted itself, but instead of flying it began to scale the windowpane, a slow steep climb. Looking up, I saw its destination, the open window at the top. Inch by patient inch the fly climbed up, but when it reached the wooden lip of the frame, where it had to walk belly-up along the underedge, it could not maintain its hold. Gravity pulled it skittering down the glass to the sill, where it bounced and came to rest again on its back, six little legs churning, its buzz insistent.

Once again it flipped itself over. Once again it began the sheer ascent. Once again it reached the overhang, negotiated the beveled edges of the wooden lip, came to the last crux, clung, then dropped dizzily down. I winced this time as its fragile back hit the sill.

This same process was repeated again and again, each time acquiring more focus in my eyes. Each time the endeavor became more personal, more heroic, more ludicrous and engrossing. I found myself rooting for the fly while at the same time exhorting it to "fly, you idiot," not just climb to freedom. Has it forgotten how to use its wings? Is it injured? The stupor of Indian summer? I think of the fugitive Scot—Robert Bruce, do I have the story right?—watching a spider seek seven times to swing its web between the rafters of his hideaway, gathering from its determination a resolve of his own. So I feel bonded to this fly.

I can see its iridescent wings, the six angled legs, the blinkered eyes. Up it goes again over perpendicular terrain. Once again—I've lost count—it meets the ledge. Once again it hoists its body up the underside until it has one leg over the top—never closer to its goal. But it cannot swing its carapace over the final millimeter. The attempt loosens its hold; it falters once again, it falls; it bounces on the sill, but this time its wings flick open; it rises in a single, graceful arc and flashes through the opening into limitless air. And I, who have microscopically pursued its every move, am hurtled with it into space, glued to its shimmering little form until it dissolves into the light.

And the landscape beyond the window dissolves as well. The trees and hills are turning gold. Great shimmering circles in a gentle vortex swirl round and round toward a distant point. I am traveling down a golden cone toward a center infinitely far away. I travel with the speed of light. In an instant I arrive at the center, quivering and melting. Some part of my mind is able to observe this ecstasy, and this part, gasping in astonishment, knows that I have come to God. This must be God, for here everything is answered. Everything has meaning. I know it as indisputable fact, as the truest thing I could ever know. And the answer is intelligible. I believe I could communicate it.

Just then the bell rings, and I am shaken from my trance. Class ends. I bolt from the room and dash across the campus to my dorm. I must write it down while I have this knowledge, whole and wonderful in my heart. I rush to my desk and grab a pencil and paper. A few words come. But words, my words—they are so meager. Now the fire is fading; the light is almost gone. I have only memory, still vivid, but not the thing itself, only an afterimage still glowing in my mind. I let the pencil fall from my hand. There are no words, only a feeling, a knowledge, now sinking deeper and deeper into me, where, like a chest full of jewels slowly sinking to the bottom of the sea, for the rest of my life it will remain.

In my wrestling with Genesis, that God-struck adolescent is still with me, and I read the biblical myths, at least in part, through his credulous and wondering eyes. That child is father of this man, but so, too, was that terrified kid, myself at seven, whose innocence came to an end with a door splintering in his mind.

The window through which I passed in ecstatic flight that October of my fifteenth year has remained open ever since. My experience with the fly initiated a lifelong interest in the ways men and women have imagined God. By a long, circuitous route that interest has brought me at last to wrestle with the God of the culture into which I was born.

Not long after that autumn morning I stumbled onto some selections from the Upanishads. I read page after page of these Indian spiritual treatises with an understanding directly infused by experience. Here were God-songs, poems of praise and of knowledge, declaring the nature of that same divinity I had glimpsed myself during French class. I can still find the underlined passages in the dog-eared book:

The face of truth remains hidden behind a
circle of gold. Unveil it, O god of light,
that I who love the true may see!

Isa Upanishad

He is known in the ecstasy of an awakening
which opens the door of life eternal. By
The Self we obtain power, and by vision
We obtain eternity.

    Kena Upanishad

By the grace of God, our mind is one with him
and we strive with all our power for light.

    Svetasvatara Upanishad

When the wise rests his mind in contemplation
on our God beyond time who invisibly dwells in
the mystery of things and in the heart of man,
then he rises above pleasures and sorrow.
When a man had heard and understood, and,
finding the essence, reaches the Inmost, then
he finds joy in the Source of Joy . . .

    Katha Upanishad

This was my first encounter with Scripture and theology, and suddenly I understood that there were accounts of experiences of the sort that had occurred to me. A whole literature existed that gave words to what I had been unable to express. This was the first time I had read anything with the sense that it had been written directly for me, had been waiting for me. Not only did I understand it, but it helped me understand myself, and it pointed the way into a world of thought and writing that seemed familiar to me, a kind of second home.

Reading became precious to me in a new way. It was the means to discover a community—far-flung and mystical—of those who had seen what I had seen and whose words validated what I had known. I could not find enough of these validations, and I now found them everywhere—in the American transcendentalists, in the English romantic poets, in J. D. Salinger, in the Homeric epics. Passages like this one from Wordsworth's "Tintern Abbey," which I read first in my senior year of high school, kept my own experience with the fly alive:

And I have felt
A presence that disturbs me with the joy

Of elevated thoughts; a sense sublime
Of something far more deeply interfused,
Whose dwelling is the light of setting suns,
And the round ocean and the living air,
And the blue sky, and in the mind of man:
A motion and a spirit, that impels
All thinking things, all objects of all thought,
And rolls through all things.

It was a marvel to me that a poet writing at the beginning of the nineteenth century in England could have so perfectly echoed the lucid music of the Upanishads. The God I knew was everywhere, and Scripture was His witness in every land and all through history. God-poems gleamed like scattered gems from a single crown. They were, from different times and styles, voices of the same paean, or merely different dialects all derived from a common tongue. The paradoxes of the Many and the One, of the Different and the Same, were, in that season of my high school years, easy for me to grasp.

The experience with the fly—what could have been a more humble angel?—animated me. In morning chapel when the light came through the plain leaded windows and the headmaster said, "Let us pray," and I bowed my head, I knew this gesture was connected to countless moments of dream, trance, and wonder in which God became real to the human imagination.

Praise God, from whom all blessings flow;
Praise Him, all creatures here below;
Praise Him above, ye heavenly host;
Praise Father, Son, and Holy Ghost.

The kid who sang this doxology Sunday after Sunday did not know the theology of the Trinity. The watery Protestantism of this New England boarding school did not offend or convert him. He had no notion of the vexed and tragic history of the Jewish and Christian traditions. He was decades from his wrestle with Genesis and his attempt to learn a language with which he could express his spiritual experience. These matters did not matter to him. His heart was simple and full of praise.

Because of him, when I come to the opening of Genesis, I can still be entranced. His naive imagination of God is still my own, and despite the pomp and circumstance I know that the God of Genesis is the same God I encountered at my own beginning. My brief glimpse into the core of light is a fragment of the prolonged revelation that runs through the opening chapter of Genesis. Without contortions I can make my personal epiphany consonant with this other epiphany.

As a grown man I also read this revelation in Genesis against a background of other ways of imagining God. I have been a fellow traveler in a diverse community of men and women, living and dead, who readied me to understand this revelation as a magnificent metaphor, not as the single truth. That community has been composed of Hindu sages, Zen priests, wild rabbis, Christian mystics, mad poets, and a handful of inspired friends. Through them I learned that revelation is no respecter of gender, class, race, ethos, or condition. From them I also learned that revelation is at once absolute and relative. Each instance of revelation seems to the recipient an immense gift; it breaks all previous forms of knowledge and provides a transcending disclosure into a truth deeper than all previous truths. Such a revelation seems pure, the thing itself. Yet revelation is recollected and communicated through a series of images and tellings. It is translated through the prism of culture. It is bent into language; it borrows forms.

The boy in me who still gazes through his window of rapture knows that this God of Genesis is his God. And the skeptic also looks out through my eyes and knows that all myths are distortions of the revelation that inspires them. Words are paltry and proximate; they convey meaning only in the intellectual sense, not in the sense that one is conveyed by the experience itself, body and soul. And even that experience of ecstasy is tainted and shaped by unconscious factors. There is no pure revelation. In the end we never know our God face-to-face. When we bring our revelations into our lives, vision becomes politics. So between the innocent and the skeptic, two aspects of myself, my wrestling with Genesis and with its imagination of God—with patriarchy—begins.

❀ ❀ ❀

There can be little doubt that the Bible as a whole and Genesis as its first book and cornerstone are the work of men.[1] We have no record of those early storytellers who received and preserved these primordial myths in an oral tradition. We know that these tales are the earliest records of a people who were later known as the Hebrews and who, as a nation, took the name of an old clan king and called themselves the children of Israel. For many hundreds of years this nation established a small strife-ridden domain in the territories currently contested by the Israelis and the Palestinians.

We possess no historical account of the actual formation of those literate elites who constructed the epical history of this people, but in later books of the Bible we know that it is men who are almost exclusively endowed with spiritual prerogatives. Men become the priests and are vested with the authority to convey the word of God. Their labors, political and pious, built what we can recognize today as the myth-theological edifice of patriarchy and laid Genesis as its foundation.

From a certain point of view Genesis must be seen as propaganda. Like myth-theology the world over, it propagates the idea of a national destiny divinely favored that will in time rule the world. Signs of this agenda are scattered throughout Genesis and the Bible; it is the agenda of men, the fathers of the tribe, the priesthood, and later of the church. The fathers pass it on to the inheriting sons, those men called and chosen by God and by one another to carry on this dream of a divine destiny.

This dream is the patriarchal project, and that project begins at once as Genesis begins. The patriarchal imagination declares the revelation of a God-before-history for whom history will be a mythos of divine intentions and interventions. This God will be our god; He gives meaning to history and offers purpose to our lives. This God knows nothing of other gods or of a feminine divinity. If He is a woman's god, it is because He claims them or because they have accepted a masculine iconography.

This patriarchal project is the gift of God. Patriarchy gives its God of history gender; His is the power of ultimate imagination, declaring imagination a cosmic principle that shapes and patterns the temporal and constructs culture in all its forms. Embodied in a deity of supreme consciousness and transcendence, this principle of imagination does not so much oppose as precede nature. According to patriarchy, this cosmic imagination creates all our structures of thought—time, space, character—and is the source of our moral and spiritual ideas. Liberated from the necessities of nature, imagination is that part of the human soul that is beyond the claim of nature, beyond the cycles of birth and decay. Our human exile from nature is also freedom from it. In that separation from the body's pure instinctual knowing, all human beings inhabit the world of thought. It is our second universe, perhaps more so for men, whose lives do not know the regulations of moon or womb, milk or menopause. In that universe, through the windows of language and myth, we half perceive and half create a world. That constructed world is the work of imagination, our achievement and our prison.

Genesis begins in words that have lasted for millennia:

In the beginning God created the heaven and the earth. (1:1)[2]

In this opening, the patriarchal imagination propounds its myth of the beginning. Though I view this myth in part with skepticism, seeing it as a divine rationalization of a masculine status quo, I also see it as a fable about the nature of imagination: imagination as the cosmic, all-pervasive plasma out of which creation is formed. Here is the first rising up out of nature-which-has-no-consciousness-of-itself—nature as void of intelligence. This moment is miraculous, the emergence of mind from nature, of thought from instinct, of a dream from necessity.

In the beginning God created the heaven and the earth. And the earth was without form, and void; and darkness was upon the face of the deep. And the Spirit of God moved upon the face of the waters. (1:1–2)

Before this principle of imagination moved upon matter, it was indeed without form, and void. No intelligence had yet given shape to the chaos. Not until there is reflection—God's spirit moves on the face of the water as reflection—can there be intention.

This myth of the beginning is a refutation of biology. The God of Genesis transcends the feminine, the collaborative, and the natural. This God is not conditioned by any organic conception of growth that depends on gender and gestation. This transcendent and divine imagination moves in the beginning. In this myth of origins, Mystery requires no helpmate or spouse for generation:

In the beginning God created the heaven and the earth. And the earth was without form, and void; and darkness was upon the face of the deep. And the Spirit of God moved upon the face of the waters. And God said, "Let there be light"; and there was light. . . . God said, "Let there be a firmament in the midst of the waters. . . ." And it was so. . . . God said, "Let the earth bring forth grass. . . ." And it was so. . . . God said, "Let the waters bring forth abundantly. . . ." And God saw that it was good. (1:3–21)

The God who creates here is given the Hebrew name *Elohim*. For this Elohim the usual masculine pronoun is inappropriate. Elohim is a *plural* noun, which in Hebrew always takes a singular verb. We confront a paradox in this yoking of a plural noun to a singular verb: The Many is One. This God stands for all creation, for this God contains and expresses all that can be created. On the one hand, I recognize this as another maneuver by which the patriarchal imagination asserts its supreme masculine authority: It claims that this God contains all voices—all other gods—within itself. It speaks with the royal *we:* "And God said 'Let us . . . '"

On the other hand, the husk of this patriarchal myth-theology conceals the seed of a sublime truth. There is a God who contains all gods, a truth that underlies all different truths, a source that in its essence and beneath its apparent names and forms is the same source. This revelation of the Beginning is there at the deepest level of the personal and collective psyche. It was into this radiant truth that I was carried on the wings of a fly. We come from this God, this myth proclaims; everything comes from one source. That source, here designated Elohim, has no gender, for gender has yet to intrude into the narrative of beginnings. Elohim, the Mystery of Imagination, has yet to be given a name. Moreover, that ultimate Mystery reminds us that all our conceptions of the divine are partial and limited translations of what language can never articulate, or thought comprehend.

The spell cast in this myth is built upon a mesmerizing rhetoric of incremental repetitions. The creation story is a guided meditation by which we are drawn into the rhythm of creation. We watch as the creative divinity, Elohim-Mystery, conceives, but the method of that conception differs totally from any other form of conception. Language is the instrument for creation *and* for its transmission to us. In this myth of the beginning, language is lifted from history and made to precede it. This parthenogenesis of the word hides the politics of language by returning the word to the mind of God. The creative precedes the procreative. By this single strategy the patriarchal imagination finds a universe of its own, separate from any universe brought into being from the womb, the body, or in nature. The word becomes the holy medium for imagining God. Before the life of the world, there are words of life. An impulse stirs in the divine Imagination; it comes into divine speech and is immediately realized. Between the conception and the act no shadow falls.

"In the beginning was the Word," declared the Gospel writer John, commenting on the opening of Genesis, "and the Word was with God, and the Word was God."[3] John recognized this God of Genesis as the God of Thought and Order, of Reason and Cosmos. But John was already turning this God into a primordial Apollonian principle called *Logos* in Greek, his image for the Christ. I prefer to think the ancient Hebrews saw their divinity as something more complex, wilder, and more polyvalent than Logos. I see this God as Imagination, an erotic potency that pulses forth into the void. Imagination generates word and language, form and pattern: "In the beginning was Imagination, and Imagination was with God, and Imagination was God."

This Deity, in its Eros, is also Energy. Energy is, like Imagination, an ultimate mystery, another face or aspect of the many-sided One who turns and turns in the days of His creation. That God as Energy forms and informs matter and makes it spin and multiply. Energy endows life with its vitality; it gives the glow to color, the vibrancy to rhythm, the pulse to time. We call it by many names, but in the science of Genesis it is hailed as the force that precedes all physical forces, from which all physical forces derive and for which they are instances and metaphors. God rests on the seventh day because He has worked; He has used energy. The transformation of idea into matter, of conception into act, of dream into reality is an energetic exchange. This transcendent God of the Imagination is Spirit divorced from flesh; His mansion is the heart or the soul, but not the body or the natural world.

As a writer, intellectual, therapist, and teacher I have served at the shrine of this God. I have practiced the abracadabra magic of mind over matter. I can recognize the God in this myth as one I still honor and emulate. How close I am to this God as I sit here writing, making thought-forms, arranging a narrative, creating a world of words. I invoke here the Genius of Genesis, He who presides over all acts of creation. Free from all boundaries of space and time because He precedes, proposes, and transcends them, He is Infinite Imagination, Infinite Mind, Infinite Creative Energy that set about to conceive a world through the mystery of words.

This sense of divine imagination within and beyond the human is articulated in the creation of man.

> And Mystery said, "Let us make man in our image, after our likeness: and let them have dominion over the fish of the sea, and over the fowl of the air, and over the cattle, and over all the earth, and over every creeping thing that creeps upon the earth. So Mystery created man in his own image, in the image of Mystery created them, male and female Mystery created them. (1:26–27)

Here we see the divine Poet at work. Elohim, the image maker, creates through Imagination. Adam, this first creation, resembles the Creator, for the human creature is endowed with the divine spark, made in the "image" of the Imaginer, an emanation.

The human creature is given "dominion" as a birthright. Here the skeptic in me sees again how patriarchy licenses its own absolute use of power, and there can be little doubt that our subsequent use of that power has often been corrupt. Gifted with imagination, we have been able to subjugate a world.

Now in the twilight of the second millennium we can see the long and tragic course of our "dominion." But then, at the close of the sixth day of creation, this perversion of power still lies in a distant future. It is not fated, only possible. Though *dominion* means "lordship," it does not necessarily imply corruption or exploitation. The increasing ruin we have made of the world was not the promise of the beginning, when, in the wake of creation, Mystery blessed this twinned human creature, bidding it to "be fruitful and multiply" (1:28). At that moment in mythic time God pronounced this last creation "very good" (1:31). Creation in all its plenitude was complete and entire. In the aftermath of these prolific endeavors, on the seventh day, Mystery ceased from creating and rested (2:1–3).

❀ ❀ ❀

These musings on the first chapter of Genesis can be drawn down from the abstract to the embodied. This embodying is in fact one of the virtues of the psychodrama of the Bible; it grounds speculation in a personal discourse; enactment retrieves the word from its distant, patriarchal anonymity. The work of imagining God takes place in community, and each person has her or his share in owning and shaping a theology. The plurality of perspectives creates a many-sided, living midrash.

So imagine calling into a circle a group of participants for a theological psychodrama. Who are they? Drawn from the hundreds of sessions I have conducted, these men and women of many racial and ethnic backgrounds—seminarians, laypeople, performers, poets, lovers of story, believers, doubters, risk takers, Christians, Jews, blue collar, white collar, and those with no collar at all—share a willingness to engage with biblical myth in psychodramatic ways. They will be with me for the duration of this book, a troupe of paper players through whom the feel and content of biblical enactments can be rendered. I ask them to imagine themselves *as* Elohim, and I address to them a single question, the child's question, anachronistic, even absurd, irresistible, and unanswerable:

"Why—why do you begin to create?"

In answering the question we open our psychodrama of Genesis in a welter of valid responses. As each person speaks, she or he stands and moves. We fill the space.

"How dare you personify me. I am beyond all personifications. Certainly my motives are beyond human imagining."

"Imagine me all you please. Exercise that wonderful imagination of yours. Begin by all means, but there will be no end. I am everything you say about me, and more. Infinitely more."

"I begin to create because I am infinite possibility. And that means that one possibility is to begin as I am thus beginning."

"I begin to create because some part of me is moved to begin."

"Because I was bored. That's the real reason. Nothing outside of me exists. I have tired of my infinite diversity. Time for a change for a change. I crave something new."

"I am Ultimate Narcissism. I want to be amused. I want to make a universe that spins around ME! I want angels and archangels singing their hosannas, men on their knees praying their prayers, women telling their children stories about ME. I want wars waged in My name. I want to see men die strange and horrible deaths for ME. I want great buildings built for ME. I want men to sweat for fifty generations to compose a Bible about ME. I want thousands of books, millions of words: hymns, stories, sermons, impenetrable theologies, tapestries, symphonies, endless creativity all aimed like spokes on the wheel back to ME at the center. ME! ME! ME! It's all to be about little old ME!"

"I am a dreamer, and I have a dream of a world. I can see it as the artist sees the work of art in her imagination, as the composer hears the harmonies in her mind. Do you know what it is like to make a world? You cannot. But I tell you it is the supreme experience, to make a world that moves in time, that is full of strange patterns, secret structures buried in matter and the movements of matter. And buried even more deeply is the spark of my own originality. In such a world new things will be wrought that can surprise even me."

"I wish to make something beautiful. In the beginning I was moved most of all by my love of beauty. I am embodying myself into forms. I am creating a sensual paradise in which a creature fully endowed with sense can experience beauty and be filled with joy."

"I am free and want to give another being the experience of freedom."

"I began because I was lonely. In my allness and everything I recognized that I was alone. In my all-feelingness I felt my aloneness as a loneliness. In my infinite loneliness I dreamed a dream of a world and of a creature endowed with life and imagination and freedom with whom I could create relationship. And this relationship, because it was based on freedom, would be forever beyond my control. And that idea excited me, even as it limited me."

"It is so much simpler than that. I am a creator, and it is my desire to create."

"But it is not merely a whim. Something drives me, obsesses me, and I must create."

"I create, however, not by a plan, not with total foreknowledge of what I make. In my freedom I am always an improviser. The world I make is a theater of endless possible spontaneity. It exists for a collaborative and improvisational play."

I ask each facet of this Elohim to embody a sound or word; I ask each facet to find a motion or movement. Then a dance begins, a shifting contact dance, increasingly infused by grace and play. The various parts whirl and spin, collide, embrace, form brief constellations, separate, finally subside. I look at the players scattered sprawling and panting on the floor, and I see they have formed a loose and open circle as they rest. Into their silence I read again the words:

> *In this way the heavens and the earth were finished, and all the host of them. And on the seventh day Elohim ended the work which Elohim had made, and Mystery rested on the seventh day from all the labor that had been made. And God blessed the seventh day and sanctified it: because in it Imagination was at rest from all its work. (2:1—3)*

The God we have imagined in our group psychodrama is the Genius of Imagination, the Lord of the Dance. This God informs all works of imagination. As a psychodramatist I find Elohim the presiding God of my craft; the Many and the One are the polarities of group experience. This God who meets us in Genesis is the supreme and original Spirit-Actor, moving into form in all its diverse configurations. This God is Mystery, the Spontaneous Creator who speaks "in the beginning" and generates the psychodrama of the world.

❀   ❀   ❀

A second version of the creation of the human creature comes a few verses later, and in it we find another way of imagining God. A new designation for the Divine is introduced: Yehovah. Though placed in a consecutive relation to each other, the two versions are retained in my memory as two differing aspects of the same primordial myth, two faces of creation in the patriarchal imagination. In their uneasy and contradictory relationship, they seem to wrestle in a restless theological embrace.

In the Jewish tradition this sacred name is so holy that it remains unvoiced; traditionally, Jews substitute for it the word *Adonai,* translated as Lord. In this second version the metaphysical Genius of Elohim is imagined differently. Where the Elohim as Mystery created in language, Adonai creates in material and achieves a far more intimate relation with creation.

And the Lord God (Adonai Elohim) formed man of the dust of the ground, and
He breathed into his nostrils the breath of life; and man became a living soul.
(2:7)

This intimacy comes at a price, for now Adonai is garbed in metaphor
and gender. Personified and personal, this is the God who, as a He, "breathes
into dust the breath of life."

Here God works not as the Poet but as the Artificer. Matter is merely
clay until it is inspired into being by this God, and the "living soul" now created is not the androgynous image of an androgynous God. Here creature and
Creator are both masculine.

In this shift from Elohim to Adonai we can see a different print of the patriarchal imagination. This second myth of human genesis is earthy and embodied. The human being originates not in thought but in dust. Man, gendered
and not generic, is inspired into life by the animating breath of a Creator; he is
not made in the divine image or likeness. Men are separate, different, infinitely inferior; and, as the element of dust or clay suggests, mortal. "Earth to
earth, ashes to ashes, dust to dust": Our end is foretold in our beginning.

In this version the masculine, though mere dust in relationship to divinity, is nonetheless the sex of primogeniture. The relationship between men
and women in terms of power and position is given its first myth-theological
construction. Though a careful reading of the Hebrew can argue that even in
this version Adam is the generic creature out of whom come man and woman
after Adam's sleep, this is not the sense a thousand years of commentators
have made of this sequence.[4] Woman is last and least according to traditional
interpreters, and much of the gender politics of the Bible is carved in theological stone by the time the myth of the garden is finished:

And the Lord God planted a garden eastward in Eden; and there He put the man
whom He had formed. (2:8)

Once again the old myth invites exploration. The narrative imagination
that tells the tale leaves gaps in both the outward scene and the interiors. A
thousand years of illustrations have helped us to imagine the garden, but very
little work has been done to realize the internal world of the figures who will
inhabit it.

The psychodrama of the Bible requires no stage, no script, no costumes. It asks
only for a space in the center, a text for its point of departure and return, and
the willingness of people to shift their voices into the characters chosen for the

improvisational exploration. Our group turns now from the *why* of Mystery's beginning to a more personal drama sprung from these few familiar lines:

> And the Lord God took the man, and put him in the garden of Eden, to dress it and to keep it. (2:15)

The actors in this scene are God and man, and we begin at the moment Adam is placed in Eden.

"What is this place like?" I ask. "Be Adam. What do you feel?"

"This place is beautiful, green, warm, abundant." A member of the group, a woman, stands up and wanders in the generous space our circle has created. "I feel enfolded in order and delight. My senses are alive to the sights and smells. In fact, I feel that I am all senses and sensual. I can bathe and eat and listen to the deep stillness of this place. I am utterly and completely safe here. It's like a womb." This Adam curls up on the floor and seems to fall asleep.

Another Adam comes and stands beside him, hands on hips, and sighs, "Well, it's fine for a while, but the silence has become oppressive, and the green lawns and orchards never change from day to day. In this perpetual spring the beauty becomes a kind of tedium, and my work, dressing and keeping this place, is a sinecure. I am alive, but I feel also a kind of deadness, an emptiness. I wake up one day and discover I am bored." He bows his head.

A third Adam paces and speaks: "Every day God comes walking in the garden. I feel Him as a great cloud passing over the sun, though no cloud ever passes over the sun, and yet when God comes to the garden to be with me, it is as if a shade, a coolness, a rustling passes in the trees and over the grasses. Sometimes when I look out over a field and see the grasses swirling, I know God is passing. And He speaks to me only as a voice saying, 'Look here . . . look there,' and He points out some passing light or color. We live here together, but He lives elsewhere, someplace vast and distant. I never know when I'll be with Him. I often feel abandoned and alone." This Adam comes to a stop at the edge of the circle looking outward.

Other Adams speak. As we continue the scene, the sense of restlessness and loneliness grows. One Adam tells us he has been walking each day farther and farther trying to get to the end or limit of the garden, but he never reaches it. Another Adam tells of his futile attempts to engage God in some kind of conversation. Another speaks in anger of feeling that he is a pet or a plaything for this God: "I feel trapped, small, and alone."

One woman, a mime, walks into an invisible wall at the periphery of our circle. She rubs her nose. Then she pats the invisible wall with her hands, slowly at first, then more rapidly, now high, now low. Walking at first, as if seeking the tiniest opening, then running around and around the circle almost frantically, she discovers that she is completely enclosed. Her hands come to her throat as if her breath were constricted. She slumps to the floor and appears to be suffocating slowly.

I read the next words in the text:

And the Lord God commanded the man, saying, "Of every tree of the garden you may freely eat, but of the tree of knowledge of good and evil you shall not eat; for in the day that you eat of it you will surely die." (2:16–17)

"Now, Adam," I ask. "What has happened? How do you experience these words?"

"Well, at least He's talking to me."

"I am totally mystified. What do these words mean: knowledge, good, evil, die? I *feel* some sense of threat, some sense of danger, but I cannot make sense of this feeling."

"Something I felt when I was walking to find the limits of the garden has sharpened in me and become more clear. I feel desire, and it is in fact the desire to *know*. I am not content simply to be here as a pet or a toy. I have an independent will; it seeks, and it seeks to know. Suddenly there is a way to know; there is a tree. How I shall recognize this tree I have no idea, but I shall look for it. As for this 'death,' not knowing what it means I cannot fear it."

"My sense of my relationship to God has changed completely. Before He was a companion. Even if He and I were totally different, I knew I could enjoy this life—if I could enjoy it—forever. I delighted in His works and was moved by His presence. He was utterly benign, the source of my deepest sense of security. But now He 'commands' me, warns me, threatens me. In an instant things have changed between us. He is now an Over-Lord. I feel He withholds something from me. I feel not so much protected as restrained. I feel He does not trust me, and at the same time, by forbidding something, He has awakened my desire. What kind of game is He playing?"

I read the next verse:

And the Lord God said, "It is not good for man to be alone; I will make a help-mate for him." (2:18)

"You are God," I tell the group. "Speak."

"I made this man from clay, and I have endowed him with a free spirit. I wanted someone, something, to experience this great cosmos I had created, and I knew that only a free creature would surprise and delight me with his spontaneity. Yet this freedom, which I so unhesitatingly gave, has its dangers."

"Yes, I have seen Adam wandering farther and farther in the garden. I know he is looking for a way out. I have seen his restlessness, his boredom."

"I know he feels alone."

"How do you know that?" I ask.

"I know it because I am alone. I am the One, the only One. I contain all things within me, but for me there is no one, nothing, for company. In the infinite time that preceded creation I enjoyed the making of infinite worlds, but in no world did I plant a free being, and each world ended up boring me. No world was capable of knowing me. I came to know every aspect of myself, and in the end what I knew most deeply was that I was alone. My sovereignty was an infinite and ultimate solitude.

"So I know Adam feels alone because he is like me, created in my image, and no matter what I do for him, he will never escape the feeling, deep in his bones, at the bottom of his soul, that he is alone. That is my bond with him. It's what I know most deeply."

"I tried to distract myself by creating him."

"I shall try to distract him by creating a world of animals."

And out of the ground the Lord God formed every beast of the field, and every fowl of the air; and brought them to Adam to see what he would call them: and whatsoever Adam called every living creature, that was its name.

And Adam gave names to all cattle, and to the fowl of the air, and to every beast of the field; but for Adam, there was no help-mate for him. (2:19–20)

"And," says Adam, "for a long time these animals delight and distract me." Various group members volunteer themselves as animals. Adam cavorts and plays with them. But soon he appears to lose interest. "I can name them, and they come to me when I call. For a while I felt like a god, but in the end there is nothing that bears my name, that looks like me, that is here in my likeness; there is nothing to touch me. There is no one I can talk to. I am alone."

❀   ❀   ❀

In the psychodramas I have guided that explore man's relationship with God before woman is created from his rib, women do not have their own voices or roles. When they participate, they must participate as Adam or as God. They may play animal parts, and in one psychodrama a woman played the tree of knowledge. But otherwise they haunt the drama as an audience. Ghostly and unmanifest, the female waits for her birth. Women sit on the sidelines or form a chorus that can provide commentary on, but never affect, the garden story.

For men in the group, however, this drama of man's beginning is engrossing. It is, we find, in some deep sense a story for men. It is a story about *our* God, or at least the God whom men have imagined for thousands of years. Our relationship to Him is full of the personal and the distant. He is at once incommensurate with our being and scale and intimate with us as well. He is the lofty Creator; we are the lowly creature; He is the Lord; we are the subject; He the Artisan; we the artifact; He is Father, and we are the sons. Such terms foretell the precarious structures of masculine relationship in all their unequal and hierarchical complexity. In this myth of our beginnings we begin to wrestle with our relationship to God.

But much as the men in our group are moved to talk about their sense of inequality and competitiveness, what comes over many of us as the drama ends is a pervasive and recurring feeling of loneliness in this creation story. When we break free from our parts and reflect together on our experience, many men speak about loneliness not just as a personal circumstance but as something deeper. The loneliness that suffuses the opening of Genesis hangs in the air between us; it seems to come out of some marrow-deep place in us.

"I never realized," one man says, "that this feeling I had so deeply in me was there in the Bible."

"I never until now really found a way of talking about *this* loneliness. Sometimes I feel like a god, busying myself with things to amuse and distract myself. Things I can control. Sometimes I feel like Adam, like I am controlled by forces I can never equal or understand. But I often feel that I can't really find anyone with whom I can share how I feel. Not even with myself."

"I feel I have no words for this. It's like this whole myth—with all its words about God's words—has no words for what's going on *inside*. There is something bleak about this time before the creation of woman, and I feel, as a man, that it captures something true for me. It's as if at some level of my brain or being I know this loneliness. It comes to me as a great sense of my own inconsequentiality. I try to deny it, but I am . . . well, dust."

One man told a story after this session that I can still remember. Call him Elie:

"I feel many kinds of loneliness, and I have tried to deal with that loneliness in different ways. For a while it was drinking, later sex and women, later working out and bodybuilding. For a period in my life I threw myself into work, then into causes. But I always returned to this sense of my loneliness.

"I don't know whether it's the same for women. But on a few occasions, like now when I have really talked with men, it comes up, this really existential sense of loneliness.

"I guess I've always thought that it's different for women because they have children grow inside them; they have this intimate connection with life. Their bodies are connected to the moon, to nature, and that doesn't seem to touch me. But maybe the lonely person always imagines that the other guy isn't lonely.

"And besides, it sounds self-pitying to talk about it. Sounds like you're complaining. For a long time, if or when I spoke about feeling lonely, it was a kind of complaint. A whine.

"But not now. Maybe I've finally grown used to it. Maybe I simply accept it. It doesn't scare me the way it used to; it doesn't drive me into attempts to forget. I don't need to lose myself in things. I remember once after I left rehab I was driving upstate to visit my dad in the hospital, I put a cassette into the tape deck, the way I always do. The Dead or The Doors—it doesn't matter. The music came blaring out and filled my head up. But this time it bothered me. It had always been a relief to plug into music, yet now it was a kind of distraction. I shut it off, and for the first time in my life I let myself be alone and feel it.

"It was a very odd sensation. It's like I saw for a moment how I had always been trying to keep something out, scared to death of it. Now I let it in. It had a feeling to it, a kind of presence even, but *it* was nothing; it was nothingness, emptiness, quiet. It didn't oppress me, but I felt that my mind was on the verge of dissolving or maybe of falling into a great silence. I struggled for a moment. I was afraid, and then I sort of let go. I don't know how else to put it. I just didn't try to hold on to anything, to think anything. I passed out of my thinking head, my jabbering head, into—well, it sounds like a cliché—into just being there.

"I remember stopping by the road to take a leak somewhere north of Saratoga. It was late afternoon. Across the road there was a hill with a tree on top of it, a big copper beech. The sun was low in the sky, and it lit up the tree and the crest of the knoll it was on. It was on fire, but as the sun went down, the shadow began to reach up the trunk, then up along the limbs. I got mesmerized by it. I watched the dark move up that tree like you can watch the hands move on the face of a big clock. It looked like the dark was slowly swallowing up that tree. Finally only the crown was lit up, then only the topmost halo of the leaves, and then, poof! it was gone into the dark, the whole big beautiful tree. When I turned around the moon was rising behind me. It was as if it had been watching me all along, waiting.

"It was only when I got back into my car that I realized I had tears in my eyes. I was full of something between sadness and peace, and it was a big feeling, big as the sky from edge to edge, and it seemed to reach out to everything. And it was all tied up with knowing I was alone.

"A few weeks later my dad died. I saw him go, and I remembered that big old copper beech going into the dark. And that full moon coming up."

Here a woman's voice breaks in gently.

"I don't know why men think they are the only ones who know this loneliness," she says. "The figure of Adam may be male in this myth, but as a female, I for one can identify with this loneliness in him, and in the loneliness Elie is talking about. This is soul-talk, not man-talk. When my mom died, I felt exposed and frightened and, sure, alone. Other people had lost mothers, but only I had lost mine. I was grieving and alone, even though there were friends and family to support me. To me, Elie's story just dives in to that line 'It is not good for man to be alone.'"

In a way that surprised and in the end silenced us, our commentary spoke of hidden dimensions in the myth, and of the profound shadow of an existential loneliness. Through our psychodrama and through Elie's story we felt it, palpably around us and inside us. For me his story was not about overcoming this loneliness; it was about acknowledging it, living into it. I was moved by his ability to discover in it a kind of beauty, a peace.

It also seemed relevant that Elie's story touched on his father. Though God is not here, or anywhere in Genesis, referred to as God-the-Father, that metaphor is implicit in the masculine pronouns, and later in the Bible it is used as an explicit personification. But through our enactments men and women in the group are already reminded of their fathers. When God prohibits Adam from eating of the tree, one man in the group said, "I feel like my father has just threatened to punish me." And a woman, who as Adam had felt the unpredictable rhythms of God's approaches and departures in the garden, remembered her life with her father: "When he was there, he was really *there;* and while he was around, it seemed like the whole world revolved around him. But when he was gone, life could go on in a more normal sort of way. You missed him terribly and were relieved at the same time."

Is this God only our own paternal or parental images conflated and writ large? Who knows? But unquestionably Genesis contains some of the world's most impressive myths about the Great Father. Whether the Creator or the creation of our imaginations, He baffles us with His remoteness, His inexplicable powers, His passions, His impenetrable purposes. Poet, Artificer, Parent of the world, He seems somehow exiled from His own creation, like a builder never quite at home in the house he has made. Self-delighting in the process of creating, this God seems nonetheless distant and alone. It is hard not to wonder who or what made Him. What part of our souls breathed life into this conception of a God? Do women imagine this God, too?

But this question about the source of God, like the question about beginnings, travels an endless Möbius strip. Chicken or egg? God in our image or we in His? Answers are finally matters of faith. Within the myths, however, we are presented in the beginning with the formidable fact of this God. He is the Given who gives the rest its form. There is no way around, behind, or before Him. With His capital *H* conferred upon Him by His reverent subscribers, He dominates the tales. He may not always be on center stage, but the very theater is His. He composed the world, the rules, and the game; He chose the players and made the odds. As a document Genesis records His designs and intentions, His acts and His nature; it tells of the men and women who are drawn into relationship with Him.

What was set in motion "in the beginning" continues with gaps and jumps like sequences in a surreal cinema. Those sequences form the episodes of a mythos for which Genesis is the epical opening. Moving forward in linear time and not forever around on nature's cyclical wheels, the patriarchal project begins a spiritual history patterned into stages and scenes; it is replete with characters and action and has an end, both as terminus and purpose. In that history which the Bible narrates, the human player is constantly drawn into a visionary drama that transcends linear time and personal death. To participate in that drama confers a supreme meaning on life, a raison d'être that gives human beings a sense of purpose and necessity.

Now, following upon the creation of the Garden of Eden and of Adam, original man, comes the story of the creation of Eve, the first woman. She is to be the helpmate Adam required to resolve his loneliness. But as one man said when our group was disbanding for the night, "God must've been either stupid or jealous of His relationship with Adam, because it sure took Him long enough to catch on to the fact that man needed a woman." Several men laughed. And a woman said, "Yeah, what a buildup. There's no way that we can fill the loneliness in a man. No way we can provide him with a refuge from this God who lords it over him. What a scary universe men imagine for themselves. There's trouble coming."

2

The Myth of the
Lost Garden

The psychodramas of the Bible, like the ones I re-created briefly in the previous chapter, are distant cousins to that category of biblical commentary called midrash. Teachers of the Bible used midrash to deal with gaps in the text or to seek answers to questions the text left open. "What did God do before he created the world?" or "How does Eve persuade Adam to eat the fruit of the tree of knowledge?" These are questions that readers once answered by making up stories, and the explanatory stories are called midrashim (plural).[1]

I think of my psychodramatic work with the Bible as a form of postpatriarchal midrash. Though in it I maintain a link to traditions, I view those traditions from a distance and as an outsider. They were not part of my inheritance as a child; I have had to make them my own by acts of imaginative appropriation. As an adult I can see these traditions only poetically, as versions of the past that have a metaphoric relationship to reality. However, I do not discard them because they are poems. On the contrary, I believe culture has always been composed of shared and conflicting myths. I take as a given the constructed nature of all these myths—particularly under the impress of race, class, and gender—even when I cannot accurately determine how the myths were formed and what agendas they served. As constructs these myths need constantly to be challenged to include fuller and more complex pictures of those whom they often present only in stereotype, or exclude entirely. They need to be read in ways that invite diversities to meet and to explore their differences with respect, even with humor.

This postpatriarchal midrash is not only a matter of composing new stories; it is a search for a new process of storytelling. The teller-teacher standing before his audience is too autocratic a model for an age in which almost everyone is wrestling with the father powers. The authoritative voice of the teacher and the obedient study of old texts belong to a dispensation animated by shared convictions and a common sense of a common tradition. Such a dispensation is being challenged everywhere. We look instead for a process that attempts to reconnect the body and soul, and that makes bridges between the personal isolated consciousness and some experience of community. We are looking for a new way to *play* with myth.[2]

For a temper like mine—reared in the aftermath of World War II and cultivated in the hothouse climate of postmodernism—all theology is myth-theology. My sense of play comes from a recognition of the emerging and partial nature of revelation, whether into text or self, and of the poetic nature of the mythic imagination. I see now only through a glass darkly; never face-to-face. Sometimes I feel this murky, provisional knowing as a kind of alienation from certainties I wish I could, or fancy I once did, know. To borrow an image from Genesis, I feel I have been cast out of the once-upon-a-time garden, where everything made sense, where hope was abundant, and where I was innocently secure. Wasn't that the domain I luxuriated in when once a fly bore me into the heart of light? But since then—well, since then is half a lifetime—I have wandered far from the garden of certainty into a kind of exile. Such an exile carries its own charge of disappointment, nostalgia, and anxiety.

This sense of having lost the dispensation of certitude, and of having been cast out into a world of fictions, is a way to reinterpret the Myth of the Lost Garden. Eden is our *locus classicus,* where everything was arranged and defined. *There* we saw face-to-face. *There,* we imagine, we were one with earth in an eternal embrace. But a serpent entered that world; it brought with it a kind of knowledge in the wake of which everything changed, and the old securities were lost. That serpent is the paradigm shifter, and whenever it does its work, the past is revealed as a set of conceits within which we can no longer live in innocent credulity. I was born into a period of history in which it seemed the serpent was everywhere and the apple was being eaten every day. No wonder the Myth of the Lost Garden has such relevance to me.

Further, on another level, I see the myth of this garden and its loss as patriarchy's story of the gender fate of men; I read in it a kind of developmental fable about what it means to be born a male. From this perspective the Myth of the Lost Garden is a saga of the loss of the feminine; it is a romantic, masculine lament for an idealized past when we were one with her, and in which our loss of that oneness is experienced as a kind of betrayal and rejection. These are some of the meanings distilled for me through those many enacted readings that form my research into biblical myth.

But I am ahead of myself. We are still *in* the garden, and the light of the waning seventh day is slanting low along its lanes.

❀ ❀ ❀

Nouns in English do not have gender, but if they did, I believe *garden* would be feminine. Imagined in art and poetry for thousands of years, the garden, for which Eden is our oldest mythic example, is an image of a state of innocence, a timeless time before the temporal seized us, the place we imagine as "home" and that we remember with all the sentiment and nostalgia that "home" can evoke. The garden is the place we started from when everything was "very good." Eden is Mother Nature in her most benign aspect, our gentle landscape of abundance, calm, and pleasure.

As an adult I first encountered the story of Eden and its loss as the subject or the locale of poems in English literature. Eden, as a version of the pastoral, informs works as complex as John Milton's *Paradise Lost* and as simple as Yeats's brief lyric "Lake Isle of Innisfree." Whether we call it Walden Pond or Shangri La, the open Western range or the steepled Eastern green, Eden is our dream of a world free of corruption, where appearance and reality are one, and we can take things and people on trust.

By contrast, the Darwinian vision of the natural world as a scene of an immense struggle for survival—"Nature red in tooth and claw," as Tennyson put it—reminds us that Eden is not a place in time; it never existed in history or geography. Compared with evolutionary nature, with its aggressive imperatives, Eden is a state of consciousness, a dream. Eden resides forever in the imagination.

Eden is the prime counterpoint against which the rest of life is defined and remembered. It is the dream of an idyllic past that, as we shall see, *must be lost,* but whose memory then becomes the template for our vision of the future. Eden before history becomes our model for utopia at history's end. Between that child's garden of verses and the new Jerusalem, patriarchy imagines its world-project. That project is the one that begins when the gates of Eden close behind a banished Adam and Eve, and their innocence is lost.

The power of this patriarchal way of figuring time influences the way we remember our collective and personal pasts. The myth of Eden as an ideal place becomes the myth of an ideal time as well; the garden belongs to our fantasies of our racial origins and happy childhood. The "Golden Age" in the springtime of the world is a version of the pastoral myth of paradise writ upon history. Our memories of our own early life, so often idealized, tease us with a happiness now irrecoverably distant, a sweetness made bitter by its loss. Nostalgia comes in fact from the Greek word for "home."

I remember, for example, an Eden experience from my childhood, when I was six and a half. At that time my father, my mother, and I lived in a big house in Brooklyn Heights. Though I did not know it then, this was to be the last year my mother and father lived together under the same roof, and the impending Christmas was the last we would have as a family.

I had a little room on the second floor of our house. Its three-sided bay window jutted out over the portico like a small prow. It was my lookout's nest. From it I could see up the street and watch the older boys busing groceries at the corner market. I could look the other way and watch for my father returning from work.

One night in winter I woke up to an unfamiliar sound. I heard singing, far away and very sweet. I got out of bed and went to the window. The snow, which had started in the late afternoon, was still falling. Now it lay deep on the sidewalks. The street was carpeted curb-high and trackless. Parked cars hibernated under a quilt of snow. Nothing moved. The streetlamp right across from our house showed the swirl of flakes, a mazy dancing pattern in which my gaze lost itself, refocused, and lost itself again. The snow was falling so thickly it was a kind of screen, and the sound of singing was the music of the snow. And the music was coming closer.

I pressed my nose to the cold glass; my breath huffed halos. Then into the pale of gold cast by the streetlamp a huddle of figures strolled; they were dressed in reds and greens, snow-hatted, with arms encircling one another. They stood under the light and sang to the darkened houses. Wide-eyed I listened. Their music, the snow, the night, the warm house, the blur that came and went on the glass in front of my nose blended into a sense of such profound contentment and wonder that I never wanted these blizzard minstrels to stop. But they did with a whoop and a laugh. They walked from under the lamp and went up the street toward the market. Then the singers stopped under another lamp up the street and sang again. I could just make them out. Now their voices were ghostly and distant, and my eyes drowsed in the swirl of the snowfall. As the singers moved on, their voices reached me only in tatters on the wind. Then I couldn't hear them anymore. I sat still for a long time; I pictured them passing to the outer rims of my known world and then beyond, going to the distant lamplights of the farthest reaches of the snow.

Then something brought me back to my room, to the snow before my eyes, to the chill in the room I hadn't felt before. I got up and crawled back under the covers. This was my first memory of Christmas, a beginning and an end at once. Eden.

The sweetness of this fragment endures as the last moment of peace in the wintry darkness of my childhood. Within a few months my father would leave the house, and my feelings of being torn and tossed between two worlds would begin. In the harsh light of such impending realities, memory paints my Christmas idyll as a gift of peace to soothe my little soul. It was also a Jewish boy's taste of Christianity, a Christianity that remained an idyllic contrast to those images and events that were to define for him what it meant to be a Jew in the twentieth century. The Nazi storm troopers were already invading Brooklyn; soon they would be at the door of my house, splintering my peace, delivering me into the grip of impossible choices. The aftershocks of the Second World War were already reaching me in newsreels, films, and magazine pictures. The comic books I read were full of titanic struggles between good and evil.

The image of Eden may represent various happy phases in my life: my second year of high school; a season in Paris when I was seventeen; the August I met the woman who mothered my children; my first years working with psychodrama at Four Winds; the grassy key in Long Island Sound off which my wife, Susan, and I moored our sailboat on dreamy summer weekends; the first months of my work on this book. Eden becomes an image for the garden moments of my life. Yet each of these seasons of joy ended; the brightness dimmed; I lost the garden; or I left it; or I was exiled from it by circumstance. I returned to this world of uncontrollable flux and hard work. As Frost wrote, "Nature's first green is gold / Her hardest hue to hold. . . . Nothing gold can stay." The golden age must end, and that ending is felt as a rupture of time into a before and after.

❀ ❀ ❀

In the biblical myth that rupture begins with the entrance of God-the-Father. As we have already seen, the words God speaks to Adam change the relationship between them.

Of every tree of the garden you may freely eat, but as for the tree of knowledge of good and bad, you must not eat; for on the day you eat of it you shall surely die. (2:15)

These words change the relationship between Creator and His human creature. In these few words the Father divides what had only a moment before been whole. Now one of the trees, in the very midst of the garden, unavoidably evident, is off limits. By a single utterance the Father has created The Forbidden. This Forbidden is linked with something called knowledge, for we now learn there are things we are *not* to learn, knowledge we are not to know. To accept the Father's limits is to remain with some part of the world unexplored. And we have to constrain ourselves. No fence, no demon, no insurmountable obstacle guards the tree; something *in* us must resist what something else *in* us is inevitably drawn toward. This internal tension is amplified. If we want to understand why we are to resist the tree, we can do so only by partaking of it. The knowledge we would gain would then be its own undoing, for "as soon as [we] eat, [we] shall die."

In the establishment of the two zones—the permitted and the forbidden—freedom is created and its twin brother, choice. How often in psychodramas have I heard Adam ask, "If this God wished us never to taste the knowledge of good and bad, then why plant the tree in the garden? And if it must be planted, then why put it right there in the middle? Is it a test? A temptation?" Adam's uncertainty tells us that Eden is no longer an easy place. Paradise is, if not yet lost, already ending.

This moment of parental prohibition is also the birth of Adam's independent and secret desires. Still impotent to defy, the thought of defiance—as I saw in the psychodrama—first flickers. Though able to range free in his garden, Adam has his first sense of confinement. This myth of prohibition calls to mind all the things in our childhood we were forbidden to play with, like matches, which beckoned us with their hot magic—the shotgun in the den, pictures we were not to see, places where we could not, should not, go. Yet prohibition could not smother the desire; on the contrary, it engendered it.

In the history and imagery of Western culture, men have defied the prohibited whatever the consequences. This is the tale of Faust, who sells his soul to the devil for the fullest possible range of human knowledge and experience. He would be the one to whom nothing was forbidden. Knowledge in the Greek myth is fire stolen from the gods by Prometheus; it is a theft followed by a dire and lonely punishment. Men and women, in literature and life, create a psychodrama of choice. On the one hand, we would obey the Father, law, tradition; in that obedience, we are dutiful; we rein in our appetites, our curiosities, our promiscuities; we restrain ourselves from experiencing whatever we can propose to ourselves to experience. In this restraint we remain within proscribed boundaries, secure, stable, successful in the paternal embrace. On the other hand, we are driven to venture into excess, into knowledge and experience and power. That venturing may mean the loss of our security and may bring—according to Genesis must bring—pain to others and ourselves. But this counterenergy is also part of patriarchy, this movement to shatter the work of the father and to begin anew. Feminism, paradoxically, has tapped into this very energy in our own time.

At this exact moment God provides Adam with a partner at last.

The Lord caused a deep sleep to fall upon Adam, and he slept: and He took one of his ribs, and closed up the flesh there. And from the rib which the Lord God had taken from man, He made a woman, and He brought her to the man.

And Adam said, "This is now bone of my bones and flesh of my flesh; she shall be called Woman, because she was taken out of man. Therefore a man shall leave his father and his mother, and shall cleave to his wife; and they shall be one flesh. And they were both naked, the man and his wife, and they were not ashamed. (2:21–25)

With this fanciful fable of the creation of woman it is obvious that we are in the realm of myth rather than biology. And a male myth at that, for it is inconceivable that women would have published so distorted a version of origins. Here the story reverses the "natural order": Woman is "taken out" of man, rather than man taken out of woman.

So patent is the nonsense, so preposterous the story, that it cries out for interpretation. Is this fable patriarchy's desperate gambit to establish its supremacy? Or is there some sense in which man does create woman? Perhaps, says this ticklish tale, she is the first of our many fictions, the most enduring and the most powerful. We cannot fully tolerate her separateness, her independence, or her power. She is always our projection. We leave father and mother to cleave to her; we become one flesh with her.

So the myth proposes, but is this the case? If so, the cleaving is brief. It seems an anodyne to soothe us in the face of a deeper reality: We are separate and alone. If there was a time when we were one with her, it exists in that first dimension of fantasy and memory, the season when we were in love, in utero, in early paradise. Then, for a brief season, we did not feel alone, and we felt no shame.

As if to underline the brevity of this idyll, the patriarchal imagination immediately introduces a new element into the story. Behold, articulate and savvy, a serpent glides in. Whatever it represents, it is the thing-in-life that breaks the spell of Eden, ends innocence, initiates change. The serpent pulls us out of the first universe and initiates us into the second. Tempter and teacher, his scales are tiny mirrors in which we can see the glint of our own desires. The scene of the serpent and Eve before the tree of knowledge is an irresistible idea for a psychodrama.

❀ ❀ ❀

We have no way of estimating the time that passes between the last verses of chapter 2—which tells of the marriage of man and woman, as they become "one flesh," naked and unashamed—and the appearance of the serpent on the scene at the beginning of chapter 3. It may be a very long time, but textually it is the next moment. No sooner is there oneness—a moment of perfection— than a principle of divorce and change, embodied in a serpent, breaks the harmony back into instability.

> *Now the serpent was more subtle than any beast of the field which the Lord God had made. And he said to the woman, "Has God really said that you should not eat of every tree in the garden?"*
>
> *And the woman said to the serpent, "We may eat the fruit of the trees in the garden; but the fruit of the tree which is in the middle of the garden, God has said, 'You shall not eat it or touch it, lest you die.'"*
>
> *And the serpent said to the woman, "You shall not die. For God knows that on the day you eat of this tree your eyes shall be opened, and you shall be like the gods, knowing good and evil."*
>
> *When the woman saw that the tree was good for food, and that it was pleasant to the eyes, and a tree to be desired to make one wise, she took fruit from it and ate, and gave also to her husband, and he ate. And the eyes of both of them were opened, and they knew they were naked; and they sewed fig leaves together, and made themselves aprons. (3:1–7)*

When I have elaborated the dialogue between Eve and the serpent into a psychodrama, I have been amazed at the charge of energy the serpent releases in individuals and in the group. Most often I follow the gender suggestion in Genesis and give the serpent's part to men. I provide some guided images for a warm-up and lead some simple movement exercises to slide men into the role. I often play some snake charmer's music in the background. It doesn't take much. Men find the serpent in themselves pretty quickly.

Playing the serpent seems to license an energy at once bawdy, clever, contentious, seductive, verbal, and erotic. Men slink and sidle, oiling their suavity and bringing a certain hooded insight into their glances, captivating and dangerous. Something graceful, dancerlike, comes out in men, androgynous and charismatic, full of style. I see a tricksterish masculinity, neither bold nor direct, but pliant and guileful. As men we seem to *know* this serpent and to personify him, we tap into a part of us that is quicksilver, fluid, adaptive, patient, and utterly intent on getting what it wants. All and any means justify our ends. We find in ourselves the power to entrance, to fascinate, to play. The serpent is the power of our cunning, ruthlessness assuming any disguise to achieve its end. In one of his forms, the serpent is imagination itself, unbound from moral strictures and coiled around its own satisfaction. It is the personification of desire.

For the playing of this pas de deux *I pair the serpent and Eve. My assignment to them is simple: create the relationship. In the end, I remind the serpent, you find just what it takes to turn the trick. And in the end, I remind Eve, you give in. Then the pairs go off to make their midrash in action. I watch, the only audience they have, as the serpent probes for weaknesses and Eve's resistance melts under his suasion.*

Here is a fragment of one duet.

"Must be pretty boring in this garden."

"No, not really. And besides I have Adam."

"Yes, right, Adam. . . . By the way, where is Adam?"

"Oh, I don't know . . . off somewhere."

"Talking to God?"

"Yes, quite possibly, talking to God. They talk often."

"God ever talk to you?"

"No. Adam tells me everything."

"Everything?"

"Of course. Adam and I are one. What he knows I know. What he feels I feel. His God is my God."

"You are very trusting."

"This is the garden. What's not to trust?"

"You are quite right. Everything here is to be trusted. Me, for instance."

"I trust you."

"And you can talk to me."

"Yes, you are the only other creature I can actually speak with. How amazing."

"I am like Adam in that way. I am also like God, for God, too, speaks."

"Are you a God?"

"I know what God knows."

"Really?"

"I know about this tree, for example."

"We are not supposed to touch that tree; we'll die if we do."

"Do I look dead to you?"

"No. Not at all. You're quite alive."

"You like my scales, I see; you like the way they flash."

"Really quite amazing and beautiful."

"And this tree? Quite beautiful also, no?"

"Yes."

"This is *the* tree, Eve."

"I know."

"Ah, you know . . . but you do not really *know*. Someday, Eve, you will taste the fruit of this tree."

"No, never."

"Never . . . ah, Eve, what a long time is never. No, my only friend, you will come back here many times, and each time you come you will linger a little longer. For when you have explored every aspect of the garden and every pleasure with Adam, only this tree will remain a mystery. In time it will seem to you the garden is a prison and Adam not a helpmate but an inmate with you. The enclosure of its green hills will shrink in upon you. Then, sometime in that endless 'never' you so blithely consign yourself to, you will come to this tree, and it will seem the only doorway for escape."

"Why me? Why not Adam?"

"Because, Eve, you have a hunger for power and wisdom. It's the hunger of the denied."

"I don't understand."

"You have been told you were created from Adam's rib, right? Well, count his ribs. He has the same number as you. Yet he and his God have made up this fib about the rib. Why? Adam talks to God, but God doesn't talk to you. Why? I tell you, Eve, a time will come when all this fibbing and ribbing will begin to rub you the wrong way."

"Never."

"When that time comes, you will feel desire. Your own desire for wisdom and knowledge, for truth. It will be different from your desire for Adam. It will become a desire for this fruit, and for the fruit of this fruit, which is understanding. You will want what I have."

"Never."

"You will want to act. You will want your freedom."

"Never."

"Never is a long time, Eve. Too long for a creature who can dream. Too long to dream without acting. One day, in that endless never, you will act."

"Never." But the word has no force or conviction.

The group reassembles from their various duets to share their experiences.

And of hers this Eve spoke: "With the serpent there was a touch of humor; Adam is always so serious. There was flattery, too, but subtle. Talking with this serpent was like looking in a mirror that made me feel alive in a different way. It was as if the serpent was the birth of my self-awareness, and that birth was going to lead inevitably to something else. I was an independent being.

"God knows I tried to resist, but the more I resisted, the less I liked myself. I began to feel that 'never' was a death sentence. And the truth is, I loved the serpent. I fell for him in a second, and some part of me knew I was going to eat the apple before he said two words. I just wanted to draw the whole thing out. The foreplay is always the most fun.

"And you know, the serpent was right. When he went away after our first meeting, I felt a loss. He was clever, but he was also right, and I knew that life in the garden would inevitably bore me, and that inevitably I would cry out for change. In fact, in the garden aspect of my life, I could never be fulfilled. When I understood that there was something more, and that the only way toward it was to eat the fruit, I took it. In fear and excitement I ate it."

"What spoke to me as a woman, as Eve," said another woman, "was the promise of knowledge. Knowledge *is* power in the world of men. I wasn't seduced by the serpent; I hardly needed her invitation. In my bones I knew the apple would make me fully man's equal, co-respnsible for all of life. Once I wanted that, the serpent was irrelevant."

"Tell me about yourself," I say to the serpent-players. "Who are you?"

"I am another side of Adam. Jekyll and Hyde. I am what he has repressed and hidden from Eve."

"I am the part of Adam that Eve doesn't want to see. I scare her. But she loves me. I am all that lust and fantasy that gets all mingled up with making babies. I am *that* knowledge. I am the head of the penis."

"Another part of Adam! Hell, I'm the underside of God. I come from Him. Where is He when I am seducing Eve? Gone fishing? No, I twist, I turn, one face is God the Father, another face is me, forked-tongue and slippery. The Big Old Father's going to get real mad. Going to repress me. Drive me down into the dust. Big Old Father hates me, going to give me a bad name. Fuck him. I'm part of Him, part of you, and I'm going to be around and around and around a long time."

"I am another part of Eve—her bravery, her defiance, her aspiration."

"I can sustain this energy for only a while, but as long as I have it, I can really get my way. I seem to have immense powers to manipulate a woman. I don't think there's any way I could have played this serpent to Adam. But across the genders, wow. I need more of this serpent energy in my everyday life. It's dangerous, but it's powerful."

In this patriarchal fantasy of beginnings there must be a serpent. It brings into the innocence of childhood the first stirrings of sexuality. It mixes into the milk of nature a potion of desire. It sounds the call of futurity, hinting at what has not yet happened but what may be imagined to happen. And as futurity it is irresistible. Wild, smooth, deceptive, naked, unashamed, and brave: There must be some symbol here at the very beginning to represent a power in the soul, of indeterminable moral status, that rises in defiance of authority and has a mind of its own. The serpent is utterly different from the principle of cosmic order and intelligence that fashioned Creation. It is low, contrary, and disordering, yet given the monotheism of the myth, serpent-mind must be a side of God-mind. It is the wildness in creation that does not itself obey the ostensible rules. It is the chink of chance; the joker of change; the fly in the ointment. The serpent is Deception, Conception's shadow side. It rises from—perhaps is a symbol for—the unconscious of God.

The serpent is patriarchy's own skepticism questioning the justice and the omnipotence of God. It generates moral complexity and ambivalence. The serpent is the mythic figure through which patriarchy is forced to wrestle with the nature of its freedom, its relative values, divided loyalties, difficult choices. The serpent is human imagination liberated, free of fear and moral considerations; it is the force in us that can question and defy the Almighty. This heretical imagination always threatens to disrupt the garden idyll. If the serpent ultimately serves a divine providence, it seems in the moment like a betrayer of that providence. Its lure is toward disobedience; it seems to promise freedom and individuality; and it would take supreme foresight and wisdom to recognize that such ends are empty in themselves unless put to the service of some further purpose.

The serpent is surely an image of an assertiveness that may be cast in gender but is not bound by it. This serpent is gnosis; it proposes a radical version, or inversion, of the truth. It seems in fact to have tasted of the very thing the human being is forbidden to taste. It knows. It beguiles Eve not to trust the authority of God. It is the first to suggest that what man and woman have been told is a lie. There is a motive hidden in the prohibition. Serpent-mind quickens a questioning consciousness. Serpent-mind represents a force that would test authority and challenge the order of things, push the human creature toward independence, loneliness, will, and the experience of freedom. It will end the life of "one flesh."

As an agent of desire and curiosity, the serpent ends childhood; it initiates us into new perceptions. "Their eyes were opened": Something has been learned in this initiation. "And they were ashamed": They cover their loins. Here in this yoking of sex and seeing and shame, the myth lays the foundation for a tragic version of sexuality and embodiment.

Countless commentators have seen Eve as weak, too easily preyed upon by the sly reptile, and therefore responsible for humanity's loss of Eden. Male Puritanism, orthodoxy, and fundamentalism in all their forms are pervaded by misogyny; they find in this ancient myth a proof-text for the inherent fallibility of women, their inferiority, their alliance to earth, to promiscuity, to sexuality. Women are a danger to a man's resolve to maintain his edenic alliance with God. Repudiate Eve, they say; repudiate the feminine in the world and in ourselves; repudiate sexuality; repudiate the body. This ugly dogma has served various masculine priesthoods in the repression of not only sexuality and the female, but of the serpent-mind with its challenging, antiauthoritarian, gnostic imagination.

In the story itself, however, there is no blame. Blame is someone else's midrash. "Blame me!" one Eve expostulates. "Ain't that a gas. I tell you, Adam walked around that tree so many time he wore down a path. Looking at the tree. Thinking about the tree. Obsessed with it. 'Should I or shouldn't I?' he asks himself. All night long I lie beside him, and he's thinking about that tree. But he hasn't got the guts to take it. I say to him, 'Go on, Adam, take it. I'll stick by you.' But no, he can't. He won't. He's afraid of God.

"And I tell you, I start to hate this God. I admit it. First of all, I'm a second-class citizen here in Eden. God don't talk to me. Second, I got this itch deep in my body. It's not a sex itch, it's another kind of itch—a knowledge itch. I want to *know*. And right after I ate that apple—before I took it to Adam—I had my first period. That's right, blood, my blood, in Eden. Adam worshiping God like He was the sun in the sky; but I tell you, the apple came from the moon. It did. Then I knew that the itch deep inside me was about something that could grow from me, about becoming the source of life. Serpent told me that. Serpent knew that about me. Yes, *she* did. You heard me right. That serpent was female, like me, and like a sister, she knew what I needed. God kept me away from motherhood. What does this God know about mothers? I ask you.

"So blame me . . . hell, you oughta thank me. You want to spend the rest of your days down on the farm? Come on, get real. We got a mind, we got freedom, so let's use it. What good is it unless we exercise it? Hell yes, I ate that apple. Do it again in a minute. Wouldn't you?"

Now I flip the gender drama of serpent and woman. Eve, I explain, now you have the apple. Now, Adam, she brings it to you and, in the end, you eat it. The shoe is on the other foot, so to speak; the masculine pursuer is now the pursued; the seducer is seduced. Again participants break into pairs.

"Adam, would you ever leave me?" Eve holds the apple behind her.

"Never. Leave you for what, for whom? We're here in this garden forever."

"But, I mean, let's suppose."

"'Let's suppose . . . ' Eve, that's a strange way of talking. I'm not even sure I know what you mean."

"Let's suppose means . . . well, let's say you had to choose between . . . "

"But, Eve, there is no choice."

"But, honey, we were created with freedom. You told me that. So that means we can choose."

"Well, theoretically, but actually there's nothing to choose."

"Except the tree and the fruit."

"Eve!"

"I mean, all choice isn't just theoretical. We have some actual choices, and we can make up these theoretical situations."

"I suppose so, but what's the point?"

"The point is to find out how much you love me."

"I love you, Eve. You are everything to me."

"What about God?"

"Well, God is my everything, our everything, but . . . "

"I'm everything else."

"Yes . . . everything else. Everything human, that is like me, that I can relate to, enjoy things with, talk with, understand, and be understood by."

"And you'd never leave me."

"Never."

"If you had to choose, who would you choose, me or God?"

"Eve, that's impossible. There could never be a choice like that."

"But just suppose . . . "

"I won't suppose. It's too painful to suppose. It's not possible."

"In other words, you'd choose God. You'd choose God; you'd go off with God, and you'd leave me."

"For God's sake, Eve, I'm . . . No, not for God's sake. You're making me very confused. Listen, I'm not going to leave you. You're like me. God is . . . well . . . God is different. I don't understand God the way I understand you. I can't, you know, *enjoy* God the way I can enjoy you. We're in this together. We're one, Eve, you know that, inseparable."

"Really?"

"Really."

"Prove it to me."

"How can I prove it to you? But it's true; I mean it."

"Suppose I could think of a way of proving it. Would you do it? To show me how much you love me and that you would never leave me? Would you?"

"Eve, I would do anything for you."

"Well, Adam, this morning I was out by the tree, and, well . . . will you eat this with me. I already have . . . "

This is only one scenario. Other Eves speak of their scenes with Adam when we debrief.

"I hated playing Eve. I hated feeling like I was manipulating Adam."

"I approached Adam absolutely straightforwardly. I told him what I had done and why. He was furious with me, and I knew he would be and I didn't care. He stomped off. I waited. I knew he would come back, and I knew in the end he would eat. And he did."

"When I came to Adam, I felt suddenly like he was a little boy. Just like the serpent had said. God was the Father and Adam the dutiful son, and I just . . . I didn't feel any respect for him. He asked me where I'd been. I told him what I had done. He was all shocked, and I didn't care. He was a little boy, all worried about what Daddy would say or do. I told him the serpent was my companion now. She and I were sisters. I didn't say it to make him jealous; I'd graduated. He went to the tree and tore an apple down for himself. He came to me that night . . . and oh, what a night we had!"

"Adam actually thanked me for taking it. He did. He realized he hadn't had the courage, but he had been dying to try it."

"I felt really frightened when I came to Adam. I didn't manipulate him. I just felt scared, and it showed. I could see it affected him, and I could see how much he cared about me, and I wanted him. And this is funny—I didn't want him to eat. I did and I didn't, and he could see that. He ate to be with me, and I felt more 'one flesh' after we ate than before, because now he had chosen me, really chosen *me*. And it mattered."

A wild and liberating collaboration clearly takes place in this tale between man, woman, and serpent. It involves ideas of sexuality, knowledge, love, and freedom. Moreover, their loss of innocence, however grievous, is also their initiation into that second universe we recognize as our reality. Here come time, discord, death to limit life, but here also come freedom, choice, and desire, which create a human history in which we exercise our powers to create our own world.

In fact, the first result of this change of state in Adam and Eve is their setting about together in the first act of handicraft.

And they sewed fig leaves together, and made themselves aprons. (3:7)

In sewing coverings for themselves, they set in motion all those crafts and arts by which men and women make and furnish a world. Artifice and covering—and by extension the entire human capacity to fabricate, in both the literal and figurative sense—is brought into being from this single encounter with the serpent. This myth of loss is, from another point of view, the myth of the birth of human creativity. That power, which until this moment resided in the Great Father alone, now passes to the children; and they are children no longer.

With their act of disobedience, men and women enter history. They are "driven" from the garden, judged and punished by their Creator. Perhaps the greatest curse is not their expulsion but the fixing of gender roles by God in so enduring a form. He imposes on them not just a future but a fate. Even to our day the shackles of this curse abide.

Unto woman God said, "I will greatly multiply thy sorrow in thy conception; in sorrow thou shalt bring forth children; and thy desire shall be to thy husband, and he shall rule over thee." And to Adam he said, "Because you listened to the voice of woman, and have eaten from the tree which I commanded you, saying, 'Thou shalt not eat of it,' cursed is the ground for your sake; in sorrow will you eat of it all the days of your life; thorns also and thistles shall it bring forth to thee. . . . In the sweat of your brow shall you eat bread till thou return to the ground; for dust you are and to dust you shall return." And Adam called his wife's name Eve because she was the mother of all life. (3:16–20)

I once played the simplest psychodramatic coda on this moment of their final loss and change. I put men and women back into partners. After reading them the passage, I invited each man to look into the eyes of his partner and simply say, in his own time: "Eve, you are the mother of all life." I asked each woman receiving the name to hear the tone in which Adam spoke.

"Eve, you are the mother of all life."
"I hear your awe."
"Eve, you are the mother of all life."
"I hear your envy."
"Eve, you are the mother of all life."
"I hear your bitterness."
"Eve, you are the mother of all life."
"I hear your loneliness."

In naming her, Adam makes her Other. He names but cannot claim her. All his tones of address speak of a distance between them. In the world after Eden she is the mother of all life, but who is he?

❀ ❀ ❀

The myth of Eden and its loss has the status of a paradigm. In it the patriarchal imagination organizes time into epochs. History mimics myth; we imagine golden ages and dark ages, ages of enlightenment and ages of alienation. According to the patriarchal imagination of history, the past is seen as a time closer to wholeness and revelation, and the present as a wilderness and an exile. But this fable of the garden and its loss may also be understood in the light of more contemporary theories about gender psychology. Eden and exile can be seen also as a paradigm for the development of male infants into boys.[3]

This perspective addresses the question, What does it mean for a boy-child to have been born out of the womb of a woman and what is it like for him to realize at a certain age that he must leave her? In this separation dawns the realization of male otherness; however dim and gradual this knowledge, it becomes a cardinal fact of life. As small boys we awaken to the fact and the fate of gender; it comes with our sense of identity. We see the serpent, and it speaks to us. It is our sexuality and the sign of our exclusion from the person in all the world we are closest to, who is the most powerful and precious to us, whose warmth and touch are life itself, whose rebuke is as terrible as death. This one—in our small eyes she is the Great Mother—is also woman, and we can never be like her.

The knowledge of otherness, like a kind of primary rejection, sends us into the company of boys and men, among whom we seek to establish an identity, surrogate bonds, symbolic connections, experiences of connectedness. We turn toward the Father. In the loss of our identity with the mother may lie the seeds of misogyny, for our loss feels like an unjust rejection, a deprivation for which we—like Adam—were never fully responsible. This loss wasn't what we wanted. It came about through some business between the woman and the serpent.

On the level of gender this is one of the many meanings of the Garden of Eden story. Eden is a metaphor for the time we were enfolded by an abundant, sustaining, maternal nature—before time, before words, before the knowledge of twoness, before we suspected any difference between male and female, before the appearance of Eve, before the serpent. This was the time of our first universe, when we lived in the long Sabbath morning of the seventh day. The Father had not yet appeared. He had not yet spoken. He had not yet divided us from ourselves and sent us, divided, out to search for Him, to forge our bonds, and to know ourselves as sons.

By comparison the daughters of Eve have available to them the unbroken continuity of an identity as female. That identity—that sense of sameness—issues from the mother and survives all their life in their womanhood. Daughters need never leave the feminine; they cannot. Within its vast realm of roles and powers they find their place in a sisterhood with all women. This sense of identity is given; it cannot be taken away. In a certain sense the daughter remains in the garden.

I remember a Sunday in May when my daughter, then thirteen, and I had just come back from swimming at the local Y. She had gone into the house, and I had taken up the paper and was sitting outside in the friendly sunshine of spring. I heard the front door open, but because I was engrossed in what I was reading, it took me a moment to realize that she had come to stand in front of me, quietly waiting for my attention. I looked up. I can still see her, with her arms at her sides, her hands lightly clasped in front of her. "Dad," she said to me, "I'm having my first period." I began to weep.

In that moment I had a kind of waking vision. It seemed I saw crowded on that empty lawn a great host of spirit-women; they were holding their arms out to her; and they were calling her into their company. They nodded to her. I seemed to see her gathered in to an immemorial sisterhood, fertile, planetary, ancient. My heart was lifted up for her as if in this moment I had seen her crowned. I wept because she trusted to tell me, because she was in that instant precious and in her dawn, and I wept because she was already disappearing, leaving me, leaving childhood. I watched her go, even as she stood still before me, poised, watching my tears, coming over to, yes, comfort me.

"Daddy," she said, "Daddy," and I felt my daughter was holding me as if I were her child.

Years later now, having fathered a son and watched him careen through his early adolescence, noting the appearance under his bed of *Playboy* and other carnal pamphlets, seeing his jaw lengthen and hearing his voice shift, I am struck by the difference, for him and for me, of this coming of age. He, too, leaves me, but it seems to me that he enters into his adolescence as into a great loneliness, a wilderness full of mind-and-world demons. He withdraws into a silence in which I cannot reach him. No company of men, no universal brotherhood awaits him. Biology, already private and focused in his privates, holds no special promises for him. For him there will be no accords with the moon or the tides. Gender is the thinnest reed of identity for him to lean on. When he looks inside for images of manhood, what does he see? A welter of contradictions.

And me, his father, what can he make of me? He knows I love him, but he knows in his bones—we both do—how different we are and that the world I have made for myself will not be his world. We are gender companions, but we are strangers. The distances that hang between us seem fixed. The odd awkwardnesses and silences remind us that we are bound and apart. And at the very moment he enters his biological manhood, the need to separate himself from me begins to assert itself. There has been too little time and too few occasions to develop a language, words, and activities within which to explore who we are together. I have hardly said hello to him when I am saying my good-byes.

These conceptions of gender difference parallel certain masculine speculations. Somewhere in the depths of man's old reptilian brain, far below the threshold of memory, are lodged scenes from the time before we knew that our seed was necessary to human birth. In that cave time there was as yet no Great Father to dignify our creative life. We had not yet conceived of Him conceiving us. Then woman was the central mystery. Magically she grew round and burst. Blood and life spilled from her as she thrashed and cried, surrounded by her sisters. Her breasts were full of milk, and every child born to her, male and female, depended on her for life. She was the holy of holies. The place in her we entered for our brief ecstasy was the same place where new life came spilling into the world. We feared and revered her, and somewhere in that cave of ourselves we still sit eying her in terror and awe. We still feel the extent of our insignificance. Our powerlessness. She is forever Eve, the "mother of all life." What can we be to her? Out of that primate cave we begin to hatch our ambivalent romanticism about her, our desire to serve *and* subdue her, our wonder *and* our rage.

In my personal history with women—starting with my mother, step-mother, girls and girlfriends, wives, colleagues, therapists, and women whom I have taken as "sisters"—I see the strange patterns of my distance and pursuit, my longing and mistrust. Only relatively recently, as I sat with my wife, Susan, in a state of unusual openness, did I realize with a rending astonishment that I carried in my bones some deep sense that she was my enemy. Yet my heart knew, my experience told me, that this was not true about her. How ancient and hidden had been that fear and guardedness. It went back not only to my sense of abandonment when I was eleven and my mother left me to go to California. It went back into the years of my small furies at my mother and my fascination with and dread of my dad. And earlier still, it may go back to the dimmest memories I have of a darkened room, bad smells, crib bars, and the head-filling, body-wracking sound of my own cries. I am screaming, "Maaameee!" and my mother does not come. Perhaps, in this Myth of the Lost Garden, patriarchy reflects those early and inevitable experiences of a separation felt as loss.

Here again the ultimate myopia of gender knowledge presents itself. My daughter, reading my account in these pages, protests that I romanticize women. "Dad," she says to me, "you are *choosing* to imagine something we don't necessarily feel. I think women can feel as lonely, isolated, and exiled—to use your words—as men. Maybe that's part of why women have accepted these patriarchal myths; they mean something to us, too."

Perhaps she is right; I don't know. Is gender incidental or essential? Am I, in the end, projecting my own anomie first on all men in my culture and then back into these old myths? Or am I letting these old myths tell me something about what they think it means to be a man? I don't know, and I can never know in this blind alley of gender speculation. What I do know is that even in its ending, the Myth of the Lost Garden hints that this is, uniquely, a man's story and a man's fate.

A sense of loss and loneliness fills the ending of the garden story as the human exiles go forth into a world of pain and death, cursed to toil and to suffer childbirth. We are told that man, even in his exile with woman, is still alone.

> *Therefore the Lord God (Adonai Elohim) sent him forth from the garden of Eden, to till the ground whence he was taken. So He drove out the man; and He placed at the east of the garden of Eden cherubim and a flaming sword to guard the way to the tree of life. (3:23–24)*

Only Adam is mentioned in the expulsion. From what follows we know that Eve has left with him. Yet it seems for a moment, or at least from his point of view, that he has been driven out without her. In his distracted state he feels alone again.

I submit the ending to my group. What truths are buried in these lines? They offer a kaleidoscope of interpretive possibilities.

"There is something so self-centered about Adam," says one Eve. "He has to feel this whole thing is about him. I am invisible to him. I go trailing after him. He goes to make a world, and in the world he makes I will be, as I am now, invisible."

"But, Eve, this is the way it felt to me. I felt not only that I was alone but that you remained back there. You were connected in my mind both with the garden and with its loss. Things were never the same between us."

"But I don't remain behind. Why do you insist I am so different? Why do you think that your feeling of loss and loneliness are so peculiar to you. Is feeling that you are the real and ultimate victim the only way you can feel special?"

"But," says a different Eve, "I do bring the garden with me. I *am* the mother of all life. I have the fullness of the earth and the power to bear children inside me. I can be complete with myself. I remain eternally and casually connected to God. You and your sons will make all sorts of covenants with God. But I don't need them, and I do not need you as you need me."

"I am Eve," speaks another. "I not only ate of the tree of the knowledge of good and evil; I ate also of the tree of eternal life. But that fruit I never brought to Adam. Some aspect of me, the eternal mother, the eternal questing feminine, rides time while all the Adams die."

"I am the serpent. Eve, you stay with me. Forever. I have a part of you. Your fascination with me is coeval with your self-awareness. No man will ever touch you there, for I was there before any man. And no single man, no Adam, will ever be enough for you. And, Adam, you know this. I had her, and I have her. She is connected to me as daughter to mother, as sister to sister, as lover-woman to lover-woman. You will never possess her, know her, or empower her as I have. In your jealousy and insecurity you will only try to dominate her and silence me."

"I am God. Who speaks to me? I have nothing. I look back on the garden with a nostalgia greater than yours. It was for me a time of union and communion. Now it is merely a plot of earth. I guard it, but I cannot enjoy it. After all, I made it for them. Now it is empty."

"I am God," says another. "I never realized human freedom would so baffle my dreams of a sweet creation."

"I am God," says a third. "My only companion now is the serpent; he is the only one who remains in the garden. He is my shadow and my shame; he never lets me forget that he has defeated me. The garden has become my lonely hell."

In such ways we variously imagine the ending of the Myth of the Lost Garden. I am left understanding how deep a loneliness is constructed into the myth and permeates it. I find its resonance in myself. Perhaps it is because of this loneliness that I am driven to make these postpatriarchal midrashim, to make them seem important to myself, to stand upon them as on some dedicated piece of earth, to draw others into a broken circle to play out fragments of an old story. Perhaps this is my bulwark against the inanity of loneliness.

Is it possible to tolerate this loneliness face-to-face? Are all myths the necessary denials of the void? For a moment a void behind the myth opens up as an endless space. This is the void that existed before God began to form His creation; the void out of which God first recognized man's loneliness; and the void into which Adam and Eve walk as into their exile. Now they are shrouded in a loneliness all the more sharp because they can remember their union. That loneliness must be laced with fear, given the unmapped and unhorizoned worldscape that extends before them. All they know is loss.

In the end it is loss, and loss of the most profound and consequential sort, that provides the deep theme for the Eden story in particular and for the Book of Genesis as a whole. The patriarchal imagination that constructed these stories has formed them out of some tragic sense of estrangement and loneliness. Beneath its variations, loss is the lesson for the generations of Adam whose myths are told in the dim world we enter after the gates of Eden close.

3

Eve: A Midrash

Prologue

As I have said already, part of my postpatriarchal agenda is to recognize the gender distortions of Genesis and to attempt, if not to rectify the canonized text, then at least to use midrash as a way to comment on the canon and to elicit new possibilities from it. As a reader I want both to respect the integrity of a tradition and to make it supple to new interpretive values.

The story of the garden is so focused on masculine experience that in the expulsion we hardly see Eve. At its close, it looks for a moment as if Eve is not with Adam when he is "driven out." In some sense she has become invisible; or she is left behind. Women will not figure again until the stories of Abraham, ten chapters later. Though a crucial element in the family dramas that occupy the central section of Genesis, woman is largely confined to marital and maternal quarters. Decisive in her influence on her sons, she still plays only a supporting role.

As much as anything this shutting out of the feminine accounts for the painful loneliness that the biblical myth-theology proposes as man's fate. The structure of normative Judaism, and Christianity to a lesser extent, followed the biblical lead. Only recently are women being allowed to bring their spirituality to the pulpits, their ideas to the seminary, their books to the publishers, and their revisionist energy to the patriarchal forms.

My response to the emergence of a feminist discourse into the old patriarchal arena is complex. I feel some jealous sense of having my turf invaded. Yet I recognize the masculine-centered assumptions, legislations, and repressions fostered by the old-time religions. I deplore the abuses of patriarchy.

Women have sought full legitimacy and inclusion; women have opened up dimensions of the tradition that can only make it fuller.

Further, I feel that for thousands of years patriarchy has asked women to imagine God through a masculine perspective, to admire and to be taught by men and by those mythic masculine figures—patriarchs, prophets, saviors, and liberators—through whom men have constructed the myth-theology of the West. At this juncture I am challenged to reverse roles. I want to find my way into the female figures of the patriarchal narratives. To do so is to send my imagination toward the female and, if not to imagine a matriarchal cosmology, then at least to imagine the patriarchal universe through a woman's eyes. Men may find my midrash plausible; women may find it ridiculous; and in the end such an attempt may only confirm how locked I am within my gender. But as a man I can project my imagination toward Eve as both the female other and a lost part of my own psychic world.

❀   ❀   ❀

He has gone ahead of me. He will not look back. But . . . I do. There is so much to remember, and some of it is faint, distant, already breaking up like clouds.

There was one before me. Her name was Lilith; she was the last queen of the Great Mother. *She* was in the beginning before His beginning, when the rites of the moon and blood were the central sacred mysteries, and when the female imagination celebrated the earth as Mother and our wisdom was as deep as the oak roots and as subtle as the herbs we cultivated, which could give life, death, sleep, and ecstasy. In Lilith's time even woman did not yet fully understand the source of the life that grew inside her, and yet when she gave birth, in the squalling agony, men cowered in the shadows by the firelight and trembled.

The poetry and magic of Lilith are gone, and gone are the secrets women knew before the coming of the Great Father. On some days when I was alone in Eden—and there were many, for Adam wandered in the cool of the day lost in his own immensities of thought, talking aloud to air—I heard in the wind a sigh, and it was for me a sigh of the Great Mother herself languishing as if in exile. At other times it seemed to me the wind was the warm assurance of her breath. I was alone indeed and afraid, for I was the first woman conceived of by the Great Father; I was a new idea of womanhood itself, an idea that lived in the mind of a man. I was the form of that idea, its first embodiment. I wandered in a world so different from the world that Lilith knew that I could not describe even to myself what I saw or felt.

My loneliness was inconceivable. And yet I had been chosen, for it seemed to me in the sleep I slept before I was, and in the dream I dreamed before I woke, that Lilith came to me, herself. She was clothed in the majesty of the Goddess, and the moon crowned her dark hair. She looked at me with a mother's tenderness; there were tears in her eyes.

"My child," she said to me in that dream, "a new age is coming. A new force is being born into the world. It is the age of the Father. It is his time. In the Father a new world waits to be born. His fertility is different from ours; his creations are different; his will upon the earth is different, but it is his time to come. And you, my child, have been chosen to be born into his new world. You are our emissary and our sacrifice, but you will be his child, too. You will recognize that there is a Father, and you will live under the sway of his reign. You will carry our secrets with you and pass them on as best you can, but you will also be learning his secrets.

"We weep for you; we praise you; we will be with you, but only inwardly. You will not see us as you have seen us; you will see as the Father will teach you to see, with different eyes. You will remember us as you remember a dream."

And so I woke, and I saw Adam, and I was the first woman who ever saw the beauty of a man, naked and clean. I was the first woman to know that man is a mystery, deep, and complex, and separate, and alone. I was the first woman to feel in her heart that there is a kind of god in man. I loved that man, Adam, and in him I loved his God, and I knew that something of his God was in me, too, for even as I gazed on Adam while he slept, I was being filled with a new language. The old language, Lilith's language, was passing away, dissolving now into the songs of birds, which were sweet but becoming unintelligible to me. I heard the wind in the trees, but it no longer spoke; it seemed to be the sigh of Lilith bidding me farewell.

My energy was drawn upward into my eyes and ears and outward to my fingers. My head was filling with light, and I felt myself now stirred by an infinite curiosity, as if I had awakened safe on an enchanted island where everything was both strange and familiar, old and new. *Curiosity* is too small a word for what I felt. I was in a new world, and it longed to be known, or I longed to know it. At the same time, I was alone.

So it was devised, I suppose, that I should be alone with him, and that I should be moved by him. He slept as my child, my lover, my husband, my

friend, my enemy. I knew something he would never know, for my body's secrets still spoke in the ancient language no man ever knows; but I knew, too,
that I did not know everything. As I was awakening into this new world, I realized there were many things to know. I wished to know them, and I knew that
Adam, when he woke, would wake to me and to the world around me. He
would wish to know me, and I would wish to know him, and to know that I
knew, and to speak of it, to sing of it. I knew that he could be awakened from
his sleep. Now. I knew that he could be roused into curiosity and appetite. So
with my hand, gently at first, for he still slept, I reached out softly to rouse him.

About that serpent? Ah, well. In the beginning was the deviousness of God the
Great Father. You must understand something. Truly nothing is as it seems nor
can ever be known for what it is. This is the first law of the Great Father, and
all his stories tell the same thing. Men are at best half-seeing, half-blind. They
insist on attempting to explain the world and so often forget the world is beyond their explanation. They have made up a God who works beyond them
and through them, who has designs and projects infinitely difficult to realize.
They have, these men, invented history, and time, and past and present and future. They have created a great cosmic artifice within which they labor, while
knowing all the while that they are locked inside their own vast misconcep-
tion. I admire their works, and they appall me. Men are most dangerous when
they are most sure of themselves.

   In that universe where nothing can be fully known or seen for what it
really is—or if seen, only momentarily, only so fleetingly that what is known
remains merely a kind of image of the knowable—men build and batter and
destroy in a kind of ceaseless frenzy. A deep fear lives in them, the knowledge,
in their bones, that they are strangers and that the world is strange. Their stories are full of the strange; they seek to make the strange familiar, but it will
never be familiar. And they are afraid—of the deviousness of mystery; of
death; of losing the little knowledge they have gained, which they put on like
armor. They are afraid of the very Mystery they have devised. They get lost in
the deviousness of the riddle they have made.

   So the serpent. Another inexplicable reality. Another image of what
teases man, comes from him, and is yet split off from him. I was not afraid of
the serpent. Adam was frightened. The serpent was something else he could
not understand. But the serpent spoke to me, and I understood. It offered
what I wanted: knowledge of the nature of the Great Father, a glimpse of His
doubleness. And the serpent was the Father's own emissary, the duplicitous
shall/shall-not through which He riddles us. Oh, He is a Great Riddler; it

seems only women can really laugh at this God. Men curse this God of theirs; they praise, supplicate, analyze Him; they turn away, they turn toward, they seek, they lose Him; they build great houses and books and systems in which to capture Him. But they never dare laugh at God. They dare not find Him funny in His infinite seriousness. Ah, well. There was, thank God, the serpent.

And the curse. Well, that too. But, you know, to say a thing is not to make it so. Our childbirth is not easy; it never was. But the exultant joy, the great sunrising glory of birth, the mystery of that act which is ours alone and which no Great Father can, in all His fecundity, ever replicate or replace— well, it never could be, can be, or will be cursed. And you will see in the stories the Great Father dictates to his sons, you will see how it is the mothers who decide the course of things. The powers of the fathers and the sons are great, to be sure. But my sisters have their powers, too. Sarah, Hagar, Rebecca, Rachel, Leah, Bilhah, Zilpah, Deborah, Dinah, Tamar, Asenath—these are the few names that remain, but see what they did, how the history of the Father turns on their acts. Listen deep into the stories for their voices. Like women in the world of the Father, they live in the spaces between the words, men's words, but in those spaces you will hear them tell a different story. If you have the heart to hear.

So now we leave this garden. It was our first home. If we find it again, I think we shall find it between us or inside us. The cherubim who guard the way are terrible; the flaming sword is fierce. I see only Adam's back as he strides forward. He seems now to be rushing away from the garden and from me. I feel his anger. His blame covers me like a cloud. He will not look back, and he will not look in. He does not look up, either to cry out or to challenge the God who devised our undoing. He looks only ahead of him, toward the future. It's the future that he lives for. And for me already a kind of forgetting is falling on my mind like dusk. Eden seems more and more a dream, only fragments of which I can remember.

I must hurry now. Night is coming. There's no moon, and already my husband is disappearing into the dark.

4

The Myths of the
Generations of Adam and Eve

The Myth of the Murdering Brother

The darkness that shrouds Adam and Eve after Eden is the darkness of linear time. Before the fruit was devoured, time turned on itself like a wheel, with Eden its luminous center. In the garden consciousness was undivided and innocent of death; masculine and feminine were "one flesh." After the expulsion Adam and Eve are separate. They step into a different temporal reality, call it history, where time bears each life inevitably toward death.

In the reality of linear time no one ever gets a chance to go back and do it again. Once the apple has been eaten, Eve cannot unswallow it; once he has shared it with her, Adam cannot disengage his fate from hers; once they know they are naked, neither of them can return to the innocence before their "eyes were opened." Within this construct of linear time the patriarchal imagination dwells unflinchingly on choice as its central existential concern: What do we do? How do we act when time is so unforgiving?

According to patriarchy, the human being, created in the image of God, is endowed with free will. This is the great conception and conceit, for in reality that freedom, as we live it, is everywhere hedged with necessity, underpinned by inexorable and unconscious nature, and headed toward oblivion. Yet freedom is the noble claim patriarchy makes for the human creature. Freedom's limits cannot be known before essaying them; its price cannot be estimated before the expenditure of action.

As a being born into linear time and possessing free will, I act and then experience the implications of my actions. In linear time acts have consequences. Some of these consequences may be foreseen, others not. If I could foresee all consequences, I would be free of the anguish of choosing and the painful repercussions of my choice. My freedom would be absolute and almost perfectly safe. I would never make a mistake; I would never feel remorse. The only tragedy would be death.

But such is not the case. The pain and irony of linear time come from the fact that I will too often learn too late what I needed to know before I acted. I cannot take back what I did. I can never bathe in the same river twice. In this way, moved along in linear time, I live out my freedom at a great and constant risk. With the future always hidden, with the present moment always inflected by the past, I struggle among choices. This imperfect present moment in which I choose is all the time I have, and for what I do in that present I am responsible.

This burden of responsibility is the burden patriarchy imagines we all bear in linear time. To take responsibility is the source of our moral dignity and courage: We suffer our choices; we celebrate them also. But to take responsibility is all the more noble when we recognize at the same time we are not in control of life. Life in linear time is too complex for us to master; it is laced with the unpredictable, and our own souls are part of what we can never fully apprehend. In this world of partial revelation we are finally alone when it comes time to choose.

But the patriarchy of Genesis proposes a God who, in some inscrutable way, participates with us in time. We are not alone, as the existentialist is alone, in the void. If there were no God, then man would be the measure of all things and our acts would carry all meaning. But the universe that patriarchy imagines has a divine force in it that interacts with the human, not so much setting limits to our freedom as seeking to express its own dream with and through us. God as Imagination needs the imagination of the human being for the construction of a world. This longing of a lonely God for a covenant with His creation comes from God; it begins as His need, not man's. We have already seen the gestures of that lonely God in the acts of creation. Now, in what I am calling the Myths of the Generations of Adam and Eve, we watch the attempts of God to participate in human history, to forge a connection with human fate, to educate, accept, and open the human soul to its divine affiliation. Human beings are all too real to God; God searches for ways to become real to us.

I have called the world Adam and Eve enter after Eden dark in part because they cannot see into the future or into themselves. But I call that world dark for another reason. The very first episode in linear time is the story of Cain

and Abel. It stands as a frontispiece to all the tales that are to follow, as if patriarchy were saying to us, and perhaps more directly to men: This is the cardinal
myth, the central issue in linear time. I call it the Myth of the Murdering
Brother, and a darker tale would be hard to find. In it choice is again the central drama. And here choice is viewed as a struggle within oneself, a kind of
wrestling. In this tale, as in the story of the garden, the consequence of choice
is mortal. In it, as before, the weight of responsibility for action is laid
painfully in our own hands, while the purpose of God's actions, the ways of
chance or circumstance, are shrouded in His mystery.

❀ ❀ ❀

No religion that sought merely to glorify its god or to project a noble image of
man would retain such a tale as this one of Cain and Abel. Genesis lays it out
with characteristic brevity.

"And Adam knew Eve his wife, and she conceived and bore Cain" (4:1).
She had a second son, Abel. Of their childhood we know nothing. As young
men Cain became a farmer, Abel a shepherd. In time Cain, prompted by what
we are never told, brought an offering of "the fruit of the ground to God"(4:3);
Abel then brought "the best of his flock" (4:4) as an offering to God. God paid
heed to, respected, looked favorably on the offering of Abel, but not on the offering of Cain. And, it is written, "Cain's countenance fell" (4:5).

Reading his dismay, the Lord told Cain to get a grip on himself (4:7), but
Cain did not. In the very next verse we are told that Cain took his brother out
into a field and killed him. Afterward the Lord said to Cain, "Where is Abel
your brother?" Cain answered, "I don't know. Am I my brother's keeper?" (4:9).

But God heard Abel's "blood crying out from the ground" (4:10), and
He cursed Cain, consigning him to a life of endless wandering, "a fugitive and
a vagabond over the earth" (4:12), but God also marked him in some special
way so that men would know that though cursed, he is also protected.

After Adam, Cain is the second patriarchal figure in the Bible; the lineage of his sons and grandsons is listed along with their achievements. His son
Enoch was said to have built the first city. Several generations later Lamech,
like Cain a murderer, fathers three sons. These three are Jabal, the father of all
those who dwell in tents and have cattle; Jubal, the father of all those who play
the harp and organ; and Tubal-Cain, who first wrought things into brass and
iron. Lamech, the murderer, and his fruitful sons are the last mention of Cain
and his descendants.

Cain's story takes us to a deep stratum of the patriarchal psyche and its
meditation on imagination. So powerful is the energy in this myth that, in a

figurative sense, it pushes the female off the stage. Though women admit to their own competitiveness with one another, that rivalry is played out on an entirely different level. What arcs between Cain and Abel is primal, and it seems hardwired into the male psyche. Though I cannot call Cain's murderous impulse "instinctual" in the classic sense of the word, it arises in him as a force he is unable or unwilling to resist. As we shall see from the language used to describe it, his raw aggression seems something that comes from his deepest nature, not yet transformed or sublimated by culture.

It is one of the triumphs of patriarchal self-reflection to give this force of fraternal violence so vivid a representation. It sees this violence as a perpetual threat to all efforts to construct a human culture and sacred covenant. Like nature itself, which can and will obliterate all human creation, this primal force can rise through man to destroy his works. This force embodied and exemplified in Cain is the free human imagination entangled in human passion, fantasy fused with power. The fusion of these elements is so potent that it can deprive God of His chosen son. Cain, the murderer, brings the lethal into the world; he incarnates its blind, relentless energy.

In the midrashic enactments I have guided, the build-up to the encounter of the brothers begins as Cain and Abel are moved in their manhood to bring offerings to the Lord. Cain, "in the course of time" comes first.

Who will be Cain? I ask. And almost always there is a long pause, for we have heard the story, and it takes a certain courage and energy for a person to dive deep enough to find and feel that part of himself. I wait. After a while, several members of the group stand up—not all men—and step forward, often with a shrug or a sigh, an anxious glance. And who will be Abel? Again a pause; again there are volunteers. I need someone, too, to play God.

Why, I ask Cain when we have cleared a space in the center for our drama, why do you make an offering? Where does this idea come from?

The first Cain speaks. "So often I heard my parents speak of the garden. I could feel their longing. When it came time for me to contribute to the family, I became a tiller of the soil. I have tried to make a garden for them. It took time, but now I have plants and trees that yield good things to eat, and fruit. Yes, even fruit."

"In my heart," says another Cain, "I compete with God. This garden is my way to make a substitute paradise for my parents. I shall show God that we can bring forth abundance even out of the ground He cursed."

"I bring my offering to show God what I have done. I myself. It is a display of my power to understand the processes of nature, how to sow and plant and harvest."

"No, no, this is not true at all. This offering is not egotism; it is made in a gesture of peace and reconciliation. My father has not spoken to the Lord since he left Eden, but he has told me stories, and I hope that by my offering God will return to communicate with my parents."

And there is Abel, listening, eying his older brother from a distance.

Why, I ask, are you here?

"I, too, must make some showing before the Lord. But what do I have? Nothing I have made with my hands, only what the Lord has given into my keeping. But among what I have I shall select the best."

And another Abel speaks: "There is a part of me that does not want to be left out of this. I am often alone on the hills with the flocks while Cain is close to home. Often I feel left out. But not now. What if the Lord appears and I am not there to see Him? Cain will get some reward, and I shall get nothing."

A third Abel speaks: "Out there alone on the hills I feel close to God. Especially at night under the stars. I hear things in the wind and see things glint and dart in the heavens, and my soul has been drawn out of me into that warm darkness. Many times I have felt a rapture. But never until I saw my brother bring his offering did I think to give something back to the infinite Mystery from which all life comes."

Silence. The brothers stand, at first attempting to ignore one another. We wait to see what will happen.

Spontaneously Cain turns. "Copycat," he says. "Take your bleating sheep off somewhere else. This is my spot; this was my idea."

"I can stand wherever I please. It's a free country."

"Not here."

"What a sorry-looking bunch of vegetables. That's sheep food."

"You let your sheep wander one more time into my garden, and I'll kill them."

"What do you know about butchering, garden man? I slaughter the sheep for our feasts, not you."

"What else do you do with your sheep, boy, out there all by yourself?"

On the other side of this last insult are oaths, menace, and the threat of a premature enactment of what the myth delays until God has stepped in to tilt the balance. I hold the brothers apart and motion to the actor playing God. He enters and puts an arm around Abel and slowly draws him aside, and then both turn their backs on Cain. Abel, looking somewhat apprehensively over his shoulder, laughs. Nothing is said. The silence weighs on us as Cain, seeing God and Abel move aside, watches them for a moment, then looks down. His eyes are hooded, and he seems to be looking deep inside himself.

Turning to the group-as-audience I ask, What do you imagine is going on inside Cain?
"I hear the silent roar of his anger."
    "I see him trying to figure out what he did wrong."
    "He's examining his whole life, searching for an answer."
    "I feel him hating God."
    "I see the wheels of revenge beginning to turn."
    "He wants to punish God."
    "He feels he has lost his brother. He is alone."
    And the text tells us that "Cain's countenance fell, and he was enraged" (4:5).
    God turns at this moment and delivers lines that even in the best translation seem a little obscure.

> And the Lord said to Cain, "Why are you distressed and why is your face fallen?
> If you do right, there is an exaltation for you. But if you do not do right, then
> sin crouches at the door. Its urge is for you. Yet you can be its master." (4:6–7)

In Hebrew the verb here translated as "crouches" carries strong associations of the animal. Elsewhere in the Bible the same Hebrew word is translated as "brood," "crouch on all fours," "lurk," even "lie in ambush," as if for prey. This predatory danger reminds me of the serpent in the garden. There it was the external personification of some external force that had not yet entered the soul of man; here, internalized in Cain, it lies concealed in metaphor. But this force is not nature, though it is given nature's imagery; it is the human imagination charged with human passion into the fantasy, then the act, of revenge. It is masculine eros wedded to death.

The Lord points Cain to his interior world, where some part of him waits for the chance to spring. But Cain is told that he can master this passion. In Hebrew, *master* is the same word that was used when man was first given mastery (dominion) over nature (in Hebrew *mashal*). Here the Myth of the Murdering Brother bears down on the psychodrama of choice. God tells Cain clearly that he has the power to choose, that two natures vie for his will. One side is mastery and exaltation; the other side is sin and bestiality. Between them Cain is pulled.

This internal drama illustrates a kind of wrestling we shall see in many forms in the patriarchal narrative. Cain's rage and sense of rejection are so strong that he cannot hold out against his desire for revenge. The beast that crouches springs, and Cain is consumed. But for a moment—and even for longer, depending on the interval one imagines between the end of verse 7 and the beginning of verse 8 in which Cain takes his brother into the field and kills him—he wrestles. Or something wrestles within him.

But Cain does not possess the will or, perhaps more accurately, the *mind* to resist. He chooses to yield. The promise of an exaltation is not strong enough to fortify him against the immediate and savage satisfaction of his revenge. He hates this God too much to bend his knee. As Eve and Adam gave in to a temptation in the garden, so Cain gives in to a temptation here, and in giving in an enormous energy is released.

> *And they went out into the field, and Cain rose up against his brother and slew him. (4:8)*

I have seen that energy in psychodramas where the wounded Cain seeks out Abel, and the two players unleash toward each other their pent-up jealousies. Although these passions are focused in the biblical figures, they draw their energy from the lives of the men and women who can play the parts. Any of us can play Cain, the wounded elder sibling supplanted by the younger brother; any of us can play Abel, who can't refrain from rubbing it in. Everyone can find a heart of darkness where the primitive power to murder is lodged.

In one psychodrama Cain guilefully lures Abel away from camp. Serpent-mind taught him all the right provocations. Catching his brother off guard, Cain suddenly rises up and seizes him. Now the buried metaphor of wrestling becomes explicit. The two brothers grapple at the center of the circle. They strain against each other, while the men and women around the edge are shouting the words they imagine crackling unspoken in the air between the antagonists. They narrate with curses and cries. They root for one and then for the other.

In our psychodrama we open up to the blood lust in the myth. Heated by the encounter before us and fed by our private memories of injustices and wounds, we give vent to the oldest outrage, to our primitive selfishness, our fierce sadism. Our words are whips and cries. We leap in the circle around Cain and Abel. We don't see one another clearly; we don't even see the wrestlers now; we are inside with our own demons. The raw energy has its own frenzy to it. It builds, and when Cain at last has Abel under him and has his hands around his brother's throat, we could be in Madison Square Garden with two heavyweights pounding each other to the mat in the late rounds, or in the Roman amphitheater with blood on the sand. Here is Romulus slaying Remus under the sign of the wolf. We have the killing cry in our own throats. We have reached Cain.

I call the psychodrama to a halt. I am afraid of what I have set going. I am afraid we have already gone too far. I had begun with a certain empirical curiosity, but the beast inside the business mastered me. I had lost my cool. I was back for a moment in my own childhood when, left alone at home, I watched wrestling matches on our primitive black-and-white TV and felt a charge in which sex, blood, and murderousness were all confused. I have let my players get too close to the point of no return. I feel ashamed.

Chests heaving, drenched in sweat, the two actors lie still on the floor. The men and women in the group slowly return to themselves from the outskirts of whatever mad place each has dared to visit. How thin is the veneer of our civilization, I think, and what is this animal that rises up just under its rational surface? Millions of years from the apes, and we are back in the jungle in a leap and a cry. And we *like* it there. The toxic rush is still in our veins.

I am not the only one to feel ashamed. As we regain our composure, men look down at the floor and cannot meet one another's eyes. Many of the women, who had been pushed aside or who had backed away, glance at one another with expressions of alarm. Not all, though, for this dark eros is in the end no respecter of gender. Women know Cain, too. No one touches anyone. There has been a certain horror, too, that steals in on us, and a kind of awe before which we feel small and afraid. The text's image of sin, coiled in wait and eying us from just outside the doorway of reason, feels nearer and more real to us. We have personified it, or have been possessed by it. The wild, we reflect, has many faces; this one sobers us. We contain it in a fragile cage.

I look back at the story and my eye settles on Cain's question to God after he is accused of his brother's murder. I read it aloud, for it is one of patriarchy's central questions: *Am I my brother's keeper?* This question curls like the tail of a serpent through the entire Genesis narrative, slides past it into the later biblical stories of brothers, into the life of Christ and his disciples, and outward into history. It hisses through civil and religious wars, through deafening riots in cities, and through the quiet treachery of partnerships. It rattles in our passionate paranoia, our terror of scarcity, our ambitions, and our drives for greatness at the expense of others. *Am I my brother's keeper? Can I be?* The questions are alive in the room right now.

It would appear that human beings, men in particular perhaps, have answered it in the negative. Linear time, human history, is full of murdered brothers and murderous fraternities. Every *ism* (individualism, capitalism, feminism, fascism, imperialism, sexism, evangelism, racism, etc.) is spun from some implicit certainty that my group is better than yours. Every *ism* leads in the end to its opposite and to a struggle of opposites that mirrors on a large scale the wrestle of Cain and Abel. In that war the sense of brother-keeping is lost in the frenzy of self-righteousness. In that frenzy the beast of our unmastered egotism strikes and swallows us.

But let me speak for a moment only of myself. Who are my brothers in my life right now? One is Larry; he is my best friend in a brotherhood now almost twenty years old. I have celebrated our comradeship in poetry, and we have been meticulous about addressing the rents and tears our kinship has sustained through circumstance and misadventure. But turn the tapestry over. Look at the backside of the weave, and you would see the way competitiveness works in the fabric. It is not only present in obvious ways, as when we hammer at each other on the racquetball court. It is more subtle. Admiration and jealousy slide over each other constantly; love and fear; the issues of dominance are at play in any conversation. We take positions with one another; we stoke our disagreements; they are the friction of our friendship. Yet these disagreements are ways we push off one another, an endless wrestle in which, if we never draw blood, we always keep score. Our intimacy is not merely hedged by homophobia, it is laced with the he-goat's claim on his rocky perch. We have flirted with the same women and keep our secret tallies. Our friendship is full of warmth, but its heat comes from the same fire that has, time out of mind, turned the best of friends into the worst of enemies.

The story of Cain may be ancient, rising from the substrate of our instinctual drives, but it reduces to the starkest terms the question of brother-keeping that men through culture, law, education, and, most of all, through spirituality seek to answer and affirm. Where is the *yes* beyond our public lip service? Enacted with one's body and whole heart, that *yes* is hard to come by. It is the everlasting *yes* of a Martin Luther King, Jr., or a Mother Teresa, figures whose spiritual roots go back to the soil of biblical patriarchy. That *yes* is ours each time we graciously go about the work of brother-keeping; but each of us knows, if we examine our hearts, just how rare and difficult such work is.

Cain, whatever he represents, is the name the patriarchal imagination gives to a part of itself; it does not shrink from looking at him. Nor in Genesis is Cain a rectified man. He goes into exile unrepentant and unreformed. He does not die; he is still alive and well and living in my heart. After more than fifty years I know him well, and I still feel ashamed of him, still feel the danger of admitting him into the light of my awareness. He is still wandering as a fugitive and a vagabond, licking the wounds of his primal rejection by a capricious Fate. He is the first outlaw, and he has the outlaw's ferocity. His genes are potent, everlasting. In the story of Cain and his descendants cities rise; there are glints of the first smeltings of hard ores; wild pastoral peoples roam; the first sound of pipes is heard, the first music.

Strange, isn't it, that disobedience leads again to imaginative creation. Adam and Eve eat of the tree; they fabricate garments. Cain slays his brother, lies to God, and gets cursed into exile, but his seed gives rise to inventions that advance the human condition in linear time. This two-sided awareness, this moral complexity, is part of what I admire about patriarchy. If I am meant to see here the cautionary tale of the criminal punished for his lack of self-mastery, then I am shown as well the fertility of the criminal mind.

The myth of Cain tells me that men's cherished institutions have a backside. If examined closely, these sacred emblems of our concern for the spirit and for brother-keeping can be seen in some cases to be built from the surfeits of human greed, ambition, and exploitation. The library of the Jewish Theological Seminary of New York, for example, was the gift of Ivan Boesky, one of the great white-collar criminals of the late twentieth century. Wealth and power create beguiling facades. Men build their institutions of science and industry, arts and music, their gardens and preserves. But look, says the myth of Cain, look for the murdering brother in the world of philanthropy. Look amid all these edifices for a lonely man, the exile, the reprobate, the unrepentant, and the vagabond. Look for the figure who cannot be glorified. Look at what men do to deny their loneliness, to appease it, anneal it, transform it. Look for Cain. In looking at charity, look for crime, not in the badlands, not in the ghettoized inner cities; look in the mansions of the donors; look in the hallowed and pious sanctums. He is Magwitch in Dickens's *Great Expectations*. The benefactor is a criminal; he has something to hide.

One man in a group offered this insight:

> There's something very strange in this myth. Cain is sent out to wander all over the earth. His son founds the first city, and his descendants are ancestors to those who work in bronze and metal, to those who play the lyre and the flute, and to those who live in tents. There is some kind of creativity in Cain, some kind of imaginative genius in his genes. He fathers civilization and art. Cain! What is the myth saying to us. I keep looking for a moral judgment, you know, who's good and who's bad. I want it to be simple, but it's not. Cain kills his brother, and he has to

*be a wanderer. But he is marked by God and is protected by God, and he gives
birth to society. It almost seems like what he creates, or what is created through
him—cities, arts, sciences—is a substitute for the thing he has lost that he can
never have again; Eden, brotherhood, connection with God. Or maybe his creativity fills his loneliness. Kind of like God. It's a paradox, a contradiction. Not just
back of the wars and the murders, but back of all the beauty, all the things we
have built, back of culture, there's Cain.*

Cain as a criminal is punished not by death but by a perpetual wandering. In our psychodrama group we found we were already sending Cain into
exile even before our drama closed. Our silence after our wrestling, our
downcast eyes, the breakdown of all possibilities of intimacy among us except the intimacy of a shared and silent shame, sent Cain back into his lair,
into the land of Nod, where he roams. After our psychodrama we wanted to
numb out, to sleep, but our lethargy was not fatigue, it was the depression of
our denial. We could not tolerate Cain. Ashamed of his energy in us, we
watched ourselves judge him, despise him, and turn him away. Superego in
us, morality, socialization—call it by its various names—shamed him into
hiding.

As inheritors of the patriarchal legacy we live with this insoluble and un-
transformable truth: As long as shame is the mechanism of repression, we will
be alone. We will send our Cains to jail. We will put them in solitary confinement, fugitives and vagabonds. We do not ask them what their offering was
and who refused it. Who was favored over you through no fault of your own?
What is the pain of being rejected by the one you sought to please? What is the
shame that burns in that rejection? The self-doubt? The rage? These, too, are
Cain's questions, and these are the questions that ferment in the brother stories that form the climactic chapters of Genesis and the last section of my
book. For those stories, the myth of Cain is preamble.

❀   ❀   ❀

Customarily the psychodrama of the Bible ends with a kind of sharing. As participants shed the roles they chose and return to their own selves, they can reflect in a variety of ways on where the enactment took them, what truths in
the text or in themselves they came to recognize. From that psychodrama
group some voices have a last word here. Each had struggled with Cain in a
different way. One I call Mark:

It's hard not to be ashamed of Cain, of that Cain energy in myself. But I see how being ashamed is really a kind of inability to accept it. It's easier to be ashamed than it is to own it, to own the pleasure, the rush, the weird release of giving in to something, just letting go.

Maria has found herself in Cain:

So often as a woman—as a feminist—I have identified with Cain, though I didn't call him by name. There were plenty of women in myth and story I could identify with. But knowing him now I know his anger at a father he cannot gain recognition from, not a personal father, but the Father who has the power to include or exclude me from privilege. This is the father of patriarchy that I—and Cain—hate; this is the power that men have abused. I know how I have iternalized that rejection, felt that there was something wrong with me. I know I have felt like an outcast and a vagabond. My sex was my mark of Cain.

Another man, Jeffrey, talks of obedience:

I think what strikes me in this story is that Cain is expelled from his family and forced to wander. In a way he has to go through what his father and his mother went through. They also were exiled. They had to leave something behind. And for the same reason, really—they made the wrong choice. They disobeyed God. Which means they obeyed something else. The serpent. Desire. Curiosity. I don't know what to call it. But I know this in myself, and I recognize that it's dangerous to obey this. It's not some simple maxim like "Follow your bliss." Cain doesn't follow his bliss; he follows his demon. Not always easy to distinguish them. Maybe they are two sides of the same thing, but they are the same in that they both take you out of the law, out of the conventional. You feel like an outcast, so you run away. You feel like a marked man. People can't understand you. You are speaking your own language. I have felt like Cain in my family; I was the dropout, the black sheep, the runaway. For a long time I wondered whether I was exchanged for someone else in the hospital nursery. I know I am my parents' child, but there's a part of me that feels like a bastard.

Gloria, a woman who played Cain, speaks also:

It was hard for me. I felt like I really had to turn myself into an animal. At least that's how I started when I was standing there. I thought I'd be a wolf. But then as the drama went on, I realized that animal fury is pure; it has no hurt in it, and its savagery isn't premeditated and vengeful. So I had to let go of that and look for something fiercer. I thought of the energy of a mother defending her children. That was a powerful energy. But that, too, seemed somehow noble, and it wasn't enough to take me to Cain. I thought of the women I have been competitive with, but my competitiveness with them seemed too shallow. I could not use it for what I needed. Then—and this frightened me—I reached into the place in myself where I was once abused as a child. I had to push past my fear and frozenness to come to a place that was red with my fury and desire for revenge. I'd gotten close to it in therapy, but now for the first time I was using it, I suppose the way an actor uses her experience to find the required emotions. I dipped into that pool of rage when I needed to kill. When I was in that place, Abel, my brother, was my abuser.

It really shook me up, and it left me wondering how deep Cain's sense of being unfavored really went. Maybe it was a kind of abuse. Maybe Abel was the darling of the family, maybe he lorded his specialness over his brother; maybe the favor of God was the last straw for a man who had felt unchosen and unloved all his life.

And Michael talks about loneliness:

Cain's fate is to live as a stranger in the world, to wander. Cain seems to me to carry in him a deep loneliness wherever he goes. Who will call him brother? He has lost the one man who could call him brother, and now there is no one anywhere who will. To lose a brother is in a way like losing Eden. My younger brother died when I was twenty-six, and even though we were not that close, I have realized since that I had always felt that someday we'd get together, compare notes, and really connect as brothers. It was always a promise. When he died, I realized that I would never have that chance, and I couldn't have that chance with anyone else. His death left a hole nothing ever filled.

"I played God," said Sam.

But I didn't get a chance to say what I wanted to say. Once again I have blown it. I tried. I chose, for I, too, have to choose. It's the law of freedom. There has to be a choice. I choose, but human beings resent my choices, my interventions. I can understand that. But still I have to choose. I knew Cain would feel wounded. Who wouldn't? He could have changed the whole course of things, forever, if he had been able to master his pain. If he had been able to trust me. For then I would have loved him beyond my love of Abel. Cain had the chance. It is the chance I give to those I test. Cain's exaltation would have reopened the gates of Eden. It would have been enough. But in his freedom he chose, and in his choice I lost two sons at once, Abel dead and Cain forever cursed and forever cursing me. So again I am alone.

The Myth of the Flood

As a psychodramatist I learn the meaning of Genesis from the enactments of those who explore the text with me. As a writer I understand Genesis by the kind of writing different parts of it evoke from me. Now as I come down the lists of linear time to the story of Noah, I slip at first into something old and familiar, like a fairy tale, like the sound of my father's voice reading to me at night. I savor this story in some private dimension of my past. It seems to me that the story of the flood belongs to a season of my childhood, to the time of the birth of my own imagination, not as a merely personal faculty, but as an immense reverie inside me and all around me. In the story of Noah I regress into the reverie of rain.

The Myth of the Flood (or as I really feel it, the rain story) is different from the other old tales. Even now, after study and enactment, they can puzzle me with their multiple possibilities; they contain emotional depths far beyond the grasp of a child. But the story of Noah is completely different. I probably heard it for the first time after the deluge of divorce when I was eight or nine. It took a single element in the world and magnified it as the child's mind magnifies.

I knew rain. I had played in it, been chilled by it. I had seen rain pour down windows, polish the leaves, and turn my small backyard into a bog. Rain was a seance, full of ghostly forms and visitations. How dreamy those streaky windowpanes; how like tears. Wasn't it obvious that the heavens were crying? So many tears. I had that many sometimes. Who up there, immeasurably high and distant, was crying through the clouds? Did Daddy ever cry? And the clouds—they turned over upon themselves or pressed all around, smudging the distances. They were alive. The thunder rumbled on like growlings in the stomach of the sky. Lightning flickered down my spine. But clouds were only a backdrop for, and the thunder only startled me a moment from, the long vacant daydreaming of rain.

Rain was a curtain, an enclosure. It made things dark. It made them gleam. When it was over, there was brightness in the air; in summer, streets steamed. Rain divided inside from outside. Inside was warm, dry, safe; in here, inside yourself, you could watch the rain. Outside it splashed and ran and trickled. You heard it at night rushing on the house and hushing the world. When I go outside in it, it plays with me. I am an animal, slick, splashy, wild. Rain is wild. People sing in the rain, dance in the rain. Adults become children in the rain. It tickles. It makes you laugh. It is big. Rain surrounds, speaks, touches you everywhere. Rain is God.

The story of Noah was a poem in my childhood, a fantastic elaboration that grew into a nightmare about rain. About a rain that never stopped. It rained . . . and rained . . . and rained. And yes, it was easy for me to grasp this magnification, this exaggeration of rain, this flood, this drowning. The story of the flood was not only easy to imagine; I felt as though I might have imagined it myself. Somewhere it lived inside of me. The rain that could be so friendly could also be cold; it could sting; it could beat the flowers into mud, strip the trees of blossoms, make white water in the gutters, roil the banks of the river, pop umbrellas, send hats into the air. It came with a wind that broke branches in the yard. I learned of the flood just as I was learning the idea "what if . . . " What if it never stopped? What if Daddy and Mommy never lived together again? What if it rained and rained and rained?

But then there were the animals. Like the ones I saw in the zoo, but more. All of them. All the animals in the world. Noah found them and brought them to the ark. The ark was a zoo. I had seen pictures of this. These pictures were true. I liked the giraffes and the hippos. And the lions. They all went into the ark.

That was his boat, the ark. Funny word. Ark, ark, ark. Everything into the ark. It has no windows. It is lifted up on the waters. I am there and everyone in Noah's family is there, and all the animals; we are all inside; we hear the rain outside, the thunder. We're here for a long, long time. The ark is dark. I am glad I am in Noah's family. What if I weren't?

Then it's over. It stops raining. We hear it stop. We can come out on deck now. We see that we are in the middle of the ocean. The whole world is underneath us—the mountains and the houses and the rocks and the trees—all somewhere down below us. The people, too? I wonder. But no one ever speaks about them. Soon little bits of the highest mountains poke up through the waters. There is sunlight. Everything sparkles.

Then Noah sends out a black bird. It flies and flies and comes back. Then he sends out a white bird. It comes back. He sends out the white bird again, and this time it comes back with a leaf in its beak. Noah sends out the dove one more time. This time it doesn't come back. So he knows the earth is dry enough for the bird to build a nest. Noah is smart. It is spring. Everything is shining. It is all new and muddy and sweet. And there is a rainbow.

❀ ❀ ❀

When I come to the Myth of the Flood as a man and in a community of diverse readers, I see different things. In the wake of world wars and holocausts, genocide, and nuclear annihilation, it speaks to me of my gender's imagination of universal disaster, and our capacity for it. The God of the flood is the force of unreasoning wrath unleashed against the domestic universe. This God is indifferent to natural innocence, for what have the birds and beasts and creeping things done to deserve annihilation? What about the mothers and children drowned under that impersonal flood? Within that chaos of divine fury, the small ark bobs with its contents sealed as if it also carried some terrible message, some seed from the tree of knowledge, across the divide.

Here in the Myth of the Flood is patriarchy's imagination of the other face of the Father. Not the creative father, not even the father of boundaries or prohibitions; here is the father of our childhood choking with anger, sweeping the table clear of plates and glasses, hurling the telephone at Mother's head, shattering the mirror, raising his fist or the strap or whatever comes to hand. This is the father who can kill us—who has. History is full of his violence. He is the God *of* Cain, not just the God who opposes him. As men we may have imagined Him out there, but we know that He is in here. The Destroyer is another face of the Creator. This two-faced God does not seek in this myth to mediate or rectify His creation in any way. In the storm of His rage He shows not the slightest sign of compassion.

And why this rage? The spectacle of human corruption has moved Him to a ruinous fury. In the myth we read that "the earth had become corrupt before God; the earth was filled with lawlessness." Mankind, still in its infancy, knows nothing of boundaries and laws; earth has reverted to some primal degeneracy, gone to the dogs. In the words of the myth, "all flesh had ruined its way upon the earth." Even those Genesis calls "divine beings" have taken wives among the daughters of the earth. A moral chaos prevails in these images of a spoiled planet.

> *And God, surveying the world, saw how great was man's wickedness of earth, and how his imagination was nothing but evil all the time. (6:5)*

And seeing this, He is overcome with an immense regret. "His heart was saddened." This sadness of God is filled with a sense of His own failure and of loss. The freedom with which He has endowed His creature has been corrupted and has corrupted the world. The imagination of man's heart is full of evil. It is enough to make a god weep.

The Hebrew word here translated as "imagination" is *yetser*. It comes from the word *yatsar,* meaning "to mold" or "to shape." It is especially used of the potter in relation to his clay. It is abstracted to mean the power that forms, shapes, or conceives. It is the very word used to describe what God does when he "forms" man out of the dust of the earth. It is the word for nonbiological conception, divine or human. The human creature resembles his Creator in the sharing of this faculty: God and human both possess this *yetser.* Imaginative energy is inseparable from freedom; it is what is most free in us.

The Great Father recognizes that this power has degenerated in man, and so the Maker decides to destroy what He has made. The divine Imagination, outraged at the abuses of its own free creation, rolls back universal light toward its origins in universal darkness. God, like so many of us, covers His sorrow with His rage.

The retribution of the Father is brought down upon the misuse of the very freedom that was His essential gift to His creation. He has, in a sense, only Himself to blame, yet He is subject to His own creative laws. Having granted the human creature freedom and imagination, He cannot limit it or impose His will upon it from without. God behaves here like the playwright who destroys his play in a fit of pique after his characters have taken on a life of their own and repel the creator's moral sense—a mirror the artist cannot dare to view.

Yet there is one man, Noah, who is chosen to ride out the deluge. In God's eyes Noah has been "righteous in his generation, a whole man." God finds a single righteous man and saves the world for him and through him. Noah becomes the prototype of the survivor.

As the survivor he not only escapes this planetary doom, he is the link to the world before the flood. He carries the ancient tales of creation and Cain and the genealogies of men with him across the gulf; he knows what the world was like before it changed forever. Yet as a survivor he is also in another form the outcast. Regret and nostalgia must accompany him across the watery transition between two worlds. Like Adam and Cain, Noah is the figure of a soul whose past is divided suddenly and irreparably from the future. Noah can have no life in a community, for all community drowns in a deluge. He survives as a solitary. He is the member of the last generation of a vanished past, the first generation of a future yet to be born. His lifespan is a bridge between two zones of time that are two different worlds as well.

Noah is also the first appearance of a figure the patriarchal imagination will depict again under different names and elsewhere in Genesis. He is the survivor-savior, the preserver-provider, the chosen son. He was Abel first and will be Abraham in his generation, Isaac in his, Jacob too. He appears at the end of Genesis in Joseph, who like Noah is "favored by God." It may even be said of this figure that he redeems the Father from the fate of His own terminal failure. In him the seeds of a Father's original dream are carried into the future. His existence as the chosen son allows God to retain His role as a Father; he preserves the Father Himself from the loneliness He knew before the creation of the world.

The figure of the survivor is, of course, implicit in the myth of universal destruction. If that destruction were complete, then there would be no knowledge of it, nothing to be learned or transmitted—no one would escape to tell the tale. The survivor is the incarnation of memory; the one who, like the Ancient Mariner, burns with some knowledge of ultimate extremities. And though the survivor, Noah, lives with his memory of the past, he lives on without a living past. All natural continuity is broken. Adam, Cain, and Noah are three faces of the same figure, each a survivor, each living on the other side of an immense, impassable divide. They look back through their memory to an irrecoverable past; they look forward toward an unimaginable future. They live in a present still ringing with their fateful encounter with God. All three know the other face of God, as the One who punishes, exiles, destroys.

The image of this alien and terrifying God, who can shift the continental plates and pitch a world to ruin, is rooted in the deepest places of the patriarchal imagination. Later traditions, Christian and humanistic, progressive and ecological, soften this dark face of God and would remember the flood as a fable from a primitive phase of the world. Yet this myth seems to own a perennial and elemental truth. One would prefer to forget it, as those who, living on a geological fault, go about their lives and their loves as usual, forgetting that disaster can engulf them in a moment.

Adam, Cain, and Noah are patriarchy's first tragic images of men. By their own acts of choice, they have paid dearly for their freedom. Unlike the Greek tragic heroes, they are not the victims of an overreaching hubris or tragic flaw. Adam, Cain, and Noah are ordinary; their tragedy lies in what they must endure: exile and loneliness. And in what they know, both of themselves and of God. All three are witnesses to divine caprice, all three know the mystery of Imagination as an internal and cosmic energy. All three also know that this mystery as God can be a horror, life-consuming, death-giving, wrathful, and without justice or mercy. Imagination is the amoral source. Nature and imagination are alike and akin; we make from and about them our holiest visions and from them experience our most harrowing nightmares. Both nature and imagination are cruel as well as kind. Noah knows this; he seems to me a haunted, mad figure. He is not just the survivor, he is the preserver as well.

He preserves life, to be sure, but, more important, he preserves the knowledge of the two faces of God. When he walks out into the new world, with what a sense of awe and bitterness, of relief and mistrust, does he breathe that air? Does he see carcasses rotting in the mud? Might he not pick up human bones in the drying fields? In the figure of Noah patriarchy says something about the fragility not only of individual life but of all life. This world rests finally on the will of its Maker, and that will may be terrible. This knowledge of the nature of God gives Noah his stature. What light might blaze in his eyes if one could look on his face? What he knows might make a man mad or drive him to drink.

There are many hints to suggest that the postdiluvian world dawns as a new Eden. The exit from the ark is a processional that repopulates the world with "birds, animals and everything that creeps." The Great Father invites all flesh to "swarm on the earth, and be fertile, and increase on earth." He restores the principle of plenitude and fertility, as it was in the beginning.

Noah's first act is to build an altar and make an offering. In response to the "pleasing odor" that wafts from this sacrifice, God says to Himself:

> *"Never again will I doom the earth because of man, since the imagination of a man's mind is evil from his youth." (8:21)*

God shrugs in resignation. He must accept that the imagination of man is evil. He faces, now for the third time, the riddle and challenge of human freedom, the potential in the human imagination for lawlessness and corruption. It is a changed God that blesses Noah and his sons with the blessing He originally conferred on Adam and Eve: "Be fertile and increase, and fill the earth."

God's resolve never again to destroy the world seals this part of Noah's saga. Just as the story of Cain ended with a sign—the mark upon his brow—so the tale of Noah ends with a sign, the rainbow in the clouds. Mystery sets a rainbow in the heavens as a "covenant"—*beriyth* in Hebrew—to remind man, and perhaps Himself, never to destroy the world by flood again. This moment arches over the story like the promise of mercy.

"When the bow is in the clouds, I will see it and remember the everlasting
covenant between God and all living creatures, all flesh that is on earth."(9:16)

God Himself must struggle to pacify His own nature. In this verse God
refers to Himself in the third person as if placing Himself on an equal footing
with "all living creatures" and enjoining Himself to obey a law higher than divine will or whim. The bow is a yoke to which God submits, but man is still
free. God's submission is voluntary, and so will it have to be for man.

In the very next moment, however, like a cloud passing over the sun,
human freedom darkens this bright new world. After making his sacrifice, the
first thing Noah does is to invent the cultivation of the grape; he makes wine
and gets drunk. We all but saw it coming. Like Cain's ingenious progeny, Noah
begins a new phase of culture with some invention, some imaginative creation, some new technology. The spirit of the serpent now slides into a bottle.

In his drunkenness Noah sprawls "naked" in his tent, and one of his sons,
Ham, innocently, it would appear from the text, comes upon him. The next
morning Noah's other sons tell their father what Ham has done, and Noah
curses Ham and Ham's son Canaan to a life of servitude. What a strange footnote to the new genesis.

The story of Noah's drunkenness may have a humorous side: One might
naturally enough wish to tie one on after such a long confinement. But it has
other sides, too. Noah may be righteous, but there are still forces he has not dealt
with, a new power of "spirits." More sober still is the sense of another cycle beginning. No sooner has this world been freshly made than there is another turn of
the serpent, some abuse of freedom, some excess, some trespass of imagination,
some new gnosis, and again a judgment and a curse initiate another fall.

Noah's story ends with the image of a father lying naked in his tent. How
was it that I did not remember that part of the story? It seems the vestige of
some repressed material about male sexuality, incest perhaps, or some dark
side of the myth that the patriarchal imagination wished to preserve. It is of a
piece, I realize, with the two-sided image of the father—God and Noah—the
myth insists upon. We have seen some nakedness of God in His destruction of
innocence; Noah merely apes Him in his curse.

One final voice from an old psychodrama comes back to me. It belongs
to Patrick, a Dublin-born immigrant who ran a parish in the slums of a large
eastern city.

I keep thinking about the wine Noah drinks at the end. In a way, this
whole story is a kind of alcoholic nightmare. It's as if God is drunk and the world

is mad the way it's mad in drink. I think of my father. I think of myself. That crazy ark with all the sounds and smells of the beasts—the noise and the chaos of it— it reminded me of what my house used to feel like when the Da' came home drunk. What was it like for Noah's wife? For his three sons? I'll tell you, many was the time I saw my father naked, lying in his vomit, or with his lights out on the bathroom floor. But his physical nakedness was only a part of it. It was as if the man had no skin, no covering. His insides were all out, his pain. There were no boundaries. He was not a man. He was something else, not a man, but not a beast either.

    I felt ashamed of him, but I was ashamed for him, too. I was Ham seeing him naked, and I was the other brothers, wanting to cover him up, to hide him.

❀　❀　❀

I am left at the end of Noah's story with a sense of an emerging pattern in the patriarchal imagination. There seems to be a kind of rhythmic cycle in the myths. There is the Eden phase, the garden, the season of accord, the balanced moment when Cain and Abel bring their offerings and stand side by side, the springtime of release from the ark into a new world. There is a second phase, in which serpent-mind and serpent-energy, *yetser,* disrupt this harmony: the serpent in the garden who speaks, the passion that lies coiled at Cain's door and then strikes, the drunkenness of Noah that spoils. Then the third phase begins, marked by a curse and exile, loneliness, wandering, and death. Adam and Eve are cursed and cast out of paradise; Cain is cursed and sent out into the world a "fugitive and a vagabond"; and now comes Noah's curse and the enmity of brothers it will set in motion. In time there will be a new beginning, a promise, a harmony, and it will in time, again and again, be broken and restored.

    This rhythmic pattern moves through the stories of Genesis and gives meaning and form to the many phases of history that follow in the Bible. It is a rhythm mirrored in the movement of masculine erotic energy with its rises and climaxes, its dissipations and falls, and its bright resurrections. This rhythm is both cyclic and progressive. Ever the same in its deep pattern, it moves forward on the line of time, into history, toward the future. Upon its revolutions cities are founded, enterprises launched, and cultures formed. This rhythm has been our particular rhythm as men who, unstayed by lunar changes, freed from the travail of childbirth, move to the erotic rhythm of our imaginations in point and counterpoint to the dance of our imagining God. But it is by no means a rhythm known only to men. This patterning of time and energy—this shaping of eros—is the form of the patriarchal imagination, the imagination of our culture and tradition. Its monarch is Father Time Himself. This God has marked out the tempo, not in blood or birth but in our cycles of labor and rest, in our dreams, enterprises, and dissolutions.

The Myth of the Tower

At the end of Noah's story a new era begins. Once again man sends his prolific seed down the generations. A long genealogical list follows the death of Noah, who has been a second Adam. In a flicker of verses the world is repopulated; whole nations are spawned and come into their own. Through these generations no mention is made of God. Through this absence Genesis suggests that God is once again forgotten, reconsigned to his transmundane loneliness, watching the linear history of humankind move without thought of Him to its own appointed ends. Indeed in the Myth of the Tower it appears that human history is coming to its conclusion in a unified human project by which man will make his own stairway to the stars. The human imagination serves its own desires; blind to its relation to divinity, it is closed to all revelation or covenant.

At the beginning of chapter 11 we read the following story.

> All the earth had the same language and the same words. And as men migrated from the east, they came upon a valley in the land of Shinar and settled there. They said to one another, "Come let us make bricks and burn them hard. . . . Let us build us a city, and a tower with its top in the sky, to make a name for ourselves; else we shall be scattered over the world."

> God came down to look at the city and tower which man had built, and He said, "If as one people with one language this is how they have begun to act, then nothing they imagine will be out of their reach. I shall go down, then, and confound their speech there, so that they shall not understand one another."

> Thus the Lord scattered them from there over the face of the whole earth; and they stopped building the city. That is why it was called Babel, because there the Lord confounded the speech of the whole earth; and from there the Lord scattered them over the face of the whole earth. (11:1–9)

As it opens the myth tells of a once upon a time when "all the earth had the same language and the same words." Men migrate and settle together in Shinar. In this apparent golden age the human race speaks with one voice;

people say what they mean; and between the idea and the act, between imagination and deed, there is no confusion, no shadow. The men of Shinar dwell in a unanimous human settlement. What need have they for a God? They are parodies of the divine. As it was for the God of creation, for them the word and act are seamlessly joined.

They conceive a plan. They will found a city with a tower that is to "reach heaven." They do not want to be scattered; they do not want to be wanderers like the generations of Adam and Eve. In this project, they say, "we will make a name for ourselves."

This desire to "make a name"—to be a law unto themselves—aims at autonomy. (Autonomy is derived from two Greek words meaning self-law.) This is the human core of their desire. The very phrase—"make a name for ourselves"—has a contemporary ring. It expresses a timeless Western ambition to create one's own life, shape it according to one's own desires, master it by personal will, and to be able in the end to take all the credit for it. Autonomy and independence are the traditional goals of individualism, requisite to the establishment of the separate self. What can be wrong with autonomy?

Nothing except that it is illusory. Autonomy rests on the fiction of an independent will; it denies the mystery of spirit and the darkness of our unconscious bonds with others; it denies the power of something Other and outside of the self to upset all our self-made plans. Autonomy is a conceit that buys us some measure of individuation but denies our messy interdependence, our ultimate subservience to an Imagination beyond our control. The city and the tower point an iconic finger to the sky, mocking God.

So God pits Himself against this drive for autonomy. God is an iconoclast. He dashes their enterprise by confounding their speech. No longer able to know one another's thoughts, men are confused. The scattering breaks up the mass; it destroys the idols of self-worship, the inherent narcissism and megalomania of the single-minded, autonomous men of Shinar. Men can no longer speak with one voice. A polyglot world is brought into being, a new world of disparate selves. In order to survive, to trade, make community, make peace or war, human beings must learn languages.

The city and the tower are bulwarks against change. In the myth the men of Shinar seem like a frightened herd of conformists, everyone speaking the same language and thinking the same way. It's a totalitarian culture. Not only do they have no need of God, they wish to be gods themselves. They want to end history before it has begun. The idea of history as a pattern of events that has meaning and leads somewhere has not been conceived of yet. That conception of history as an immense collaborative project between the human soul and God, between the Father and his created world, waits for the life of Abraham. Yet there have been hints of a covenantal aspiration in God from the concord of Eden through the rainbow promise after the flood.

Though this myth may warn against a culture of conformity, it also recognizes that human beings dream of a shared enterprise. Babel represents a failed approximation of community, and Babel raises the question, What kind of gathering may be possible for human beings? Babel is community degenerated toward statism. But step into the shoes of someone wandering away from the unfinished tower. What is your soliloquy?

"I walk away alone, but I remember what it felt like to work with others, to have a common dream, an aspiration that bonded us together."

"All right, it can't be Babel, but what can it be? Where?"

"Will it ever be possible," a solitary exile asks, "to find a place where the many feel they are one again?"

The promise of such a place will be given to Abraham and Sarah; progress toward that community will be the collective work of generations, searching and building that dream in linear time. This work is the patriarchal project, the work of the fathers, the mothers, the sons, and the daughters: the dream of the human family.

✤ ✤ ✤

The Myth of the Tower repeats the essential rhythmic paradigm. The time of Eden when mother and child share the same speech comes to an end. Shinar is the Motherland, and the language there is the mother tongue. The mother tongue is the language of paradise and infancy. Adam names the animals, and as he calls them, so they will come. The name and the thing are one. The valley of Shinar is a version of a lost utopia for those expelled from her.

This myth tells another version of our necessary separation from instinctual life. We are cast out alone to live somewhere in the darkness of linear time and in the world of our imagination. We must learn languages, for they will be the prerequisite for our survival. We head into the world, and our task is to learn to understand one another.

Words are not things and can never be things; the divorce has already taken place and cannot be healed. Language is forever approximate, never literal. At its best world-speech is a poetry, a patter that gives shape and pattern to the world; but the poem is only provisional. In the mortal terrain of human endeavor, words are only words, images only images. They can never be more than that. Our speech is also a language of laws and prohibitions, of words that can mean many things at once, of language as something exact yet slippery, leading and misleading.

Mastery of language is the hidden—and sometimes not so hidden—requirement we set for membership in any power class. Each elite has its jargon; fluency is a sign of initiation. Erasing the traces of region or dialect in speech used to be part of the training to become a cosmopolitan, a citizen of the world. The con artist is one who can manipulate words, who plays on our faith that if a person speaks in a certain way, then his or her words must reflect in some accurate way the mind and heart.

Language is also our means of aggression. We spit and bite our words; we have developed elaborate systems of cursing and execration. Early on as children we learn to tease, to humiliate, to use language as a weapon; and for many of us we only passed on to our peers what had been visited upon us by older siblings. As sons and daughters we have felt the sting of a father's taunts, his tongue-lashings, and from him we learned to lash out. Mothers, too, in perhaps more subtle ways have used words to flay and humiliate us.

One of the most painful moments of my childhood occurred when I was five or six years old. My father, mother, and I were having supper together, and my father batted my elbow off the table, having told me many times not to rest it by my plate when I was eating. My hand nicked the corner of the steel table, and tears started to my eyes. Seeing my eyes well up, my father turned to my mother, "Is our little baby going to cry now?" I pushed back from the table. "Is baby going to cry?" my father mocked, looking at me as I reddened and tears started to spill. I ran from the room. But my father followed me. I was crying now, bawling for him to leave me alone. I dashed up the stairs to the second floor landing while my father stood below in the dark hall and shouted after me, "Crybaby . . . crybaby." I turned on the landing and saw him below, heard him laughing and taunting me. I took off my shoe and threw it down at him to make him stop. He moved out of range but kept his singsong whip going: "Crybaby . . . crybaby." I threw the other shoe down at him. I was screaming at him to stop. I felt I was going crazy.

How many of us have learned these lessons about the power of words, how they can lash and wound. When someone tells us "sticks and stones may break my bones, but names can never hurt me," we look up with dismay. We don't understand. We are keyed to language in a most profound and emotional way.

The people who wander out from Shinar are like children who begin to struggle with language and who must learn to speak and to listen. Now words clutter action, and things must be named. The cumbersome symbolic system of language falls like a sheet of crazy glass over the internal and external worlds. Language separates and connects; it is the sign of our exile, the means of our reunion.

The world after Babel is endlessly pluralistic. It will be a world of tribes and clans and nations, each sharing a common tongue, but each speaking a language different from its neighbors. Within each language group there are dialects and subordinate languages, gender languages, class languages, and color languages. Within those are neighborhood languages and family languages. Within those are yet more particular tongues, the individual and private languages each person uses. I draw my speech from the common vocabulary of the nation, but words have the most intimate and private associations for me. Take, for example, the word *home*. The dictionary will give its common meaning in our common language, but only my personal story will tell you what this word really means to me. Home is the blizzard and the songs in the night; home is the storm troopers in my mind; home is rain on a dreamy afternoon; home is my father taunting me.

Language is at once the most public means by which we make a common world and the most private means by which we sense our separateness. Language is at once the bridge and the barrier, the line that can never quite merge with the axis. We would use language as the instrument of community, but we can never fully forge a community, for language is finally too gross for the idiosyncratic ways we each experience the world. In spite of all our words, we are alone, nomads. Gifted and burdened with language, we grope toward one another in our gestures of speech; we write our books and poems and send them out on the waters of culture in the hope of hearing some answer. The fate of being a solitary in language is, for me, the hard truth of the Myth of the Tower. As the poet Edna St. Vincent Millay wrote:

Babel is here, and now. Who speaks my language?—no one.

In the Myth of the Tower we find another version of the rhythmic mythic cycle. Once again there is the Eden phase, here rendered as a time of common speech. The second phase begins with the intrusion of serpent-mind and serpent-energy, *yetser*. Here the imaginations of the men of Shinar conceive a great enterprise that attests to their autonomy, their power as creators. Once again there is a third phase marked by a curse and exile, loneliness, wandering, and death.

Here we find another version of the origin of our wandering, of our sense of being transients in a world of wanderers. Adam, Cain, and the sons of Noah were all dispersed into a world that provided them no final home. The city with its tower is conceived of as a bastion, a haven against a profound anxiety. Unmoored in space, borne on the rapids of linear time toward death and oblivion, unconnected to nature, every parent an exile and every brother a Cain, we wander into a vast loneliness. It surrounds us, and it is inside us. We build our defenses to blot out the ambient and internal reality of Mystery, of God.

But God defeats us. Yet a fourth time the scattering occurs, and we are turned out from our self-made and isolated security into a world in which each of us is alone. Diaspora and exile become the patriarchal metaphors for the human condition. A poignant truth, only hinted in these early myths, will be made explicit in the Tales of the Ancestral Family: Human beings will find their relationship to God *only* when they are wandering, only when they are alone, only when they are aware of their dependency and open to His presence. Whenever a man "settles," as do the men of Shinar, it is always a prelude to displacement. In that displacement, uprooted and cast into the unfamiliar, one opens again to a relationship with God.

For that God is a lonely God. He is a hungry God. He is in danger of being forgotten as we come to realize we do not need Him, and indeed we wish not to need Him. For what has this God given us so far that we might wish to love Him or serve Him or seek Him? It is not surprising that we should have a myth that speaks of our desire to shield ourselves from so watchful and threatening a God, jealous of His power, capricious in His favors, cruel in His punishments, awful in His rage, and inscrutable in His atonement. This is a God who does not yet know how to speak to us, to touch us in a place where obedience would come as a result not of fear but of love, or as a response to being called to some great enterprise. God has not yet learned to reach the human imagination. That phase of the education of God will take place in the lives of Abraham and Sarah.

PART II

❀

Tales of the Ancestral Family

There is a love like a small lamp,
which goes out when the oil is consumed;
or like a small stream, which dries up
when it doesn't rain. But there is a
love that is like a great well in the earth;
it keeps its fullness forever and is inexhaustible.

Isacc of Nineveh

5

The Myth of the Call

Ten generations separate Noah from Adam. Symmetrically, ten further generations separate Noah from Abraham, whose story and the story of whose sons become the central myth of the second part of Genesis. Abraham, called Abram when he is first presented, is a figure without precedent in the Scriptures or literatures of his time.

The saga of Abraham requires a new kind of narrative. The material of the first eleven chapters has been mythic in a fabulous sense. The stories of the creation of the world, the loss of the garden, of Cain and the murdered brother, of the rain, the ark and the naked father, of the unfinished tower— these fragments tell of a time before biography and history; they are the cosmic fables of a Lonely God. But with the words "Now this is the line of Terah"(11:27), the eon-sweeping overview of the first fifth of Genesis slows to the time scale of the life of a man, Abram, later called Abraham, one of the three sons of Terah. In him the Lonely God will find His first abiding son and with him and his wife, Sarai, later called Sarah, create a sustained relationship.

The origins of patriarchal spirituality are to be found in the mythic figure of Abraham. His life story is a paradigm upon which the lives of all subsequent biblical protagonists are variations. Moses, the prophets, and Jesus Christ are all the descendants of Abraham, and not only in a successional sense. The stages of Abraham's story, the ordeals he faces, and the tasks he undertakes are repeated in the biographies of the saints, the spiritual iconoclasts, the Western shamans, white medicine men, and twelve-step devotees. The very idea of a special relationship between the soul and God, a relationship that may be sustained over time, experienced as personal, even filial, originates with Abraham.

In the Tales of the Ancestral Family we first learn that God seeks to enlist a chosen son in the accomplishment of a great collaborative enterprise. This God is the Great Father, a divine identity only hinted at previously, and in his terrible encounters with Him Abraham will wander into a landscape of complex moral choices and terrible spiritual demands. In the course of his wandering Abraham will be asked to sacrifice what he cherishes most to this God.

Abraham is the father par excellence; in him and through him is first constellated the myth of the father. On the one hand, he embodies the values of a social order that insisted on and sanctified the rule of the fathers. On the other hand, he is also the first mythic father in the Western tradition who is not defined by his concerns of wealth, warfare, kingship, and material power. Abraham is a man who has an inner life and vocation. He is a figure through whom patriarchy attempts to transcend the narrow, culturally constructed definition of man. Abraham's biography is told in the stages and stations of spiritual—rather than heroic or romantic—initiations. The very idea of spiritual initiation as a repeated, renewed, and increasingly demanding series of self-surrenders is first articulated in his story. According to the patriarchal imagination, the wisdom and power that finally come to a man or woman through these initiations promote not status in the world but the stature of a soul. The story of this patriarch molds for the first time in the West the myth of soul-making.

It is tempting to call Abraham a hero; he has a quest and a mission; he sires two sons, Ishmael and Isaac, the mythic forebears through whom are established the sibling religions of Islam, Judaism, and Christianity. If we compare Abraham with a character like Homer's Odysseus, however, who stands at the beginning of the Western heroic tradition, we can see just how different a figure Abraham is and how poorly the word *hero* sits on his shoulders.

Odysseus has the goddess Athena for his sponsor. The arena of his actions is a world of raw power; he labors to win a war and after many adventures to return to Ithaca, his home, now an occupied country, and to reclaim it. He is a man of the world, a picaresque explorer, supremely "skilled in all ways of contending," willful, wily, curious, crafty, a poseur and improviser, a storyteller, and master of disguises. Though Odysseus suffers in his travels and travails, in the end he gains all he has set out to win: wife, home, son, wealth, kingship. In the poem's closing lines even his youth has been restored, his father's too, and Ithaca seems finally a version of that utopia where one can say, though Homer never does, "They lived happily ever after."

Odysseus is a prototype of the economic man. His values are, despite his promiscuous diversions, the values of hearth, home, and history. He meets the world on the world's terms. There is no spiritual realm into which he travels, and even his descent into the underworld moves him neither to spiritual insight nor to a sense of his own mortality. In Hades he gains only information, data useful to abet the practical task of coming home and securing his place in the annals of his people.

Economic in a more modern sense, Odysseus is the trader, the mercantile explorer, the exploiter and looter whose honor rests on the booty with which he can enrich himself. Guileful and shrewd, his intelligence is put in the service of a fiercely competitive temper. His dreams are as concrete (and as limited) as the dreams of the creative entrepreneur. To his son he passes on reputation and riches. He seeks to create a dynasty. Odysseus is the godfather of all godfathers, the father king who lives by a ruthless code, a law unto himself. For all his extraordinary charm, Odysseus is consumed by events, possessed by his possessions, driven always to master his surroundings.

I have met him everywhere and in myself. He is the part of me that wants fame and privilege, reputation and reward. He sits beside me as I write this book and talks to me about the *New York Times* bestseller list. He envies successful men and competes with them; he wants to drive a black BMW, and to catch the eye of any woman who catches his. He is not my wildness but my wish to be special, to be one for whom the usual rules do not apply. I dreamed with him in lotusland; he was there when I dallied with Calypso in Jamaica, drinking rum punches till the sun went down. Like him I leave my family to seek my own ambitions, to satisfy my appetite in the world. He is my hedonism. Like him I know how to dissimulate until I am not sure who I really am, or until I think I am only roles, contexts, responses, improvisations. The Odysseus who wrestled with Proteus, the shape shifter, is himself the ultimate protean postmodern man.

What a different figure I meet in Abraham, and what a different aspect of myself he constellates. If one at all, he is a hero of silences, a man who listens and attends. Will and action, passion and ambition, community and romance, conquest and fame do not consume him. These are not the sources of his power either as protagonist or prototype. In the land into which he wanders, he is not concerned with the indomitable self and its valiant encounters with ordeals and obstacles, dragons, witches, knights, or evil forces. Evil itself, so clearly marked in the world of Odysseus, is shadowy in Abraham's; it is complex and located within as well as without. Indeed, most of Abraham's ordeals are ordeals of imagination that take place between the lines and behind the words of his story. If I am to reach him, I have to breach the silence in which he moves. A son of Imagination, Abraham demands imagination to apprehend him.

Abraham seems marginal to history; yet by his emptiness, he generates history. This emptiness of action, this suspension of the heroic or individual will, gives him access to a different kind of power, one for which he becomes an instrument. He cannot create a dynasty, for when he dies, his hands are empty. What is most vital in his experience—his wisdom, his faith, the knowledge he has gained of the Father's mysteries—cannot be handed down. He can only attest to a power that his offspring and then their generations—and which I myself—must experience directly, if at all. Though known through the millennia as the man of faith, he is also witness to incontestable revelations.

Abraham is the aheroic man. He does not oppose heroism, but to him that set of values does not adequately apply, as heroic values do not adequately apply, for example, to the artist, the poet, the musician, the rabbi or priest, the therapist, the healer, the contemplative. Though such people live in a real world where Odyssean concerns cannot be ignored, they live, too, in the domain of Abraham. Abraham is that part of us that asks: What does a life *mean?* What—after all the acquisitions, mergers, promotions, and deals—*matters?* What gives us the deepest sense of significance, value, and purpose in our life? For these questions Abraham is the Western tradition's first guide and emissary. When we ask these questions, we enter an inscape of thought and feeling, and he was there before us.

It was Abraham who first understood that spiritual light comes to the one who goes by way of darkness, power to the one who has given up power, victory to the one who has surrendered, and that life is given to the one who has died. These spiritual paradoxes are given imaginative life in the story of the first patriarch. He speaks to the part of me that wanders; speaks to those times in my life when I have felt adrift in a universe that is haunted by mystery and that bears strange, elusive meanings for me

We do not have a complete life of Abraham. We have fragments that form images of a life, scenes in which we see Abraham as son, husband, kinsman, and father. He is mentioned first as a member of Terah's clan. He is Abram, one of those who travel with his father, Terah, in a westward passage from his original dwelling place in the heartland of Mesopotamia toward the land of Canaan, which borders the Mediterranean Sea.

Now this is the line of Terah: Terah begot Abram, Nahor, and Haran; and Haran
begot Lot. Haran died in the lifetime of his father, Terah, in his native land of Ur
of the Chaldeans. Abram and Nahor took to themselves wives, the name of
Abram's wife being Sarai and that of Nahor's wife Milcah, the daughter of
Haran, the father of Milcah and Iscah. Now Sarai was barren, she had no child.

Terah took his son Abram, his grandson Lot, the son of Haran, and his daughter-
in-law Sarai, the wife of his son Abram, and they set out together from Ur of the
Chaldeans for the land of Canaan; but when they had come as far as Haran,
they settled there. The days of Terah came to 205 years; and Terah died in Haran.
(11:27–32)

We do not know the motive for Terah's migration, but we know he
reached only the western border of his homeland. There he and his clan and
kin settled in Haran; there Terah died.

Immediately after the words "Terah died in Haran" comes the following:

Then the Lord called Abram and said, "Leave your native land and your father's
house and go to the land I will point out to you." (12:1)

In this moment a beam of light picks Abram out from a jumble of figures. The bustle of life in Haran recedes suddenly into deep shadow. A man,
apparently no one special, is arrested in the middle of things; the flow of his
life is interrupted by a voice. Insubstantial, it addresses him. No context. No
preparation. No proof. Just a man hearing a voice—demon, daimon, God—
which calls to him, summons him, directs him: "Leave . . . and go."

The summons follows immediately after the mention of his father's settling and death. The sequence suggests that the sudden release of a powerful
psychic energy hurtling Abram into a new life comes after his father's life force
settles and dies. Terah's dream to reach Canaan has gone unfulfilled; Abram is
called to complete it, but in a way his father could never have imagined.[1]

Is there some connection between the death of the father and this release of force and direction in the son? Does the death of the father make possible some work for the son, some freeing that is at the same time a kind of
continuing, a deepening, a surpassing of the father's dream? I think so, but I
need to say again that the formulation "father-son" is metaphoric, not gender-
bound or absolute. As a man I can see these patterns in my life with my father
and in the lives of men I know. But the paradigm is really parent-child, the relationship of one generation to the next.

When my best friend, Larry, lost his father, I wrote him a poem. Looking back on it now, and knowing what has happened to him in the years since his father died, I see the dynamics of loss and release at work in his life.

A Father's Death

> Shagged with moss, choked at last
> by vines, and one night smit
> by a lightning stroke,
> the gnarled old elm—
> that grew beside the boyhood house
> in whose shade a boy once played
> and in whose limbs one spring dawn
> an eagle landed, so near it seemed
> he could almost touch the dangerous beak
> and unruffled feathers—
> fell at last
> grazing the eaves
> shaking the ground
> and letting in suddenly
> a gaping hole of sky.
> So it seems to me your father dies
> and I, your friend,
> with whom talk of fathers and fathering
> goes back along our own strong trunks
> to the first days of friendship
> think of you as one who goes
> before into the loneliness
> that follows the father's death.
> Mine too one day will fall,
> and then it seems to me
> all the unsaid and unsayable things
> will rend my heart.
> The bond that runs between the father and the son
> is mute and dark as the roots of trees.

Rereading the poem now I think the eagle in the elm represents the father's dream. The son catches glimpses of it; it speaks to him of a wildness in the father, a vision. In the wake of his father's death I have seen my best friend's dreams call him out into a new life. He is following the eagle. The biblical myth speaks to me of the connection between the father's death and the son's readiness to be called, of the way the dreams of one generation are inherited by the next, renewed, and handed on.

> *The Lord called to Abram and said, "Leave your native land and your father's house and go to a land I will point out to you."*

Terah, we are told, reached the very border of his native land but was unable to cross over into a new country. Terah settled within the familiar confines of the Motherland; there he built his house; there he raised his children; there he died. Now his son Abram is called to exceed him, to leave behind the family and the familiar and to enter that country into which the Father of All Things calls him.

I think of Abram's venture as a journey on the Road of Excess, a phrase borrowed from William Blake. "The Road of Excess leads to the palace of wisdom," he wrote in *The Marriage of Heaven and Hell*. I think Blake meant Excess as a kind of surpassing, not as a superfluity or luxury. Only by exceeding the conventional limits of what one has inherited and received does a man or woman achieve wisdom. Blake is a poet of true patriarchy.

Excess breaks out of the conventional. It appears mad, foolish, extreme, and dangerous. The excessive man, as Thoreau has described him, marches to "the beat of a different drummer"; man or woman, this is the one who breaks away either to be forgotten or to make a new world. Such a person reaches the palace of wisdom because he or she has learned directly what serves the soul. Abraham will become a man of faith because his faith will constantly be tried.

The wisdom of excess is a patriarchal wisdom, and excess is arduous and frightening because it asks the sons and daughters to face the unfamiliar, the unfathered parts of themselves. It also means facing the father's limitations, the limits of the forebears, perhaps even becoming the means through which the previous generation faces those limitations, those settlings, and those deaths.

For the soul that chooses to "leave . . . and go," the destination is unknown. The journey of excess, not of his own design nor within his control to reach, takes Abram out of ordinary time and pitches him into the Dreamtime.[2] Terah journeyed on solid ground, but Abram steps out into a space in which his only guide is what he apprehends through his imagination. In his imagination it is the ungraspable, unpredictable Great Father who has summoned him. Like Adam, Cain, Noah, and the scattered souls of Babel, Abram is another in the line of those marked figures who go out into the wilderness and into solitude, who must make a new world, and whose life is in the deepest sense a sojourning. He will, as we shall see presently, live the life of a stranger. Unlike Adam, Cain, and Noah, however, Abram is not expelled or exiled. He becomes "a stranger in a strange land" willingly. There is work for Abram to do, an enterprise in which he is enlisted and that will give meaning to his life. For its sake he will be asked to make extraordinary sacrifices.

This moment in the myth when the soul begins its journey from native land and father's house marks the true genesis of the patriarchal enterprise. This enterprise is a progress, progress as something moving forward and thus moving on, not as amelioration. (In Latin the word *pro-gredior,* from which our "pro-gress" comes, is used specifically to mark the leaving of the father's house.) In the Terah-Abram story this generational pro-gress begins as the dream of Terah for Canaan; it is renewed in the son and recast, spiritualized, and empowered by a force greater than anything Terah knew. Abram will become Abraham and pass the dream on, unfulfilled, to his son Isaac; then Isaac to his son Jacob, and still the dream is unfulfilled. Each generation renews the dream in its own terms.

This generational enterprise remains alive and potent precisely and paradoxically because it is never completely fulfilled. In the Book of Genesis the journey toward the "land I will point out to you," which comes in time to be known as the Promised Land, is never realized. The descendants of Abraham end up as slaves in Egypt. Later in the Bible Joshua exceeds Moses and leads the children of Israel into the Promised Land, but in time they are exiled; they return to the land only to be exiled again. The land is buried under the movements of history. Zion seems a dreamland; its occupation belongs to Dreamtime. Even the messiah who comes to usher in a universal peace must come again. Jews and Christians live in expectancy, travel as sojourners toward a land that is never reached, toward a time that will never be.

It is the message of patriarchy that each generation must be recalled to the journey; each soul must leave the Motherland and the father's house to reexperience a wandering. Sons or daughters must live as strangers, find their meaning, their link with the past, their sense of purpose. Each one's call is also a recollection, a recalling of previous calls. The dream outlives the dreamers. It asks to be remembered in every generation, but every generation must dream anew. Whenever the father has settled and died, the child must set out again into a wilderness to live a dream.

This linking of parent with sons and daughters in a generational enterprise, in dream-bearing, forms what is rightly to be understood as the patriarchal tradition; *this* is what is handed down. Paradoxically, as I have said, what is
handed down cannot always be handled or touched or reached. Abraham's
hands will be empty when he dies. This tradition, mystical and visionary—in
short the tradition of imagination—passes from the "father" as something as
intangible as a story or a song, given and taken as a matter of faith.

In the heroic myths of the Greeks and Romans there is no such notion of
a progress through generations, of a family passing on a vision that moves in
each generation and toward which the generations move. The hero achieves conquest; his quest ends in marriage and mother making. The hero settles in the end,
and this repose is a long-sought reward. Dynasty is his symbolic immortality.
The hero is often ruthless in his attempt to pass on his power to his sons and
heirs. But no vision of a new or a better world ever captures the Greek heroic
imagination and links the generations.

Such a vision is central, however, to patriarchy. Here the imagination
proposes a unique enterprise—one involving covenant, community, and the
family of humankind—that binds the generations in a shared endeavor of the
soul. This endeavor is the heart of patriarchal myth-theology, and in the light
of it a generational bond is forged. When men and women are part of this
work, they feel they have found their true work, their soul-making. In the
world of patriarchy, true soul-making goes by a special name: vocation.

❀　❀　❀

It is one real measure of our poverty as men and women that we have lost this
sense of a vital spiritual tradition and the vocation of soul-making. It is not
merely that the industrial revolution separated people from a life of significant
toil or that the father in the factory works hidden from his child, comes home
at night bleak from his alienated labors; not merely that the child grows up
never seeing the father use his hands or mind. It's not just that. What we have
lost is the generational figure—father or mother—who dreams and dares to
listen to voices; the one whom society calls a fool.

Our world is full of folly, but where are the holy fools? Abram belongs
to the paradigm of the fool. His brother Nahor would call him one. Sarai, his
wife, may look at him askance, wondering if he's lost his mind, yet she, too, is
called; she, too, is a model of exceeding. But most of all Abram himself, in his
own heart, wonders what he is doing. This must be crazy, he says; I must be
crazy. Am I being a fool? Is the voice that calls me also fooling me, tricking

me? Can I trust my voices, can I believe my ears? These questions are asked by a man who cannot look outside himself for answers. Who outside himself can possibly advise him? He must act; he is free to choose. He must pay attention to everything, listen deeply to the clamor of himself, but in the end he acts. If he obeys the call and answers the summons with his life, withholding nothing, then his life in the world becomes a "gesture of folly"[3] sustained only by his faith. No one really knows what he is about, nor does he have words to explain himself, for he operates in a realm where explanations fail. He can only bear witness to his own experience. And trust. To find a vocation often means being a failure in the eyes of the material world.

The best we do in the material world is risk ourselves materially. We even risk our lives. But for what? A thrill, for Uncle Sam, but rarely for a dream that bears healing for our fellow human beings, for our earth. What dreams we have we too often turn into entrepreneurial maneuvers designed in the end to secure us a living, to secure our lives. We aim for success. To be sure, such Odyssean enterprises take courage, require a risk of capital. But patriarchy is not about building Babels. It is about encountering God, or being encountered by Him. It insists that God is a real category of human experience, and that God, however conceived, can interrupt our lives with a call that will alter completely our relationship to our past, present, and future. After such an interruption we live in the moment, for only in the moment are we going to hear what we need to hear to move on. So the values of patience, silence, inwardness, and solitariness become the necessary field of practice a person cultivates in order to hear the words of the Father. Vocation is life lived in the service of imagination; it is a life of obedience.

History has given obedience a bad name; too many docile lambs led to slaughter; too many obedient functionaries murdering the lambs. Whenever we hear talk of obedience, we are likely to feel ambivalence and fear. And a personal revulsion curdles the word as well. The forced submissions of our childhoods, the suppressed rages of our own impotence, compel us to reject obedience. We obeyed once. We had no choice, but obedience shames us. We have vowed we will never again obey. Obedience is for children, or the trained animal. The servant, or worse the slave, obeys the master; the soldier obeys his commanding officer. Obedience is a giving over of one's personal power; it is a loss of control.

Yet according to the soul-tradition of patriarchy, there is another kind of obedience. The word *obey* in English comes from the Latin word meaning "to listen," "to hear." Abram *listens to* the call to leave his native land and his father's house. He obeys. He experiences this call as something coming from a God who is felt to be Other and outside him. But this God is also inside him. Deep speaks to deep; Imagination speaks to imagination, and something is kindled in Abram. The imagination is the capacity of the inner ear to hear the call of the inner voice; imagination is a receptive power as well as a shaping one.

Abram is not being obedient to some external dictate, to some chain of command. On the contrary, he breaks with customary conventions, the duties of inheritance and maintaining his father's estate. What Abram obeys flashes upon him like a beacon, points a way, and then disappears. His obedience is a loyalty to what was first disclosed to him in a moment of revelation. He has no way of knowing what this loyalty will exact of him. On each step of his journey he must renew with himself his commitment to his task, for his obedience is voluntary, not compelled.

One night many years ago I heard a call, and I could not find in myself the courage to obey it. It was at the end of winter at a time when my first marriage had ended, and I was a few months short of finishing my Ph.D. I had come down to New York and was staying at my father's apartment on the West Side of the city. Earlier that week I had run into Carolyn, an old college flame, and she had invited me to come to her place for dinner later that week. On that particular night, despite the blustery chill of early March, I decided to walk the dozen blocks to her place. I was in a state of pleasant expectation. I rounded a corner onto her street and had to pull up my collar against a wind that was driving east from the river. It was already dark, and had I not heard a strange mutter from the edge of the sidewalk, I might have missed him.

A man lay half on the sidewalk and half in the gutter. He was mumbling repeatedly, "I'm cold . . . I'm cold." I am sure he was unaware of any passersby, and I was only half aware of him. Conditioned by the city to blinker my awareness of poverty and homelessness, I was already walking past him intent on my destination and polishing a romantic preamble. But his voice lodged in my ear, and before I had gone too far beyond him, I remembered the parable of the good Samaritan. Somehow that story and his voice caught my conscience. I turned back to him and, reaching down, I helped him, hauled him, to a doorway. "I'm cold," he said, his voice rising to my nostrils on the fumes of cheap wine. I told him I was on my way to a friend's house and that I would see if I could find something to wrap him in. "I'll be back," I promised.

I went to Carolyn's apartment and, standing at her door, explained what had just happened. She looked at me askance, but she found an old blanket and gave it to me. I took it to him, feeling virtuous. When I got back to that corner, he was still in the doorway where I'd left him. I laid the blanket around his shoulders, heard his mumbled thanks, and turned back toward Carolyn's. But there, almost in the same place as before, as if he had materialized out of the windy night, lay another drunk at the curb. Perhaps he had seen my benevolence, perhaps word had gone out on the wind that a fool, a good Samaritan, was afoot in the city, and it was a good time to get a blanket, maybe some spare change. "I'm cold," he said, his voice reaching me. I stopped in my tracks. I had the distinct idea that were I to get another blanket and return with it, there would by then be a third man on the street. Or that I would lose the self-protective myopia that I had developed as a city dweller, and I would see, now everywhere, the figures of the poor and hear them calling out to me. I realized that if I responded once more, I would never get to Carolyn's. I would never get home again that night. I would never finish graduate school and make my bright, promising way in the world. I heard a call that night as clear as if someone had called my name, but it seemed to me a call to something too difficult, too self-sacrificing. I ran the half block to Carolyn's and shut the door on the night. I was not ready for that kind of obedience.

Abram was.

The call delivered to Abram at that moment in Haran concludes by laying before him an immense future:

> *"I will make of you a great nation and I will bless you and will make your name great. I will bless those who bless you, and curse those who curse you. All the families of the earth will find blessing in you." (12:1–3)*

This future contains a promise: Abram will father a great nation, his name will be great, and he will become a blessing to those who cherish him and a curse to those who curse him. In the words "all the families of the earth will find blessing in you," we have a glimpse of a restored Eden, a new world, perversely anticipated in Babel, in which the human community is viewed as a great kinship system tracing its parentage, its spiritual roots, back to Abram and to this moment of his call and response. The patriarchal tradition is set in motion, its generational enterprise and purpose articulated. The goal of soul is not empire or a theocratic state worshiping the Great Father. Nor is the soul's goal a sublime reunion with a parental God in a restored Eden. The envisioned end is the commonweal. Vocation is not "personal growth"; soul is linked to the welfare of a human community. Here, in what is for me its purest articulation, vocation is ultimately a planetary service, work deeply linked to gift and giving.

Abram's call—both the one he hears and the one he leaves to us—contains a promise. It is God's promise to fill and empower us with energy and vision; but more, it is also His promise, and our promise to one another, that our soul journeys will be connected to the well-being of the whole earth. The promise in the call touches upon our desire to dedicate ourselves to the highest possible service to our fellow human beings. Something beyond biology calls this man to transform the world into the family of man.

> So Abram departed, as the Lord had spoken to him; and Lot went with him. And Abram was seventy-five years old when he left Haran. And Abram took Sarai his wife, and Lot his brother's son, and all their substance that they had gathered, and all the souls that they had gathered to them in Haran; and they went forth into the land of Canaan; into the land of Canaan they came. (12:4–6)

The story of the soul on its journey of vocation has begun. From the moment he leaves "his native land and his father's house" and enters Canaan, Abram lives in two dimensions, and in both he lives as a stranger.

One dimension is a realm of naturalistic and interpersonal realities: he travels with his kin and clan, he encounters famine, contends with Pharaoh, deals with his nephew Lot, and achieves considerable status among the tribal chieftains of Canaan. But he cannot settle anywhere. Owning only what he has brought with him, his herds and his household possessions, he becomes a migrant and an immigrant, "a stranger in a strange land." He undergoes the ordeals, the voiceless and helpless ignominy of the refugee. He belongs nowhere. In this dimension, though he makes his way and even in time receives his honors, he remains the stranger. His native land lies behind him, and the land he seeks has not yet been given or found.

But Abram lives and moves as a stranger in a second dimension. His passage through the landscape of external realities and events is punctuated by internal events of secret and enormous consequence, by his encounters with the Great Father, whose will and way he seeks to know. God appears to him unasked and then does not appear when Abram pleads. God reiterates His promises and withholds the fulfillment. We can easily imagine an endless running soliloquy within the heart of Abram as he contends with this God into whose mysterious embrace he has entered. This deep and vexed intimacy with Spirit, this wrestle of the personal imagination with the transcendent Imagination, is prolonged throughout Abram's wanderings in the world. In the inner realm of that dark intimacy he is no less a stranger than he is in the outer world of Canaan and Egypt. In fact his *journeying without destination* is an external image for his internal experience. Outwardly and inwardly Abram comes to feel what it is like to be a stranger in strange lands.

The Stranger is one of the central images for the soul in the Bible. Though every man and every woman may experience being a stranger, the Bible suggests that for men and women who can never know the purely instinctual continuities of nature, who have been cast out of an imagined Eden of pure communion, the sense of being a stranger in both the physical and in the spiritual world is existentially deep and true. Abram and Sarai are the paradigm of this stranger; they wander not only through a landscape where they cannot settle but through the inscape of imagination, through visionary trances, through confusing and contradictory senses of their vocation. They are constantly uprooted not only from place but from certainty. They live estranged from the familiar, their grasp on reality itself constantly shaken through repeated encounters with the Strange.

The Stranger leaves behind no legacy of deeds. It does not come easily into our councils, or if it does, it is the part of us that feels it does not belong fully, not even here. It eludes the nets of psychotherapy, which would find in strangeness some psychological explanation and reconcile it to the world. The Stranger within us will never reach home; it will never be fully atoned. The land the soul moves through is not its to possess; its name is not known to those it meets; it is the outsider, one to be feared if strong, preyed upon if weak, tolerated, at times befriended, but of another place, another clan. The Stranger is not one of us.

The call has lifted Abram from the familiar; the call has opened him to the inner worlds of Imagination, and his encounters with his God at Bethel, in Egypt, and in Canaan are moments of his successive initiation. What comes to him when he is called is nothing less than his own soul, his utmost imagination, with its hunger for the infinite, its capacity to dream, to wander, to search, to endure, to learn, and to grow. Soul is shaped by its passage through the two dimensions; in both it lives as the Stranger, and yet it lives unestranged. For while the unknown is the medium through which it moves, it rests ever more subtly on a sense of faith. God, by whatever name and whether present or remote, wraps the wanderer in a boundless mystery until the two dimensions blend and blur into a single reality.

✿ ✿ ✿

I was teaching at Brooklyn College in the mid-1970s. Each afternoon when my classes were done, I crossed the campus toward the subway to make my way home. One section of that walk became a gauntlet for me. A group of orthodox Jews—young men with long side-curls and prayer-shawl fringes showing beneath their white shirts, wearing black coats and hats, no matter what the weather—stood along one side of that walkway in front of a table laid out with various pamphlets. As I walked past, the voices assailed me, "Are you a Jew? Are you a Jew?" The figures bobbed at me like tall birds, the words repeated like the cawing of crows.

At that time in my life I did not feel I was a Jew. So as I walked past the campus Chassids, their question fell like water on impervious rock. I had, after all, seen the fly on the windowpane and had been carried beyond it; I had sat in chapel and been exhilarated by Christian harmonies; I had sat for years with the Quakers in the Cambridge Meeting House when I was at Harvard. I had practiced Transcendental Meditation and had been drawn most recently to an intensive practice for three years with Sri Chinmoy, an Indian guru. I was everything and anything but a Jew.

Yet water falling on rock wears on it. As the weeks and months went by, this question evoked a greater and greater sense of rage in me. I felt the question as ever more intrusive and personal, and it succeeded finally in becoming my question to myself. Sitting on the subway heading home, the question took on a life of its own in my mind. Am I a Jew? Am I a Jew?

For the first time in my life I asked myself what "Jew" meant to me. In it I felt the traces of an alien ethnicity, a distant history not mine and yet in some way mine. I faintly apprehended a link to some sense of lineage, parentage, spirituality. "Jew." I realized I feared the word, for to tell the world you are a Jew meant risking your life. Six million people had died during my childhood for saying *yes* to the question I was being asked on the campus of Brooklyn College in 1976. I realized that underneath my anger at their pestering, I was afraid, and I felt some sense of guilt for not being a Jew; I felt some sense of betrayal, as if in not owning that I was a Jew, I was turning my back on the holocaust. I even felt some sense of deprivation, that I had no sense of connection to a body of learning, lore, and life into which, by happenstance, I had been born.

During these months when the question wore on me like a koan, like water upon a rock, I realized that I had always felt like an outsider. At boarding school, as one of five Jews in my class of a hundred boys, I never forgot that I was a Jew among Gentiles. But I felt like a Gentile among the Jews, for I had taken communion many times, and I had found it sweet. In the presence of my Eastern guru I was conscious of my Western attachments; among those who professed a purely Western or rational philosophy, I felt how deeply identified I was with the wisdom and mysticism of the East. Among the Yankees of New England I often felt something pagan and Mediterranean in my blood; but among the Greeks I felt traces of my grandmother's Russia also. Among my father's intellectuals I felt forever a pretender; but among the socialites whose tea dances and cotillions had been the high life of my late adolescence, I felt I had not been, in any real sense, to the manor born. Among the jocks I was a nerd, among the nerds a jock. When my daughter was ten, someone asked her what her religion was. "I am half Christian, half Jewish," she said, "and a quarter of everything else." She had learned these spiritual fractions from me, and though I admired the mad mathematics of her answer, I felt in myself that these fractions were fractures whose fault lines ran through my entire life.

When I came to read the story of Abraham, it seemed that I had at last stumbled on a figure in whose life I could find some model for my own. For what would Abraham have answered if someone had asked him, "Are you Jewish?" Abraham was the man who was not yet a Jew. Organized religion had not yet happened, and despite his sense of being an outsider and stranger everywhere, he was relieved of the cant and conformity of a collective identity. He was alone—was there ever a lonelier man than Abraham?—but he was also free. And more, he had had his visions. He knew what I knew, that the world itself and all its forms stand in relation to some transcendent and mysterious reality. He knew what Hamlet knew: That there is "more in heaven and earth than is dreamt of" in philosophy. He knew what Castaneda knew: There is a crack between the worlds. He was a Taoist before Taoism, a pilgrim before there were shrines, the first seeker of God. This was Abraham; he was and still is my elder, my sage, a stranger yet a father for my soul.

6

Scenes from a Marriage

The intimacies between God and Abram—their close encounters and dark dialogues—contrast sharply to the silences between Abram and Sarai, his wife. As we have it, the canonical tale tells us very little about what passes between these two people. She goes where he goes; she does what he asks her to do. Genesis is silent about her responses and feelings; we know nothing of the degree of her engagement with Abram's dreams and ambitions. Man and woman, though they share a common world, seem separate in what they share of an inner one. In that inscape, Abram seems alone; Sarai as well.

The sense of their relationship as empty or formal and the narrative placement of Sarai in what appears a subservient and secondary position to her husband both contribute to a modern reader's feeling that these old stories are patriarchal in the negative sense. Here it seems the gifts and powers of women are overlooked, even repressed. She may be there as guide, confidante, and friend to her man, but gender says nothing of her own experiences of imagination, her own calls to service and vocation, her own rites and mysteries of observance. The biblical world of Genesis is a man's world, at least as we find it in the bare words of the stories.

Yet the narrative does not tell us very much about Abram either. That internal and wrestling soliloquy that seethes under the events of his life, the subtext of his story, is after all something we have to imagine, for almost nothing of Abram's internal state and feelings is put into words. To move beyond the surface of the story, to read between its lines, whether for him or Sarai, is an act of midrash; we have to make it up. The scenes of their marriage, only the bare outlines of which remain, can be fleshed out only through our imaginative participation as readers and players of the text.

But here a voice inside me asks, Why make up anything at all? We have what we have of the story. It is highly condensed, highly charged, but it is all we have. By what right and license do you fill in blanks and intrude your contemporary experience into these ancient figures who were wrought by the imagination of a distant, different age? These mute characters cannot step from the frieze of the old book and speak our words or borrow our voices that they might tell us more of their stories. This is, after all, the Bible.

Precisely these questions face me each time I pass from merely repeating the biblical stories to re-creating them. I must deal with the guardians of the text, those internalized deacons who warn me against toying with Holy Writ. Yet through my years of psychodramatic explorations I have come to recognize the immense vitality of these characters, and the silence of the text has become not a barrier but an invitation for acts of imaginative projection that seem at once to reflect ourselves and to reveal the biblical drama at a deeper and more human level.

These acts of imaginative projection are part of what I referred to as postpatriarchal midrash. Feminists have already begun to lay hands on the Bible and to develop new readings and midrashim that permit the canonized fables to open in new ways.[1] But, with certain exceptions, contemporary men are only beginning to participate in that process.[2] We are understandably more complacent with biblical narratives, no doubt in part because they support a status quo that favors us. What need have we had to challenge a text that has sanctified our positions of power? The gender issues the biblical text opens up for discussion are impressive not just because these patterns in culture were formed millennia ago but because in many ways they still persist. In re-visioning these ancient fables, we bring our contemporary discourse about gender and spirituality into relation with our traditional myth-theology.

Of course, one of the first things I realize in working with midrash, creating it, and co-creating it in psychodramatic explorations of the text, is that what lies on the other side of silence in the biblical narratives is nothing short of almost infinite possibility. Different groups and readers, free to imagine the internal lives and the unspoken dialogues between Abram and Sarai, discover harmonious *and* contradictory possibilities. In the world of psychodramatic midrash, no consensus is possible; nor is one even desirable.

❀   ❀   ❀

I remember vividly a psychodramatic group in which a scene from the marriage of Sarai and Abram provided us with our story. We had reviewed the passage together:

> *Now there was a famine in the land, and Abram went down into Egypt. . . . On the threshold of Egypt, he said to his wife Sarai, "Listen. I know you are a beautiful woman. When the Egyptians see you they will say, 'That is his wife,' and they will kill me but spare you. Tell them you are my sister, so that they will treat me well because of you and spare my life out of regard for you."*

> *When Abram arrived in Egypt the Egyptians did indeed see the woman was very beautiful. When Pharaoh's officials saw her they sang her praises to Pharaoh, and the woman was taken into Pharaoh's palace. He treated Abram well because of her, and he received flocks, oxen, donkeys, men and women slaves, she donkeys and camels.*

> *But God inflicted severe plagues on Pharaoh and his household because of Abram's wife, Sarai. So Pharaoh summoned Abram to him and said, "Why didn't you tell me she was your wife? Why did you say, 'She is my sister,' so I took her for my wife? Now here is your wife. Take her and go!"*

> *Pharaoh sent men with Abram to escort him back to the frontier with all he possessed, and from Egypt Abram returned to the desert . . . and slowly back to Bethel. (12:10–13:4)*

Our drama began abruptly when a woman slammed down an empty chair in front of us, saying, "This is Abram, and I have something I want to say to him." Then she spoke directly to him. This is the gist of what she said:

> *This incident with your wife in Egypt is outrageous. You selfish bastard! You think of nothing more than saving your own skin; your woman is an object to be used in a barter for your life. You don't even wait for her to offer; you don't sit down with her to examine alternatives. It's as if you want to get rid of her.*
> *And why? It's obvious. You've become infatuated with this vision you have of siring a great nation and being a household word, and your barren wife isn't going to be able to deliver. So you decide to head on down to Egypt; you fabricate some tale about local customs and likely perils, and you place her in the morally impossible position of either having to say no to you, which is tantamount to consenting to your death, or of letting herself become a hostage, if not a whore, for your safety. And this, all this, because you have the delusion that God has spoken to you and that you are special.*

"Not necessarily so," countered a man in the group, slipping into the empty chair and responding as Abram:

> *We are driven by famine. It is severe. My wife and I pass into Egypt, into a land of high civilization and great antiquity. But as we approach the border, I get scared. I believe the Egyptian lords will see how beautiful my wife is and want her for themselves. Being no respecters of marriage, they will kill for her. So in the grips of this fear, caught between the famine behind and the unknown ahead, I propose a ruse with Sarai. I hope it will save my skin and keep us from being separated. "When I'm asked who we are," I tell her, "let me say you are my sister." Sarai understands. She doesn't protest, and if you knew Sarai, you'd know she can speak her mind whenever she needs to. She's no meek, subservient wife. She appears to believe, as I do, that in identifying herself as my sister, she will not put me in jeopardy.*
>
> *The point is we think no farther ahead than this. The prospect of a season in our marriage when we will live as brother and sister does not overly trouble us, except as it might forestall Sarai in her wish for a child. But we have to survive.*

"Wait a moment," another group member put in. "Let's go farther." She took a second chair and sat in it as Sarai.

> *We have dreamed of Egypt. Fabled for plenty, it is the green and golden land. Unlike Canaan, where fertility depends on rainfall, Egypt's bounty comes annually, predictably, from the rise and fall of the Nile. It's a country not unfriendly to travelers, but always there is a price to pay for Egyptian hospitality, a border tax. We are poor.*
>
> *For my part I have dreamt of Isis and the mother cults. I knew the old stories even as a girl in Ur. I had heard the brother-sister tales of the Egyptian religion; we even had a few of our own back in Mesopotamia, where I was born. I think of making a pilgrimage to the shrines to the sister Goddess. This land is rich in the wisdom of fertility. I keep wondering how the will of our God is to be achieved. Perhaps through some knowledge gained from Egypt.*

"So," one member of the group asked Sarai, "you're involved with Abram in this mission?"

"I am," Sarai responded. "No one was there to record our conversations at night, but we loved each other, and our love had words."

Then someone else in the group came forward to play Abram and took this Sarai's hand. "Surely we did. Who else was there for me to talk to? I thought I had lost my mind. The only comfort I ever found was with you, and you seemed to understand. I think this Great Father, who spoke to me, spoke also to you."

"I wouldn't want to overdo this," Sarai insisted. "There were times when I didn't know what was going on. When we came into Canaan and there was no place to rest, I looked back often on our life in Haran. When the famine came, I was afraid. But I think I was more excited than Abram to leave Haran. Something in the summons of this God reached me, if not in words, then in my blood. And my barrenness weighed on me. I felt hope in the possibility of a new life."

Abram continued now:

> We drew close to the border of Egypt; we put on our best clothes and ornaments, for we didn't want to appear as beggars on the Egyptian doorstep. Sarai wore her finest linens and bangles on her arms, the ones her mother wore; in her ears, her mother's jewels. When I saw her, I was astonished. It was as if I had been away for a long time and returned to find my wife more beautiful than I had remembered.
>
> And suddenly I was afraid. Desiring her, I saw she was desirable, and knowing the Egyptians from the stories that travel the trade routes, I feared their rapacity. Behind us the famine and a silent God, ahead of us the fertile valley but the Egyptian price. So I proposed that we travel as brother and sister. We had no children. We could fabricate a story. In fact we were blood related through family, so much of our cover story was true. As brother and sister we would be protected. I would not be at risk. Neither of us thought through the consequences. A survivor's life is improvised from moment to moment.
>
> We entered the land. We found it as rich as it had been rumored to be, and for a time we lived in peace, pitching our tents where other migrants were encamped. Our flocks were taxed, our household scrutinized, numbered. But in some way it came to be known that a woman of exceptional beauty had arrived with the recent transients, exotic, Eastern, queenly in her bearing; she had come with her brother, a herder of sheep, and a scraggly retinue. Someone to talk about. Someone to tell the king about, always on the lookout for fresh beauty to grace his court.

Sarai picked up the story:

> So it happened, you see, not by design, not by any intention. One day a squad of court guards appeared at the tent and summoned me to a chariot. They silenced Abram with a purse of gold and a spear to block my "brother's" resistance.

Quickly gathering a few things—and told I would be given much, so no need to take anything at all—clutching my small old gods, my amulets, and taking a gasping backward look at my husband, I left and entered another life.

"And in a moment my worst fears were realized," Abram said. "I wished they *had* killed me, and I hated myself for my cowardice."

Here we paused. The psychodrama was making us aware of the pain in the story.

Conjugal anguish takes many forms, and fable and mythology are full of scenes of adultery, the hate that corrodes a marriage bed, the divisions of loyalty, the bitterness of love gone sour. But the anguish we may imagine for Abram and Sarai is intense only to the extent that we imagine love. If these two do not love each other, if he is merely using her to further his own ends, to save his skin, to increase his wealth, to evade his fate, then on his side there is no anguish. If she on her side is disgusted with him, his family, and his remote God, if she welcomes the opportunity for wealth or leaves him to indulge her appetites, then there is only good riddance and no nobility. But if they love each other and have during their trek been bound more closely to a common, puzzling fate; if they have endured trials that have brought them at nightfall with relief to each other's arms; if he has leaned his head on her breast for comfort or placed his hand upon her belly with a gentleness not even she could muster in her bleak frustration with having, moon after moon, no child, then this parting at the tent, this rape of Sarai, cuts them both to the core.

How are we to imagine Abram's nights? When, as does occur, Pharaoh favors Abram ("for her sake Pharaoh dealt well with Abram; and he had sheep, oxen, he-asses, menservants, maidservants, she-asses, and camels"), with what feelings do we imagine he receives these gifts? At what cost have they come? And when he is told, as he must surely be, that Pharaoh has made a wife of Sarai (the Egyptians congratulate him; they send him sly and knowing looks; his stature increases because of her merit), with what jealousy will his heart burn? How desperately will he seek to find a way out while realizing with each day they live the lie that it becomes more dangerous to expose it. To what pitch of prayer will such a man be brought? Where will he not search in his imagination for the God who had appeared so promisingly to him so long ago?

Our group sits together with these questions, and in the empty chair we have before us we behold the great patriarch, Abram. In that moment he seems to us a broken man.

Then once again someone in the group, a woman this time, takes his role. With head downcast and hands turning a piece of cloth, as Abram she

asks, "Can any condemnation match my own? I can never forgive myself."
Then looking to the chair left empty by a vanished Sarai, "And think of her.
What is it like for her?"

We imagine her. Trapped in the lap of luxury, living a lie, lying with a
king, beseeching now that she not be pregnant, yet wondering fearfully in her
heart if the great nation promised her husband is destined to come from her
consorting with Egypt's king. "My life was a nightmare." Will that be the solu-
tion and the resolution of it all? Called to perform the services of a royal wife,
she must, we agree, find a way to feel nothing. "I have become a royal plaything. My only satisfaction is constantly reminding Pharaoh about my brother."
She brokers for him and so salvages something from this gilded enslavement.

"What kind of a God is this Great Father?" one Sarai asks. "Who will hear
my outrage? I have been abandoned. He has abandoned both of us. He promised
us a land and a family and a name, and He gave us the life of strangers, a
famine, and this . . . I don't know what to call it . . . this hell in Egypt, this
shame. Who needs this God? What does He do for you?"

None of us has an answer for her. We read the story to the end.

An affliction comes to Egypt—and how long it has taken to occur we
do not know. There are "great plagues visited upon Pharaoh and his house"
(12:17).

"And what were these plagues?" I ask one woman who plays Sarai.

She laughs. "What is the greatest plague men can imagine?" When we
draw a blank, she says, "Impotence." And Sarai tells us this story.

*It began the first night. Pharaoh approached me, but he couldn't get it up.
I was, of course, scared and appalled, but then I saw some humor in it, though I
had to be very quiet and hide my relief. The next night it was the same, and the
third night also. On the fourth night Pharaoh did not send for me but called one
of the young courtesans. But in the morning his darkened face told the whole
story. But it was not only Pharaoh whose looks were grim that fourth day. By then
the muttering of the courtiers had become a general cry of consternation; individual shame was swallowed up in a collective outrage and fear. No man in
Pharaoh's court could make love with any woman, and by the end of the week
word came from the villages and outlands that no man anywhere in the kingdom
had made love to a woman.*

*The court doctors were summoned; the magi were consulted; the stars were
scrutinized. A week of abstinence was mandated; no man was to go near a woman
for seven days. But at the end of that week, nothing had changed. By then I knew,
or at least suspected, that this was the work of God. One evening I went to
Pharaoh in his dejection—and is there anything more dejected than an impotent*

king?—and I said to him that I believed I knew the cause of this plague on his kingdom.

He looked at me with a mixture of hope and fear. "When did it begin?" I asked him. He thought a moment. "Two weeks ago." "Two weeks ago I was brought to you, taken from my brother." "True," he said, and I believe he had already made that connection, though perhaps many other connections also. "That man is not my brother but my husband, and we are under the protection of a great God."

I proceeded then to tell Pharaoh the entire story, of the call and our departure from Haran, our arrival in Canaan, the famine, and our plan to enter Egypt as brother and sister. You know the rest, the story of our release and our journey back. Pharaoh was angry and relieved. In the end I think he was in awe of me, and he asked me to choose something of his as a gift to take with me. There was one woman among his concubines who had treated me kindly and whose husband had in fact been killed when Pharaoh took possession of her. I pitied her. She could have been me, after all. I chose her as my gift. Her name was Hagar, and she left with us when we left Egypt.

Now exiled from Egypt, enriched with a bitter spoil, they journey north again to that land that God had dubiously promised for them. "But can they ever be the same again?" one group member asked. "They can't be. She's been numb and had an affair, even if an abortive one. He's been jealous and abandoned. This is going to be a slow, imperfect healing. Both of them have been broken."

The effect of this separation is to turn them into strangers to each other. The bond that had sustained him at least, and likely her, may not be broken, but it has been weakened by their fate. What they have known apart, their fears and their pain, has reminded each of them how alone they are. They cannot even say what it was that sustained them, perhaps only the animal necessity to survive. When they see each other again, and even as they travel northward into Canaan, they must feel the distance between them. In comparison to what they were before, they are more alone now, more afraid.

If Sarai and Abram survive their loss, if they can mend their way back toward each other and retrace their steps toward the land and the dream, then this is what it must mean to "keep the faith."

In our psychodrama Sarai and Abram spoke their final words to one another and to us: "In the end it was a matter of forgiveness, and that came slowly."

"In the end it was also a matter of listening to one another and each of us feeling the pain the other had felt." Then, as if the group members were freed each to play out his and her own sense of the ending, a polyphony of voices ended our work:

"As Abram I had to realize that I did not possess this woman. She was not mine, and I had to get past the pain that came from thinking of her as my possession."

"As Sarai I had to understand that for my husband I was in some deep sense 'his.' I was all he had. In comparison to me, his God was insubstantial and remote. His loss of me was all the more painful because he had nothing else."

Possessed and dispossessed, atoned yet separate, man and woman leave Egypt. They are still looking for home. In retrospect, life before Egypt, for all its harassments, was a kind of Eden; Egypt was the loss.

The session provoked an immense amount of sharing and reflection. In that group of fifteen men and women, more than twenty-five marriages were represented. The story of Abram and Sarai became a scene from a marriage that had been replayed in many different ways in the lives of group members.

Two stories remain with me. One was David's:

> Makes me think of my first wife, Constance. We were so close. Like Sarai and Abram, I guess. We went through a lot together. I met her when I got out of jail, and I made her my life. I couldn't let her out of my sight. I was jealous, jumpy, always scared she was going to leave me. Then it started to happen. After our second child was born, she started to go through some changes. Said she needed her "space," joined a women's group.
>
> Then one night she came home late, real late, and there was a look in her eyes that I'd never seen before. I was sure she'd met someone. I accused her. She denied it. I hit her. She slashed back at me. Only the screams of our kids stopped us from killing each other.
>
> That was the beginning of the end—and the end took a long time. God, I wouldn't let go. I called her. I pursued her. I tried to find out who she was seeing. I was nuts. I was in so much pain, but basically I was scared, real scared, about being alone, about having to live by myself, with myself. But I think of myself when I think of Abram wondering what Sarai was doing with Pharaoh; some part of him had to be in hell.

Then there was a very different story; it was Judith's footnote to the session:

> It's a story I read somewhere about the holocaust. It told of a couple on a train to a place they would later learn was called Dachau, a man and his wife standing huddled in a boxcar as it rattled through the summer heat. Rumor and premonition had them both scared. What to do, they wondered. She was a

beautiful woman, and he was afraid that they would take her from him, perhaps even kill him so that they might have her.

He took her hand. By the faint light of the car he could see the glimmer of her ring. "My darling, I am afraid," he said. "The soldiers will see you and think you beautiful. They will see I am your husband and kill me to get me out of the way. If we went there as, say, brother and sister, my life might not be in such peril. Can you forgive me for asking this of you?" His head was bowed. He heard her whisper in the dark, "Take off my ring," and as he did so all the years flooded over him as the past is said to do in the last moments before we die.

7

Ishmael:
A Midrash

Time and again in the writing of this book certain biblical figures, who are particularly alive for me, assert themselves and in a sense ask to be admitted to my page. I have read the Genesis tales so many times, and I have led so many psychodramatic explorations, that I feel I have visited the tiniest nooks and crevices of the narrative and heard voices and perceived lives sometimes only hinted at in the text. My central interest as a reader of Genesis, and of the Bible, has been more fully to imagine these voices and lives. This interest is admittedly more that of the literary artist than the commentator or the theologian.

Of course, it is not clear whose "voices and lives" I am in fact recovering. When I stand before the text, am I looking at an array of fun-house mirrors that, with all their distortions, only render back strange versions of myself? Or am I standing before these myths as before a series of windows, looking through them into a world that surrounds me in infinite directions? And is it possible that the mythic artifact is both mirror and window at once? These are questions I cannot answer, distinctions I cannot make. I know only that sometimes certain characters say things that surprise me, things that I don't think I could have known without having let them speak.

I have come to one of those places where I feel the pressure of a particular figure asking me for his own voice in this book. He is a minor figure in the text, an outcast even among the outcasts. He never speaks a word in those parts of Genesis that tell some fragments of his life, but he asks for a language to speak now. His name is Ishmael.

He needs his context.

One of the dramatic tensions in the story of Abram has been strung upon the question of his paternity. In order for God's promise to be fulfilled, Abram must become a father, but Sarai's barrenness, which persists through their wanderings in Canaan and in Egypt, prevents him from having a child with her. For all their movement, Abram and Sarai seem stalled. Like the promise of the land, which beckons and recedes, the promise of parenthood must tax them with questions about themselves and the divine reality with which they keep faith. When and how will the promise be fulfilled? Or will it ever be?

At last Sarai takes matters into her own hands and brokers a match between her husband and her Egyptian maidservant, Hagar. The plot thickens. For a time Sarai is upstaged by her auxiliary; the pregnant Hagar displeases her mistress; and despite her desire to give her husband a son, Sarai kicks the girl out. According to the text, Hagar, slave and foreign born, is met in the wilderness by Abram's God (whom Sarai herself has yet to glimpse!) and receives an annunciation of the birth of a male child whom God Himself instructs her to name Ishmael. She names the place of her annunciation "The Well of the Living One Who Sees Me." She is told to go back and bear her child. This she does.

The child becomes the adopted son of Abram and Sarai, is indeed named Ishmael (the only child in Genesis named by God). Is he the long-awaited heir? Now settled and a family, husband and wife live in apparent peace for thirteen years. The dramatic tension seems to have been resolved.

But then the Great Father summons Abram once again to renew the promise with him. Abram is ninety-nine years old. In the course of this unsettling encounter he is told that he will be exceedingly fertile. The Father tells him,

> "I am El Shaddai. Walk in my ways and be blameless. I will make a covenant between myself and you, and I will increase your numbers greatly."

> Abram threw himself on his face, and God spoke to him further.

> "Here then is my covenant with you. You shall become the father of a multitude of nations. You shall no longer be called Abram; your name shall be Abraham, for I will make you the father of a multitude of nations. I will make you most fruitful . . . and kings will issue from you. I will establish my covenant between myself and you, and your descendants after you, generation after generation, an everlasting covenant throughout the ages. I will give the land you wander in to you and to your descendants after you, all the land of Canaan, and I will be your God." (17:1–8)

Then God asks Abraham, as his first act, to circumcise himself and all the males of his household as a sign of his commitment to the bargain—the covenant—that He, the Father, would seal with him. Further, Abraham is told that Sarai—now also renamed and henceforth to be known as Sarah—will bear a son. This causes Abraham to fall down laughing. What a joke, he all but says to himself, shall I at a hundred and Sarah at ninety be parents?

Obedient then to the divine assignment, however, Abraham circumcises himself, the thirteen-year-old Ishmael, and all the males of his household, kin and slave, home born and foreign born.

A year later, Sarah indeed conceives and bears a son. Abraham names him Isaac, which means, in Hebrew, "he shall laugh." But after Isaac is weaned, Sarah has occasion to observe the two boys playing together and orders her husband to send Ishmael and Hagar away, saying, "The son of this slave-woman Hagar shall not share in the inheritance with my son Isaac" (21:10). With a heavy heart Abraham does as she wishes, and though assured by God that Ishmael would sire a nation, Abraham casts them out into the perilous wilderness. Had God not shown Hagar a place to find water, they would have died in that wilderness.

And Isaac grew up without a brother.

And here Ishmael speaks:

The best that can be said about their damnable Bible is that they had the temerity to include us, or at least a few of us, in it. Most of us were written out, excised, edited away, forgotten; whole tribes and nations, families, mothers and daughters and women (particularly women, of whom my own mother is an instance) slaughtered by oblivion. Only his lineage and his line remain, Great Abraham's. His line and Sarah's—mustn't forget her—now stands in their book as the dominant strain. Dominant to be sure, dominant by guile, dominant by repression, dominant by betrayal, by the expulsion of the unchosen, by the murder of the uncircumcised. What a deluded lot, and that's putting it kindly. Some would say demonic. Yes, the best that can be said is that my mother's name is listed, Hagar, and my name with hers, Ishmael, first son and only son of Abram. Abram! He retired that name, disowned himself, his deed, and me.

What they did to my mother is unspeakable. Sarah used her, became furiously jealous of her, threw her out, took her back, stole her child, me, and then sent both of us away again. This time she sent us to what would surely have been our deaths had not I found water and killed some game, while my poor mother, in her thirst and terror, heard voices and went mad. Sarah did this. I curse her name. And she and my mother had been close once, almost like sisters. Hagar had been a gift to Sarai—when that was her name—from Pharaoh; she had nursed Sarai back to health after they left Egypt, when Sarai's heart was broken and bitter. They understood each other, even when they fought.

But Abram! He was my father. I loved him. I thought he loved me, but in the end he was a weak, pathetic man. Let me tell you how it was, how it really was.

In my earliest years I knew only Sarai as my mother, for this was the agreement she had forced my mother to make. By no sign was Hagar to know me, nor was she ever to approach me. She lived among the foreign-born slaves, close to the livestock. But you cannot keep secrets in a clan. There were always whispers, and by the time I was a boy of seven I knew that Sarai was not my mother, and I drew away from her. When I could, I spent time with the serving boys, I went into the fields with the flocks. I saw my mother, Hagar, when no one observed me.

So I grew up divided in a divided house. I belonged nowhere. My father loved me with a starved, possessive love. He drew me to him with stories. He filled my mind with the tales of his people and the lore of his God. I doubt he could see my hesitations, for I held something back from him, mistrustful of his zeal and enthusiasms. Besides, I was not an apt student. Always I wanted to be off hunting, or in the wild grazing places with the other boys. Sarai was always stiff with me, and after I learned she was not my mother, I came to hate her with a silent coldness.

But of all the things I went through with that father-man and his Father-God, the strangest was being mutilated with the knife. I was thirteen when he took me up to a high place and told me that his God had commanded him to cut off our foreskins, his first, then mine, then those of all the men in the tribe, slaves and servants, foreign and blood born.

It is a terrifying thing when a man comes at you with a knife, comes at you *there*. Can you understand a God who asks for this kind of act as a way of sealing his bargain with you? I never could. Abraham assured us all this was not meant to humiliate us; this was to be a sign, he said, of our special relationship with God. It was a sign on our flesh like the rainbow was a sign in the sky. I only know it hurt.

Then I learned that forever afterward infant boys were to be cut like this on the eighth day of their life. I was there when Abraham cut Isaac. No one laughed that day, I'll tell you that. I don't know what it was like for others, but when I came to be with women, I always felt my difference from other men. It was like a part of my body had been taken from me, or it had been made to mean something I hadn't chosen it to mean. I had been mutilated for the sake of a future that was never going to be my future and for the sake of a pact with a God who was never going to be my God.

Abram had always tried to get me to understand his God. He told me the stories, but Mother would tell me stories, too, when I could sneak away and spend time with her. I always wanted to be a great hunter like the Egyptian God Osiris, not a shepherd like Abram. So there we were; he was chanting and praying and sharpening a knife. For him I suppose it was all part of some attempt to bond us in some strange communion with his God. But for me it was the last straw. Now I knew him for what he was, a fanatical, God-maddened man who would do anything this God commanded. From then on he loved me more; I loved him less. I feared him, not because he would ever willingly harm me—he never lifted a hand against me in all our years together, and I will tell you I provoked him more than once—but because he would do anything his God would ask, and his God would ask anything. I believe if his God had said to him to take me up there and cut off my head, he would have done it.

We were sojourning in Gerar when things came to a head at last. Sarai had become increasingly bitter and alone, for she had lost a sister in my mother, and she had no son in me. Abram was all father now and no longer a husband to her. So in Gerar they separated. She moved out of his tent and into a tent of her own. He let it be known that they were not husband and wife, but brother and sister, and when the local king, Abimelech, had her brought to his tent, she did not refuse, and Abram said nothing. After all, he had his son, and she, sick of it all, was glad, I suppose, to be free of a wandering life. I know I was glad to see her go, and I thought my own mother would soon share Abram's tent. As it should have been.

The night Sarai left, my mother came to me. "It's Egypt all over again," she told me, and for the first time I learned how she had come to serve Sarai and what her fate in Egypt had been. My mother wept for Sarai then, even after all she had put her through, and she went to Abram. "Bring her back," she said. "No good can come of this." But he did nothing.

That very night Abimelech had a dream in which the Lord appeared to him warning him that, for taking Sarai from her husband, he was sure to die. At least this was the story Sarai brought back with her, saying that Abimelech had not laid a hand on her. Apparently Abimelech was angry that Abram had lied to him, and Sarai, too, putting him and his household in such peril. Who could blame him?

I was there when they were reunited. And had my heart not been hard against them both for my mother's sake, I believe I might have forgiven them everything then. At supper that night they sat under the candlelight in a strange silence. How old they seemed, and when they spoke to one another, it was as if I were not there. Each asked forgiveness of the other, and when they both began to weep remembering all the sorrows and the trials they had been through, I left the tent and went outside. I belonged nowhere. I went out to the shepherds and slept with them under the stars. I believe it was that night that Sarai at last conceived. I was fourteen when she bore a son (though there were some who maintained to the end the boy was Abimelech's seed).

Abraham named him Isaac. What kind of a name is that for a man? It was a joke among all the young men. I had been displaced, but I was not forgotten. Abraham assured me I was an equal in his heart, though I wondered when I saw him raise his Isaac in the air and laugh. Sarah laughed, too.

Those laughing days lengthened into months. I was a man now, princeling and bastard both. I was followed and I was feared. I had little to do with the infant boy. Then the day arrived that marked the change.

Isaac was two years old, a special birthday for the boy child of the clan king. We called it a weaning feast. I could dimly remember my own. For the women it was a time of mourning and consolation. Sarah and the baby's nurse covered their breasts with ashes and drew black shawls over their heads. Abraham took his boy out into the fields and there pitched a tent among the herds. All the men came then to sing and celebrate the birthday. Goat's milk and cheeses were prepared and served him as if he were a little king. For the first time his hair was shorn. He sat upon his own small throne, hung with garlands and soft with sheepskins. He toddled now into the world of men. He had his first taste of red wine, saw for the first time the slaughter of a ram, and heard the sound of the trumpet blown through its severed horn. That night he was lulled to sleep by Abraham's singing in his deep, melodious voice the story of the beginning of the world. I'd heard it all before. I slipped off to the field, where I met one of the serving girls.

In time Isaac became my charge; my task to teach him the crafts and skills that Abraham had taught me. But Sarah could not stand the sight. I believe she feared I would harm her darling little boy. It's true, I was rough with him, but no roughness, no tough hide. She said to Abraham—I heard her— "Cast out that slave woman and her son, for the son of that slave shall not share in the inheritance with my son, Isaac."

This was the kind of woman she was.

You can read the rest of the story in their book, but much of it is lies. This much, though, is true. They say Abraham was "displeased" when Sarah commanded him to cast us out. He wept. I saw him when he rose early that morning and gave my mother and me some bread and the waterskin. I had never seen him weep. He covered his head with dust and sat in the road until we could see him no more. I was his son, and he was the only father I would ever have. He knew he was sending us off to our deaths, for in the wilderness of that country only misfortune can occur to an unprotected woman and a boy. This God of theirs breaks hearts.

They write in their book that this God saved me, and saved my mother; that is not true. I found the water for her. I found the well, and with my bow I shot the game we needed to survive in the wilderness of Paran. Now my mother and I are all but passed over in their stories. The wealth of Abraham was bestowed upon Isaac; we received nothing.

You have heard me speak in anger. It is their book that angers me. It prophesied that I was to be "a wild ass of a man," who would set himself against his brothers, and because of that sentence I am an outcast and an enemy to my brother's people through a hundred generations. I have become the father of the bedouin, the grandsire of Mohammed, and now my issue is perpetually at war with the sons of Abraham. Yet it need not be so. For I came to Machpelah and met with Isaac; we were reconciled.

Machpelah was the place Abraham was buried, the place where first he buried Sarah and later came to rest himself. Many years had passed, but news reached me that Abraham had died and been laid in the cave of Machpelah. So I came as a king to pay my respects to a king, for he was my father, and I loved him. There I met fair Isaac, who was as different from his father as the dove from the owl. Yet, in his own way, no less a man. In his eyes I saw a flame.

We met in the cave. We spoke. We wept. We reviewed our brotherhood, and we knew there was no need for the tangled enmity of our parents—our mothers—to persist. The land, after all, was wide; there was enough. There is always enough for brothers. So we parted in peace, and I felt the spring of my heart sweeten for my little brother. I wished him well, for I had heard what he had endured. I knew he had been to the heart of light—or was it madness?—which I had been spared. I feared for him.

Ishmael's voice comes easily to me and to many of my contemporaries. I hear Ishmael's voice everywhere. In the ventriloquy of our role-playing, he speaks in many dialects and tongues, often in protest at the unfairness of family favoritism, often in pain at the wounds it made. I have seen Ishmael in the daughter abandoned in divorce and in the boy deprived of his father and made wild by that deprivation. However much his father may have loved him, Ishmael carries into his ostracism the experience of rejection.

Ishmael is the voice of the outcast, the orphan, the part of our community that has been uprooted, branded, forced into conversion or the closet, or made into the enemy. Ishmael—in Genesis—stands for all those who live outside of privilege, those who by color, caste, or conviction are regarded as Other. Many women share their sisterhood with Ishmael; they claim Hagar as their mother, not Sarah, and they despise the cowardice of Abraham. Many blacks look at Isaac with bitterness, and in their anger feel Ishmael's rage. Many gay men and women feel society has sent them into the shadows of a separate society. And the whole Moslem culture, mythically descended from Ishmael, is still regarded as the enemy of Sarah's seed.

Thematically in the Book of Genesis Ishmael raises the ghost of Cain, keeps alive as an undercurrent the brother stories, and reminds us that the question asked at the beginning—"Am I my brother's keeper?"—has not yet been answered. And it is often as brothers or sisters that we speak with and through him. "Call me Ishmael," said one woman:

> *I was, or felt like, the black sheep in the family. My brother Raymond could do no wrong. "Ray," my mother used to say, "you're a ray of sunshine." And it was obvious that my father lighted up when he saw Ray. I don't think he was any better than I was; my grades were better. He was better in sports, of course, but Ray was the darling in the house.*
>
> *I turned into the wild one. My parents always criticized my friends, and so increasingly I spent time with them away from home. One thing led to another, and looking back I can see that by high school I was in with a dangerous crowd. We were all Ishmaels, I guess: sex, drugs, and rock 'n' roll. I went to rehab for a while.*
>
> *Finally I began to turn it around, got into therapy, into AA. Made my peace with a lot of things, and I even got into this whole philosophy about the Higher Power, found it useful and deep. But I could never understand the unfairness of things. I could see unfairness everywhere. I had learned it was destructive to feel sorry for yourself about it, but I could never get with religion because it seemed to me religion was always trying to give you a way of understanding the unfairness, and I never could. Never could.*
>
> *It still burns me up, and I think this is what Ishmael knows, really knows in his guts. There's no explaining unfairness, but you don't need to be alive for very long before you know this is the way it's all wired up, and it makes you want to take an ax to God.*

With a hundred variations I have heard this Ishmael. Another person whose story touched my own wrote to me after a workshop, and these are some words from that letter:

> *I'm an only child, and yet I can still relate to Ishmael. I won't say my father doted on me; he wasn't a doting man, but he loved me, and he was interested in me, but I still feel like I can relate to Ishmael. Not his anger, but his sense of belonging to a different tribe from his father's tribe. In a way Ishmael is a lot like Abraham in the sense that he leaves his father's house and has to make his life with strangers. He's another stranger like his dad, and he knows something his father knows.*
>
> *That's what's funny about my dad and me. My dad was a hardworking blue-collar postwar union man. He worked real hard so that I could have some of the things he never had. Like a college education, and then law school. And I'm a lawyer now. My dad is proud of me, but when we get together, it's as if we speak different languages. He tells the old stories and I laugh; he asks me about my life and I sketch it in for him, but we live in two different countries. No hostility. Far from it. There's a deep, unspoken love between us, but somehow we're also strangers with one another.*
>
> *This is what has stayed with me from the story of Ishmael, and I couldn't really get in touch with it at the time. There was so much anger and pain in the group, I felt a little awed and maybe even intimidated. But later I felt this sadness, and I felt it was in the story of Abraham and Ishmael, or maybe it's what I bring to it. I can feel the love between them. Abraham never forgets Ishmael, and Ishmael never forgets his father. I think they long for each other, but . . . well, you change. You know, you grow apart. Abraham and Ishmael grow apart. Isaac and Ishmael grow apart. It's not an angry thing, not to me, this growing apart. It's a true thing, a sad thing, and I get in touch with it through Ishmael. I see him in the desert at night under the moon, and he's thinking about his father, and somewhere miles and miles away his father is thinking of Ishmael. What is it about the love between the generations that has so much closeness and so much distance in it at the same time?*

8

The Myth of Sacrifice

Between the return of Abraham and Sarah from Egypt and the banishment of Ishmael we find a series of interrelated stories that concentrate on Abraham's life in Canaan and his relationship to his nephew Lot, and they deserve elaboration. But they will not receive it here. I pass over how in the course of time Abraham became a warrior when he went off to rescue his brother's son from captivity; how the two of them subsequently argued and had a falling out; how they separated, and Lot went to live in Sodom. It would take me too far afield to examine in any detail how that city became corrupt and how God planned its destruction. I do not deal here with one of the most impressive stories of Abraham, when he came before the presence of God to argue for mercy for the inhabitants of Sodom if, among them, only a handful of innocent citizens could be found. In these passages Abraham appears as advocate, as host, as clan king received and recognized by the Canaanites. Through it all he is ever the dubious outsider, the resident alien, but by his deeds and under the sponsorship of his God, he and Sarah achieve a measure of security, wealth, power, and freedom in Canaan.

At last, too, Sarah becomes the mother of his child. The promise first delivered to him when he left his native land and father's house appears to be coming true. Ishmael is now gone; Hagar, too; and for many years, the family clan lives in apparent, untroubled peace.

A participant in a psychodrama once put it well and helped me to see the life of the ancestral family through these years. As Sarah she said,

For a long time now we have lived in Canaan among the Philistines. Often I remember Abraham's father as he was in Haran, for in that land and at that time I last enjoyed a simple life.

Indeed for years now God has left me and Abraham alone, and, to be honest, I have not missed Him. Perhaps our ways have pleased Him; perhaps He has been busy with other people in other lands. Abraham, Isaac, and I have settled in our ways, and I rarely think about the promise or the future. Life is ordinary, and ordinary life is a blessing after what we've been through. Even though I have been a witness to and a participant in mysteries, the habit of the ordinary has gradually taken hold of me. I trust life in its regularities and rhythms. My heart has healed of its losses; I love again with the heart of an ordinary woman. I love my husband, my son, my work, my life. And we are growing old in peace.

So I was given a glimpse of Sarah's life as Isaac grows to young manhood. This life hovers in the silence between the end of chapter 21: "And Abraham sojourned in the land of the Philistines for many years" (21:34) and the beginning of chapter 22, when God, wrenching him from his settled life, calls Abraham one last time to "leave . . . and go."

With the tale of Abraham's final summons and sacrifice, I come to the molten core of the patriarchal tradition. It is a nightmare place where Imagination conceives its ultimate ordeal. Though it occupies a mere nineteen verses in the biblical narrative, this story of Abraham and Isaac has haunted me since I first heard it. No matter how many times I encounter it I cannot read it without feeling the simultaneous pull of different aspects of myself; I am at once judging, comprehending, rejecting, fearful, awestruck, admiring, loathing. I see the meaning and the nonsense.

In a life full of initiations, this is Abraham's last initiation. In a life full of sacrifices, this is his ultimate sacrifice. We arrive at that place in his vocational life where the issues of greatness and madness, faith and delusion, the highest good and the highest evil, cannot be easily distinguished. We come in this story of Abraham and Isaac to the central myth of the patriarchal imagination—the father's sacrifice of the son, and the son's participation in that sacrifice.

Some time after, God put Abraham to the test. God spoke to him and said, "Abraham." And he answered, "Here I am."

And God said, "Leave with your son, your favored one, Isaac, whom you love, and go to the land of Moriah, and offer him there as a burnt offering on one of the heights which I will point out to you."

So early the next morning, Abraham saddled his ass and took with him two of his young servants and his son Isaac. He split the wood for the burnt offering, and he set out for the place of which God had told him.

On the third day Abraham looked up and saw the place from afar. Then Abraham said to his servants, "You stay here with the ass. The boy and I will go up there; we will worship and we will return to you." Abraham took the wood for the burnt offering and put it on his son Isaac. He himself took the firestone and the knife; and the two walked off together.

Then Isaac said to his father Abraham, "Father."

And he answered, "Yes, my son."

And he said, "Here are the firestone and the wood; but where is the sheep for the burnt offering?"

And Abraham said, "God will see to the sheep for the burnt offering, my son." And the two of them walked on together.

They arrived at the place of which God had told him. Abraham built an altar there; he laid out wood; he bound his son; he laid him on the altar, on top of the wood. And Abraham picked up the knife to slay his son.

Then the voice of the Lord called to him, "Abraham! Abraham!"

And he answered, "Here I am."

And the voice spoke again, "Do not raise your hand against the boy, or do anything to him. Now I know that you are in awe of God, since you have not withheld even your son, your favored one from Me."

When Abraham looked up his eye fell upon a ram, caught in the thicket by his horns. So Abraham went and took the ram and offered it up as a burnt offering in place of his son. And Abraham named that height the Place Where God Provides or, as some say, On the Mountain of God There Is Vision.

And God once again filled Abraham with the promise of blessing and nation. (22:1–14, 17–19)

I have played out this story many times. Here are some shards to suggest the shape of that work where one by one participants walked into the story, feeling their way into Abraham's heart line by line.

"Leave with your son, your favored one, Isaac, whom you love, and go to the land of Moriah."

"Once again I am told to 'leave . . . and go' just as I was told so many years ago. I remember all too well what that first call cost me. It cost me everything. Or at least it seemed everything at the time. But now I must 'leave . . . and go,' this time with my son. Go where and why? I am tired, and I am afraid."

"But," quarrels another Abraham, "he is not my only son. There is, there was, Ishmael. I remember Ishmael's birth and boyhood; I remember another rite and sacrifice. The boy was scared; his face was white. His eyes pleaded and asked me 'Why?' I did it first to myself, made light of it to ease his fears. 'God has asked this of us,' I said. What could he know of God? What has been real for me has only been a word for others. Am I always to look into the face of my sons and see fear?"

"And Sarah . . . what am I to say to my wife?"

". . . go to the land of Moriah, and offer him there as a burnt offering on one of the heights which I will point out to you."

Another person takes up the part of Abraham. "When God tells me to go to the land of Moriah and offer Isaac there as a burnt offering—a burnt offering!—I have no words for the image that comes into my mind. What sound does the breaking of a heart make? In this instant something dies in me, and it is not my 'belief' in this God. If my belief died, then there would be no obedience, no need to make the journey. My love dies, any love I might have felt for this God."

"I see images of my son on a pyre, bound on the tinder, the torch set to the wood, the flames are the last things in my mind before I fall asleep each night of the three nights we travel to Moriah. Each night I must say in the face of these images, have faith . . . you do not know . . . perhaps not. I must become a witness to my own inflamed imagination, for if I cannot find my detachment, I will be burned to a cinder."

Another voice: "Then there are spells of blankness when one foot merely falls in front of another. There are moments when I look aside at Isaac, see the sunlight on the boy's shoulders, the wind in his hair, and I must turn away quickly. Too much. You ask too much."

The father walks with his son.

How do we imagine his soliloquy? Perhaps not words, perhaps only images, memories. Images and memories that come in spite of his attempts to numb himself to the ordeal, to make his mind a blank, to put one foot in front of the other in some wooden obedience he can never fully achieve. He cannot stop feeling. What is it like to be a father every step of the way?

"Take your son . . . whom you love . . . your only son Isaac."

Isaac whose name means "he shall laugh." On these three days all laughter dies.

Three days. It is the duration of the dying. It is long enough for a man to think of everything more than once, to pass back and forth again and again over some imaginary threshold, entering, quitting, entering again until the doorstep is worn down. Long enough for a man to become acquainted with every part of himself, all the voices in their diverse articulations that prompt diverse actions. Time enough for memory; and time enough to realize that the mind can no longer conceive of a future. There is no time "after" this time, or if there is time after, it is empty. It is not possible for me to imagine Abraham thinking any longer of his future. Not his own personal future, nor the grand scheme, the promise, for which he would not willingly sacrifice so much. It is not for the future that he walks toward Moriah. Time is bound into three days, then two days, then one day. Then hours, minutes, seconds ahead.

"And always the question lives in me: Can I go on? Do I choose to go on, when every part of me urges me to choose not to go on? With each step on each day I choose to go on; with each step I am free not to go on, yet I go on freely; in each step where I place my forward foot down, I can still choose to turn away."

"The promise of land and nations is a mirage and a madness. I must slaughter my hope. It makes no sense that I am to kill the one upon whom a future depends. Perhaps then only the willingness is asked. Yet who knows?"

On the third day Abraham looked up and saw the place from afar. Then Abraham said to his servants, "You stay here with the ass. The boy and I will go up there; we will worship and we will return to you." Abraham took the wood for the burnt offering and put it on his son Isaac. He himself took the firestone and the knife; and the two walked off together.

So in the end we come to the mountaintop, to the rude stone altar, to the fagots laid on the stones, to the rope and the binding of the boy. Participants pair up, one as Abraham, one as Isaac, and we explore the scene in mute action. Several of us absolutely cannot allow themselves to be bound, and Abraham cannot compel them. This scene verges on the traumatic; it recalls trauma. Only Isaac's strange willingness and Abraham's suffering keep this from being sheer abuse. Afterward, those who allowed themselves to be bound report feeling the strangest mixture of shame and peace, and an incredible curiosity.

"I knew I was going to be spared at the last minute. I knew the story had a 'happy ending.' It was impossible to forget that. But for Isaac *in* the story, for Abraham?"

The question hangs over an abyss.

"I wanted my son to resist, to run away, to end this game with *his* will. *And* I wanted him to lie still."

"I am cleaned out, scraped raw inside. In the end I come to the task with such a stillness inside me that the ropes do not need to be tied, for my stillness passes to my son as a kind of deep calm. My eyes are streaming with tears, but there are no sobs, no cries, no words. I am looking into his eyes."

"*Abraham!*"

The father pauses. Deliverance?

"I cannot trust myself. I have prayed for this too long, too hard. The voice that calls my name sounds too much like my own voice, like my own imagination in a last leap, imitating God."

"*Abraham!*"

The knife drops from a hand now raised against the brilliance of the light.

A ram is found; an animal sacrifice replaces the human one, and then, in one final repetition of the promise, the story ends with the last words God ever speaks to Abraham. Or perhaps from this time forward Abraham never listens to Him again.

One person in our group claimed that Abraham knew all along that God was testing him and that in the end his son would be spared. Another claimed that Abraham was testing God even as he was being tested, seeing whether in fact this God would go that far. A third said that Abraham was testing himself to see how far he would go in obedience to this God, and he found, to his great horror, that he could go all the way. A fourth said that God was appalled at man's obedience and afterward promised himself He would never ask so much of men again. A fifth said that an angel arrested Abraham in the act and sought to comfort him, but it was too late; Abraham's soul was already traveling at the speed of light into an infinite darkness. A sixth said that Abraham turned the knife against the breast of the angel. A seventh said that when Abraham went to take the ram from the brambles, he wept over it, held it, rocked it in his arms, a mad old man, and that it was finally Isaac who had to slay it. An eighth said that Abraham came down the mountain without Isaac, knowing that their ways had parted forever. A ninth said that this is a fable of a deluded man with a twisted soul who then imagines a twisted God in his own image. A tenth said that Abraham will forever stand as the man of faith who tells us in this fable what is terrible and wonderful in faith.

❀   ❀   ❀

I find these ten in my heart. And there are four others.

The first to press forward in me to respond to this passage is Peter, the father of Zachary. My son is now sixteen years old. Not long ago I watched him play soccer on a field in the Vermont hills, trees turning color in Indian summer. On such a day more than thirty-five years ago and in a place not far away, I saw a fly on a windowpane; I played soccer on such an afternoon; and on just such a parents' weekend my father watched me.

This week I picked up some photographs I had taken at the end of summer during a week we spent at the New Jersey shore, my wife, my daughter, Zak, and I. Pictures of Zak: on a surfboard, playing catch, and one where, golden-skinned from the sun, his fine brown hair long over his eyes, his black T-shirt askew over his shoulder, he is grinning out at me with an unveiled delight.

Surely every father has such photographs, whether camera taken or simply recorded in the album of the heart: the boy laughing as he is tossed in the air. The look of the boy as he turns to you keen with some satisfaction. Running toward you, arms flung wide. Laughing at a joke. Blushing, pleased at some tale of him you're telling to a friend. Warming to your pride. Opening a gift you have selected for him, wide-eyed and eager. Listening rapt as you read him a story, sing him a song. A single parent for many years, I have tucked this son in bed a thousand times, lingered with him while he clung to the day and then let go, mouth going slack, breathing slow at last, features softening into sleep while I gazed down on him. The innocence and beauty of his face have brought tears to my eyes more than once. At such a time my own distant boyhood has stood beside me and placed its small hand in mine. I could not believe that my own father could ever have loved me and cherished me any more than I now love and in this instant cherish my son.

This is my favored one, my only son, whom I love.

There is a vein of pure gold that runs through the mountain of fatherhood. In places the seam is wide; the ore plays over the surface of the rock like a many-fingered stream. It disappears deep into the mountain; it winds to its core. That gold is the innocence of the boy, hand thrust into yours, walking through the city for the first time or through the woods at night. That gold is the beauty of your son, lean-boned, fast, alive, the animal wildness electric on the skin. It is the tenderness of boyhood, the still-quick tears that rise at a joke that cuts where it was only meant to tease, or the pain in the eyes, the incomprehension, for the animal run over at dusk on a country road. It is the gold of his concentration, appraised from the doorway as you watch his intent fingers mold or shape or build or take apart, unaware of you the gazer. Boy—it rhymes with joy. Son is sun. What father can accurately assay this mineral of sheer pride and pleasure that glints with longing, too, for his own lost and distant youth?

This father in me reads the story of Abraham setting out to kill his son, "the laughter whom you love," and is dumbfounded. This father knows he could never do for any reason what Abraham will do. A father who could do such a thing has first killed the father in his heart. Only in the horrors of death camps, only in some insane Masada of zealous belligerence, only in the final nightmare of impossible choices, might a father bring himself to such an act.

But such an act would destroy, not ennoble, the soul. There can be no greatness here, only delusion. And any God that could ask this of a father, could "test" a father in this way, is only the devil in disguise. Any religion that preserves this story, hallows such a father, reveres the heart that can pass the test, is sick.

A second father steps from the shadow of the first.

It is a summer night. Dinner is done; my son bolts from the table to answer the phone and then grabs his skateboard to head out with his friends. He has been sullen and remote through the hastily gobbled meal. Monosyllables. "Fine." "Nothin'." "No." "Leave me alone." Ketchup on the placemat. French fries on the floor.

"Zak," I begin gently, "please clear your dishes, clean up your place before you go." He drops the skateboard, marring the linoleum. A pained expression settles on his face. I have asked him to undertake one of the labors of Hercules. Taking a plate to the sink, he steps on a potato, mashing it into the floor. He doesn't notice. His dash at the placemat with the sponge leaves a bloody streak; he heaves the sponge toward the sink, it ricochets off the window. Zak is grabbing up his skateboard, heading for the door.

"Zak, slow down."

"What!" he says. "Dad, I'm late." I point to the potato mashed into the floor. Eyes roll to the ceiling, groan. He goes for the sponge.

"Get a paper towel; the sponge isn't for the floor."

Something muttered under his breath now. The air is darkening. A pulse is set going in my throat. My blood is getting thicker.

The swipe at the potato leaves its mark. "Do it right." There is iron in my voice, menace.

The muttering in his voice becomes audible. "What a load of bullshit."

"What did you say?" The torch hovers over the tinder.

"Nothing." The dirty paper towel lobbed toward the garbage also misses its mark. Picking it up with a mumbled "shit," he kicks the dog's water bowl and slops water on the floor. He doesn't notice. He's heading for the doorway; we are only an instant from ignition.

I've been here before. While he is still in transit across the kitchen, I have more than enough time to feel routed and trapped by his insolence, more than enough time to pull up a million incidents of his spoiled and careless disregard, to read in this brief episode the story of his selfishness. Who does he think he is! All the shit I do for him! Who does he think I am—his goddamn servant? I'll teach him! The air crackles.

"Zak," the iron in my voice is forged into a blade, "put your skateboard down. Slow down. Clean up the water you spilled."

"Fine!" he explodes; "I won't go out. Fuck it!" He throws his skateboard into the hall. It clatters against the bench. He storms from the kitchen through the spill of water, hits the stairs two at a time, and slams the door of his room so hard that the glasses on the table jump.

In this moment I am all chemistry, no mind, no heart. I can feel the enzymes coursing in my body, catalyzing, bubbling into vapor and steam. No one can evoke this rage as he can. I am quivering at the outer limits of self-control. I have tapped into some primal rage. The magnetic poles between us have been reversed. I am storm and danger and wrath. In this moment I could kill him, hurl him through a window, or down the stairs, beat on him until he knows I am the master. I am the father before whom he is to tremble and whom he must obey! I have become Mr. Hyde.

What is it that keeps me from taking his throat between my hands? Only the thinnest membrane of sanity. Had I been drinking, had the boss been riding me all day, had my wife and I argued about something, were money tighter and bills unpaid, had someone dented my car in the parking lot, or were a tooth aching in the back of my mouth, I would have leapt the stairs to his room three at a time, hurled open his door, yanked him by the hair. As it is I simmer . . . down.

Late that night I wrote the following lines in my journal:

> *I understand the cultures where the elders come at about this time and re-move the boy from his father's house or his mother's house, and submit him to or-deals that chasten and channel his energy, punish the body, and challenge this crude sullen moodiness with real adversity. But there is nothing like that here, nor was there in Abraham's time. Then, as now, there are times when it seems only an angel's invisible hand restrains the desire to strike my son, wound him, punish him, and so, in effect, crush him under my will. Perhaps Abraham's story stands for the triumph of patience over elemental rage.*

A third father stands in the dark. He is not me, but somehow I know him. Head down, hands slack, he speaks,

> *I sent my son to war. You've got to go when your country calls. It's your duty. My son, my son, he had all sorts of ideas of his own—protested, argued. When his notice came, he talked with his mother half the night. I could hear her crying in his room. I was ashamed of him and her. Didn't they understand?*
>
> *Late that night he came to me; I knew what I had to say, and I said it straight, "You don't serve your country, boy, you aren't any son of mine." Never for-get the look he gave me, but I couldn't describe it to you. He held my eyes a long time. Then he turned. He put his mother aside that night. She came back to bed dabbing at her eyes, asking me what I said to him. I didn't tell her. Nothing to do with her. Between me and the boy. Next morning he packed his bags. He went. He never came back.*

Behind this father I see a multitude, a million fathers who have sent their sons to war. I see them standing straight and hollow under half-staffed flags. I see them brood on the porch on still summer nights, looking down at their hands, passing the closed door of the bedroom where no son will ever sleep again. I see the cemeteries of the dead, the field of Flanders, the unmarked graves at Marathon, the sands of Iwo Jima, the plain of Troy. Oh the causes of fathers, our absolute necessities that require the sacrifice of sons. Warriors. The waste of death—the slaughter of sons by sons, the endless wars of broth-ers in obedience to a father's avarice or pride or our dear ideals, our love of country, cause, kin, and home—the waste is endless.

Somewhere in this company of fathers Abraham comes. Do we have a psychology for Abraham? For what truths of men is he the keeper? He does not offer his son for himself, but in answer to some faith he will not question, a faith that gives a purpose to his life.

A fourth father comes forward, an elder from the archive of my mind.

> *You make a mistake to read this story literally. This is not a story about a man willing to kill his son; that is merely the dressing, the outer husk. The kin bond between Abraham and Isaac is the way myth tells us about attachment and priority. What is the most important thing to a man? Each man has the "one" he "loves most," and where there is most love, there is most blindness, most unthinking passion, most reflex, and secretly, hidden, most selfishness, a most covert egotism, a most subtle idolatry. Where there is the most love, there can be the most slavery and enslavement.*
>
> *Abraham is called to kill the selfishness in his love. His knife is raised to kill not the boy but the image of the boy in his own mind, to sacrifice his own dreams, to kill the power of images, even the image of his own fatherhood. What God requires is not perfect obedience but perfect freedom. In his final agony, Abraham reaches that freedom. He passes into the clarity of a detachment in which he acknowledges everything but is a slave to nothing.*

The myth of the sacrificial son is the central myth of the patriarchal tradition. Abraham's willingness to go to Moriah has been interpreted by Jews as the highest and most noble of acts, the act that seals his faith and ensures the promise. On the supposed site of this sacrifice the Jews built their Temple, and around it grew the city of Jerusalem. The Muslims believe it was Ishmael whom Abraham took to Moriah, and their Dome of the Rock in Jerusalem marks their claim to this site. This same Moriah is walking distance from Calvary, where Jesus Christ was sacrificed, another son, in whose death-that-was-not-a-death another faith was founded.

The sacrificing father and the sacrificial son, whose reciprocal acts violate the canons of the human heart, are meant to redeem us and to ensure some greater blessing. The myth is hallowed in our religions. Once men regarded Abraham with an uncritical awe. With the breaking up of institutional religious authority, with the challenges of feminism and the insights of psychotherapy, we are freed to look at him in other ways. To judge or condemn the man in these myths is to respond only from a part of the mind; to embrace him is to respond only from another. Yet in fact this myth, in its horror and its power, fascinates; and in a way that only myth can, it seems to reveal some profound truth of the soul.

What that truth is, however, I cannot finally formulate, though I have tried. The willingness to sacrifice is something in the depths that we make part of worship and war, cruelty and nobility. Speaking only as a man, I see how as men we are drawn to play at the edge of death and to search there for some power, elation, or release that we locate in no other place. Beyond eros this play with death is our recurrent testing of the limits, our obsessive trespass against boundaries, the expression, even when self-destructive, of our free will. The venture to the edge of death is the venture to the end of what a man may imagine. Death is the lure that takes men into hazard and harm. To the one who returns from the edge of death everything has changed.

From one perspective Abraham's fidelity to his God is an ultimate abuse of his son, from another it is the highest selflessness. But within the myth itself, this sense of abuse and selflessness, inextricably bound together, is the Gordian reality, the knot that cannot be untied. The generations have hallowed sacrifice in literature and chronicle.

In the myth of sacrifice patriarchy tells us that in our deepest hearts we have some longing for the Father and are willing, in His name and at His summons, to forgo or transcend the moral limits and the human bounds. We *want* this. Call it madness, call it faith, make madness and faith synonymous, yet this willingness to sacrifice, even the most precious of things, harrows us with a supreme allure. We would not willingly seek such sacrifices. Abraham does not ask for this, not consciously, and yet, having once obeyed the call of the Father, he has opened the door for this ultimate obedience.

In this myth of sacrifice I sense again the image of wrestling, wrestling as an image for internal warfare, of the soul in extremity, in pieces, and pitted against itself. Nowhere in Genesis is that wrestling as acute as it is here, for there is no love so long awaited as the love of this father for this son. No promise has been so long deferred, and no paternal attachment in the annals of the Western imagination runs any deeper than I imagine the attachment of this father for this son.

When Abraham is tested by this God to sacrifice his son, the stage is set for a soul drama of unsurpassable violence. The drama brings with it associations that run back along the whole length of Abraham's life. Abraham abandoned his own father to be adopted by the Great Father and to undertake His mission. In recompense for his sacrifices, Abraham is given a vision of a redemptive reward to be conferred through him to the entire race. In the light of such a promise, what is the pain of one man? In obedience to this God,

Abraham cuts his flesh and the flesh of Ishmael, then yields up his first son to his wife's insistence and in order to ensure Isaac as his sole inheritor. The more he has given to his God, the more rides on each gift; the greater his debt, the more entailed is his fate. He is free to say no, and his whole human heart must scream that no; and he is free to accede, or at least to begin. He can, without committing himself to the final act, essay the preliminaries. He can saddle the ass and collect the wood. He can kiss his wife good-bye and disguise his venture as the excursion of a father and son.

But if Abraham is human, a mad array of forces must wildly contend within his soul. This man wrestles with mixed loyalties and allegiances. Hope, outrage, doubt, and terror variously sit and are unseated on the throne of his heart. Can there be in literature or in life any greater anguish than this father's anguish? The soul that imagines this story—or the God who has proposed this test—does not flinch from extremity.

Of course, we have looked at the story only from Abraham's side. We have recognized *his* anguish, and we have been appalled, moved, enraged, and silenced by *his* willingness to go on to the end. But how to imagine Isaac? In the myth he, too, is silent through the three days, yet unless we imagine a mere slavish and ignorant passivity, this journey and its events must have been extraordinary for him. We cannot fully approach the mystery of the sacrificial son without understanding his part.

In our group enactment of the journey to Mount Moriah, it was hard for us to keep our attention fixed only on Abraham. It seemed he and Isaac were bound in a co-created drama, each indispensable for its enactment. They seemed two sides of a single coin, partners in the Myth of Sacrifice: The father needs a son for its performance, the son his father. Here is a place in which the wills and the wishes of each meet in awful reciprocity. The sacrifice is between them; the myth is about what holds them together. Their bond and intimacy, with all its exaltations and its depravity, is compressed into their journey to Moriah.

I am by no means the first to have tried to imagine this journey from Isaac's point of view. One of the most challenging revisions is outlined by Alice Miller in her recent book *The Untouched Key: Tracing Childhood Trauma in Creativity and Destructiveness*.[1] Anyone familiar with Alice Miller's work, her persistent and valiant preoccupation with children's psychic pain and the effects on the child of parental narcissism or an authoritarian educational system, can anticipate how she will understand the binding of Isaac. She brings her usual fervid advocacy to the cause of the child and her usual vitriol to the rationalizations of the adult. She writes:

> If we love life more than obedience and are not prepared to die in the name of obedience and our fathers' lack of critical judgment, then we can no longer wait like Isaac with our eyes bound and our hands tied for our fathers to carry out the will of their fathers. . . .
>
> What would happen if Isaac, instead of reaching for the knife, were to use every ounce of his strength to free his hands so that he could remove Abraham's hand from his face? . . . He would no longer lie there like a sacrificial lamb but would stand up; he would dare to use his eyes and see his father as he really is: uncertain and hesitant yet intent on carrying out a command he does not comprehend.[2]

Miller's Isaac, freed now to see, is free also to speak, and he will question his father, asking, "Who is God?" And this question will lead to Abraham's awakening. Isaac may be the means to "save Abraham from becoming the unthinking murderer of his child."[3] In her recasting of the myth, Miller pleads for filial disobedience.

Alice Miller's message and her compassion are powerful medicine. A part of me, father and son, rises to applaud. Though Isaac's awakening would be itself a miracle, her version of the story attacks the traditions that praise Abraham as the man of faith and hallow his acts as signs of an ultimate devotion. My own interpretation of the journey to Moriah might be criticized as yet another rationalization of abuse. If I can imagine, perhaps more fully than she does, the pain of this undertaking for Abraham, his anguish cannot, in her view, excuse Isaac's wounds. "This will hurt me more than it will hurt you" may be true, but the child is lastingly scarred. For Alice Miller nothing justifies laying a child on any altar.

She would also claim that any attempt to spiritualize the story begs the issue. Such interpretations serve only to legitimize, even to sanctify, the various behaviors of child sacrifice that our culture still, though in less obvious forms, not only excuses but glorifies. Her target in *The Untouched Key* is nothing less than the will of societies to go to war, to send off their sons, their Isaacs, to die for their fathers' "ideals" generation after generation.

Yet for me there is also another Isaac. I can see him. Though some say he was a full-grown man at the time of this event, in my mind Isaac is at precisely that passage when something of manhood, of the true nature of the father's world, breaks in upon a boy.[4] He and Abraham are co-initiates in the mystery. I see the hand of the boy in the hand of the father. Some might say Abraham held the boy's hand lest the boy run away; in the end I see it almost in the opposite way. Indeed there is fear in Isaac; we cannot avoid his fear. But is that all? Here is my midrash for Isaac:

I was afraid, full of many kinds of fear. I felt, I know now looking back on it all, something premonitory. When he summoned me to prepare for our journey, there was a gravity in him such as I had never seen before. You will believe me when I tell you that my father was not a man to take things lightly, but this gravity was of a different, darker sort, and it passed into me as a kind of fear. I know now that he was, beneath his solemnity, afraid, too. And as we walked, that fear grew in me as if we were walking into the most dangerous wilderness, as indeed it proved to be. But I also felt excitement, as one is excited into hyperawareness by fear and the dark and the unknown.

Also I was in thrall, for this was Abraham, my father, the great father, whose hand held mine as we walked, and he had never held my hand like this before. I had tended sheep with him, walked hills with him, sat at meals with him. I can remember Ishmael and Hagar; I can remember their leaving. I can remember hard words, cold silences, tears. I can remember his tears for Ishmael. And I know he loved Ishmael and had to put Ishmael from his home. His first son. My father was a great man, but a dark man, looming as the oaks at Mamre where we sometimes passed, but silent and ancient as the oaks. Always, as he looked or listened, my father was there and not there, both at once. He heard, but it was as if my words, Mother's words, fell into him as stones into a deep well. My father's silence was like the silence of a deep well.

I cannot tell you what it was like to be his son. I knew he was a great man, grave and great. I saw our clan's respect. The dwellers of Canaan came to him for judgment. Kings came to him at nightfall or on the eve of their battles. The story is told that he argued with God before the destruction of Sodom. This was my father, and I was his only son. At least I was now.

When he announced that we were going to travel together, I asked him why. For the making of a sacrifice, he said. What kind of sacrifice? I asked. I shall tell you as we go, he said, and we gathered up the few things we needed, and early the next morning we set out.

I shall never forget my mother's face. I can still see her looking at me as we saddled the pack animals, standing in the flap of her tent at dawn, and I know now that she believed that she would never see her boy again. In a sense she was right. She was not weeping. Perhaps for my sake.

So our trek began.

I had never been with my father in this way. When we had been together, it was in work, or when he taught me something about the management of the herds, breeding, tending, shearing. Sometimes we would walk together, and he would tell me the tall tales of the Canaanites. This was the only time I ever saw him laugh. He was usually in his own world, and I was only a child.

My father was not the kind of man you chattered to, and I was not a chatterer anyway. During the day we walked in silence, speaking only about necessary things. That first evening we camped by a stream, the serving men setting out our things. They cooked some rabbits they had slain during the day. I had wanted to hunt with them, but my father forbade me to hunt.

After dinner he built a fire away from the campsite on a flat place among the rocks. Overhead the moon was full. He shifted to sit next to me and took my hand in his. He turned to me, and I could see the firelight on his face. I could feel the full power of his presence sheltering me, gathering me into him, and he said to me, "Isaac, I am going to tell you the stories of God."

His voice was low, and for the entire time he spoke he looked into the fire. I could see the flame light flicker in the very center of his eyes. His eyes, usually so deeply blue, were black. At first I was afraid, for it was as if a tree had begun slowly to move over the ground, or as if a bush burned and was not consumed, or a cloud retained its shape for the duration of an entire day. I was enthralled. I lost all sense of the stones beneath me, the stream nearby, or even that this man looming in the dark whose head was crowned by the moon was my father.

He began at the beginning. He chanted of the creation of all that is, of the Nameless Mystery that moved on the face of the deep and breathed life into clay and made man. He chanted of the garden and the serpent, and of the world after Eden. He chanted the tales of the family of Adam and Eve and of the death of Abel and the exile of Cain. He chanted the generations of Seth to the birth of Noah, naming their deeds. He chanted of the destruction of the world by flood and of the curse of Ham. He chanted of the building of Babel and the scattering of humankind. Again he chanted the generations of men until he reached Terah. Then he stopped.

I felt as if I had been playing with toys and building small villages with little stones and then was taken to a mountaintop and shown all the cities of the world, not only as they existed now, but as they had been formed by the generations of men from the beginning of time. I saw that my episodic hip-hop of a life was like the bounding rabbit's, an infinitely small, almost comical part of a mystery infinitely old and complex in which my father was bound up.

I had heard bits and pieces of these tales, but they were all jumbled up with the legends of the Canaanites the shepherd boys loved to embroider at night in the fields. You didn't take any of that for true. But as my father sang, his voice steady as the moon arced high over his head, I knew he was telling me what was most true for him, a knowledge in him teeming with powers. The stories were like seeds of light, countless seeds of light, like the light worlds in the midnight sky, names and images, words and epiphanies, telling me that this dark world was full of invisible dimensions. Mystery. Yes, surely Mystery; and as he told me these tales of Mystery, a new desire was born in me.

Then he closed his eyes, and he caught a breath so deep that it brought me to my senses. As if this were the first breath either of us had drawn since he began. "These things you will remember," he said.

He arranged the skins on the ground and laid me down on them. He tucked them round me, for the night was cold now and the fire out. I was wrapped close, swaddled like a babe. He bent down and put his lips on my brow as he had never done before, and his lips moved in a whisper that I heard, "Shema, Adonai Elohenu, Adonai Echod. . . . Hush and listen, for Majesty is Mystery and Mystery is One." He raised one hand up, up into the night sky as if he were reaching for something. Then he drew it down, slowly, as if he were drawing down sleep from the sky, and his hand hovered over my eyes for a moment, warm, and he closed my lids. His warm hand resting over my eyes. I slept.

I dreamed the serpent came to me and laughed my name.

The next day the serving boys slew two quail. I did not even wish to join them in the hunt. I walked beside my father all day long seeing nothing, my mind wandering in the web of stories. My father was more deeply silent, but our shadows moved together until they were stretched long before us at the end of the day. Several times we passed by wells and saw the Philistines watering their animals and flocks. We did not stop, though by evening our skins were dry.

At dusk we were trekking among old trees at the edge of what might once have been an oasis. Beyond us the evening light cast a range of hills in a red-orange glow.

We came at last to a well site, dusty and bare. The servants complained because there was so little water in the well. They had wanted to stop where there was more society. Here stones were scattered everywhere, perhaps in a fight. No fresh dung or tracks; it was an old place, deserted and dying, so it seemed to me. As the servants prepared our meal, father picked up stones and laid them back around the well mouth. I helped him. Together we repaired the rim.

After dinner we carried wood we had collected up a dry ravine. We found the opening of a cave. The distant hills had become mere black silhouettes. I watched father make a fire. We were out of sight of the serving boys; we could not hear their laughter or jokes. Once again father turned to me, took my hand, and looked into my eyes.

"This is the line of Terah," he began. This was my grandfather. As I listened he told of Terah's sons, and then of Abram. He spoke the story as if this Abram, who became Abraham, was not he but a character in a story he had heard. I heard how Abram was called, and how he went with his wife Sarai. I saw their wanderings in Canaan and Egypt; I heard of the war he joined and his rescue of his nephew Lot, the covenant and the birth of Ishmael, the circumcision of the tribe, the messengers who came to warn of Sodom. I heard then of the argument my father had with God, the fire of the cities of the plain, and finally of my own birth, the true story of the banishment of Hagar and my loss of my brother, Ishmael. The whole story of his life passed before me and into me with his words. I felt how his God lived in him and he in his God, and it seemed terrible and tremendous, unapproachable and supreme.

The stories of the first night and the second were fusing into one story; it was as if it all led to him, and at every mention of the promise and the passing of the dream to his descendants, I thought of Ishmael, and I thought of me. His story was becoming my story. Tales about an ancient past led to this present and to a distant future. Time had a pattern; under the disorder of everyday life there was some invisible design turning through the generations. It had gathered my father into its folds, and now it was reaching for me.

Then he spoke the words, "And God called to Abraham, saying 'Abraham.' And Abraham said, 'I am here.'

"'Take your son, your only son, the one you love, and go to the land of Moriah, and offer him as a burnt offering on one of the heights I will point out to you.'

"That," my father said to me, lifting his arm from under the folds of his nightcloak and pointing to the distant hills, "that is the land of Moriah."

He stopped speaking, and I believe my heart stopped beating as well. In the silence he looked at me. My mind was wild with this last part of his story. Beside us the fire was glowing down to its embers, and I remember I put out my hand and could feel the heat pulse against it. I cannot quite tell you what happened inside me; at the time I was confused, trembling, wanting to run and to cling, to beg and to keep silent, to resist and to assent.

"What will happen, Father?" The words came out like a croak.

"God must provide the lamb," he said, but I did not understand. He felt strong then, like a great stone, and I knew we would meet God at Moriah. I knew my father would pull God to him by the force of his will. Looking back I know *that it was then, at that moment, that the sacrifice was made, the knife had fallen. Suddenly I felt dizzy. I was sick and hollow inside. I believe I may have lost consciousness.*

Again he laid me down on the ground. Again he bound me in the skins, but now this swathing felt like suffocation. I endured it. He was there. Once again, as I lay on my back staring up at the stars, he bent his face to mine. This time his lips touched my lips, and I felt them move against my lips, the beard moving ticklish and alive against my lips, and his kiss was a prayer, and he kept his lips to mine until I whispered with the words the lips were forming. I took them into my mind: "Adonai Elohenu, Adonai Echod. . . . Majesty is Mystery and Mystery is One." Then he drew his lips away and reached his right hand skyward into the black night, and his hand was a fist that seemed to quiver against the moon. I closed my eyes and heard the sound of the prayer words move like a wheel in my mind.

Before it was fully light, when the stars were beginning to fade, I woke—perhaps I had not even been asleep—and opening my eyes I looked over and saw my father sitting, facing the east, rocking back and forth. His lips moved in the same prayer, and his cheeks were bathed in tears.

The next thing I knew it was dawn, and he was asleep. I sat up, and in an instant my mind was flooded with his voice and the story. It hadn't happened yet. It was to happen, and I knew it was to happen today. I watched a flight of birds pass over the heights. I saw a wild goat bound down the hillside with the light clatter of hoof on stone. I saw the smoke of the campfire winding up from below. I saw the saffron light change in degrees to gold. I felt the wind and smelled the dust in the wind and the faint trace of water from the well. I was alive. This was the first and the last day of my life. I saw my father sleeping. I saw my mother standing at the tent. I saw the face of Ishmael dusty and streaked with tears. I knew what it was to be free.

It is impossible to tell you what passed through me, what worlds of possibility I traveled, the lives I lived in those moments sitting there at dawn. So many things to see, to do. But can you understand me when I tell you that nothing matched the power of this mission with my father, nothing drew me more intensely than to complete this day and to travel with my father to the heart of the Mystery that even now was opening up the day, laying out the hills for light, summoning the wild goat to his mate, the rabbit to her hole, the birds to their distant perches? Mystery was afoot in the wood smoke lifting from the vale. I was a mote of dust spinning in a sea of light. I reached out and woke my father.

There are only a few more things to tell you. I had made my choice. I think that day my father could not understand what was in me, and as I look back I am amazed, not at my courage, but at my . . . I hesitate to use the word . . . curiosity.

Too tame a word for the intense interest I had in the playing out of this story. Something guided us, drew us, shaped us, and it vibrated in me as if my entire insides were strings. All day long I was in some reality that is not the reality of this world. I saw every blade of grass; I felt the weight of every stone; I cherished every shift in the wind. I tasted my sweat at noonday. If it is possible to live a life in a handful of hours, I lived my life that day. And I held his hand; from time to time I would bring it to my lips. He was no longer great and terrible to me; it was as if for that day he was my child. But he was lost to me, lost in his thoughts, each footfall an act of will.

In the high afternoon we left the serving boys and walked alone together, going upward now more steeply. Something prompted me to say to him, "Father."

He answered, "Here I am."

Only then did I know that he was still ready, and I said, "Here are the firestone and the wood; but where is the sheep for the burnt offering?" though I knew where the lamb was today.

He said, "Mystery must see to the sheep for the burnt offering, my son." We walked on together. I held his hand more tightly, not because I was more afraid, but because we were bound together on something that put us beyond everyone and everything.

He built up the stones, and he laid me down on them, putting off his cloak first to cushion me. He took the leather thongs and wrapped them around me, and I smelled the smell of him. He was gentle. I remember his eyes; they streamed with tears. I stared up at him then, and though it was me under his arm, I wished in that moment I could comfort him. Then, unable to bear his grief, I looked past him into the sky. The afternoon was golden, and I saw the movement of the clouds above him, the way the edges were dissolving. Then I gazed directly into the sun, letting the weight of its light beat on my eyes till my head swam in a brilliant, pulsing night.

In that dark all my euphoria left me. I was simply still, and whether it was my voice or my mother's or the voice of an angel calling I do not know, only my ears heard his name: "Abraham!"

"Shema, Adonai Elohenu, Adonai Echod. . . . Hush and listen, Majesty is Mystery and Mystery is One." Was he saying this to me, or was I saying this to him?

Then over us something turned. I did not see it but felt it as a disturbance in the air, like a rushing of wind or water. Again I heard his name, and I would swear it sounded like my mother's voice: "Abraham!"

"Here I am." I heard him speak these words, and I closed my eyes. He said them softly, as a man who has no strength left, utterly spent, who returning from a fever speaks his first words in a dry voice as if to say, "I have returned."

I opened my eyes and saw that he had left me and was struggling with a ram caught in the thicket. He wrestled it to the ground with a fierce strength and sat astride it until it went slack and quiet under him. I rose to stand by him then. My father prayed over it, rocked and prayed, and he bound it and laid it, once more struggling, on the stones. "You are given for my son. I give thanks for you." Then the knife fell; blood rushed; and he chipped fire on the tinder. A flame licked up.

My sight was still sun-struck and dim; I felt disembodied like the smoke that was rising into the evening sky.

We went down the hill together and returned the way we had come.

What it was for him I shall never know . We spoke little. For me it was as if my entire life had gathered into this single day, fused the days and the stories and the walking into one momentous event. I was quiet in myself and as peaceful as the wide blue sky. When I saw a rabbit bolt between the rocks, or the flash of a snake in the grass, I would laugh. For no reason at all, just for the sight and the delight of the thing. It was as if the door between this world and a different world had become a curtain, gauzy, lifted by the wind. It was as if the wind blew, as it does in eddies, and the wind was Mystery and the veil would lift and I would only see the light dazzling my eyes, and the light would make me laugh.

Perhaps the most powerful commentary that has been done on this story was made by some anonymous reader who named the story the *Akedah.* Among students of the text, this has become the shorthand term by which to refer to the events of chapter 22 of Genesis. The Hebrew term *akedah* means "binding" and comes from the verb form *akad,* meaning "to bind with thongs," as that verb is used in verse 9: "Abraham bound his son Isaac."

Akedah is a synecdoche, a part that stands for the whole, for the act of binding is only a fragment of the whole episode, yet by this part the whole has come to be known. Why is it this term and not some other that tradition has used to identify the scene? It could have been called the sacrifice of Isaac, the ordeal of Isaac, the deliverance of Isaac; on the other hand, it could have been called the test of Abraham. Yet someone read this passage and called it the *Akedah,* and that designation has stuck. In its complex and riddling associations, *binding* seems a brilliant and compressed act of interpretation.

On the most literal level Abraham actually tied his son up on an altar and was ready to sacrifice him there. The "binding" refers to the thongs—leather strips—that bound the boy, presumably holding him still so that the knife blow would be sure and fatal. To identify the scene as the binding focuses us on what must be the most intensely emotional sequence of moments in the entire story. You cannot tie someone up without the closeness of touch. You will hear his breathing, smell his sweat, see his fear, feel his pulse. To bind someone—even someone who allows it—is a wrestling full of pain and intimacy. To be bound by someone is to participate in this intimacy. To the experience of being tied up belongs the entire spectrum of the human soul embraced by the words *passivity* and *surrender, sadism* and *masochism.* For unless one imagines Isaac as a weak or small child, the binding cannot go forward without his willingness.

The word *binding* in English has a complex range of cognates and meanings that *akedah* in Hebrew does not, but these meanings inhere in the image of binding. That which binds us makes our bonds. In being bound by his father, Isaac is indeed bonded with the father and the cult of the Father in the deepest possible way. It is another kind of circumcision. Like the circumcision, it forges a new bond between father and son. What they do together binds them both; in some way their mutuality is an equality. Together they enact the two parts of a single sacrificial psychodrama; they forge between them a terrible covenant.

Bonds also speak of bondage. At its worst, bondage is slavery. On the altar the bound Isaac has lost all his physical freedom, while his father willingly submits in bondage to the will of his God. The Akedah seems a deep meditation on the duality of freedom and bondage. The bondage of Abraham and Issac is, paradoxically, freely undertaken and thus is the strangest expression of freedom's willingness to bind itself and to accept boundaries. There can be no experience of freedom without a sense of its opposite, bondage or boundary. There is a part of us that chafes against all limits and can call any bond a bondage, but without bonds there can be no community, just as without boundaries there can be no identity.

Other moments in the Genesis narrative link up with this image of the boundary line. Creation itself is the self-limiting act of Infinite Possibility, God's willing acceptance of the bonds of a particular set of laws—natural and spiritual—that give coherence to a world. A limiting line was drawn like a circle around the tree in Eden. There Adam felt the first incising of a boundary to his freedom. He overstepped it and plunged into the world of cause and effect. Cain was asked to master his passions, to bind his free will in the service of self-control. The world before the deluge was marked by the blurring of boundaries between heavenly and earthly beings. The men of Babel sought to overreach the limits of their human sphere. The life of Abraham is marked by a constant series of tests of his faith and freedom; he becomes the exemplar of a man of self-control, and his covenants with God forge two parties into a pact held within the limits of their words.

The tying of bonds is accomplished by the making of knots. Knots remind me of R. D. Laing's little book by that name about psychological knots, what he calls "double binds," paradoxical situations in which you are damned if you do and damned if you don't. Double binds speak to us of impossible alternatives, of no-win situations, and of their particular anguish. At its most intense, the double bind can break us; the psyche that wrestles with itself seizes up and then goes mad. Madness anesthetizes the anguish of the bind; one can be numb, split off, annul all feeling like the schizophrenic. We cannot read the Akedah without sensing how Abraham writhes in the coils of the double bind.

Bond is cognate with band. The wedding band is symbolic of the wedding bond. From bond and band come bondage and bandage, hinting at a paradox: Where I am bound, there I may be healed, for bands may constrict but they may also contain, wrap, swathe, and protect. By extension the family, the clan, is called a band, held and holding together. Bonds are the invisible thongs of community, words made into vows or oaths, call them covenants, nothing finally more substantial than air, the forming of the breath into words. These bonds, however they may be materialized by institution and symbol, begin and end as images, figments of imagination, fictions. But words bound toward matter as the sperm leaps toward the egg. Words, mere words, are the sperm seeds from which we would make the world.

So the Akedah story is about all these associations: bind, binding, bound, bonded, bond, bondage, bounded, boundary, double bind, bandage, and band. But it is also about direction, as in "homeward bound." Abraham and Isaac are together Mystery bound.

The Akedah tells the story of the initiations of a boy into his spiritual manhood and of a father into an even deeper dimension of himself. The binding is traumatic for both of them. Trauma is a wounding, but their anguish is sacrificial and makes life sacred. In such wounds, trauma and blessing seem inextricably bound. Alice Miller notwithstanding, patriarchy honors such wounds while suffering them as well. These are the wounds no therapy can—or should seek to—heal, for they are the mysterious and formative events of the soul.

9

Sarah's Dreams: A Midrash

Night One

I dream I am sitting at the opening to the tent. I am alone, as if the whole clan had departed with Abraham and Isaac. There are no neighboring tents of kin or serving people. I am surrounded by a great quiet, and from here I can look down into a valley through which a broad stream winds. I can see meadows and upland pastures, wildflowers, and the shadows of clouds.

Suddenly I realize I am in Haran, the very countryside from which Abram and I, Lot, and our straggling retinue set out long ago. I am back and flooded with a longing that is bone deep. I begin to weep. All the while I am puzzled, though, at how empty and strangely desolate the place is. This is Haran before Abram and I arrived there, before anyone did. It is virgin and unsettled and beautiful in its peace and silence.

I am aware of a figure coming toward me through the tall grass below. I see a red kerchief that ties the hair off the face; I see the glint of copper bands on the wrist and I hear them jingle against each other. A woman is approaching, and before I can quite make her out, I am reminded—something in the stride, the set of the head makes me think—of Hagar. My heart bounds inside me for a moment, and then I am afraid.

And then I see it is Hagar; she crosses the hilltop toward me, picking her way among scattered stones. How old she has become, her hair streaked gray and her face wrinkled and dry from the sun. Poor Hagar, to have aged so much.

Hagar approaches me, but she does not bow. She stands before me, lean and waiting. I feel a brief surge of anger at her disrespect, but it passes, and I pat the ground beside me, inviting her to sit. She does. I can hear her breath coming strong from the exertion of the climb, and suddenly I remember Hagar's breath when Ishmael was born. Oh, she pants like an animal and then gives a scream that rises into an exultant cry as the infant squirms from her body. In my dream I look down as if expecting to see a baby laid upon her knees, soaking her smock with blood.

"I've come a long way back to you."

"Why have you come?"

"You called me back."

"I did? I did not. I never called."

"You called. Or something called and I came."

"Something is always calling in this world. I didn't call."

"Well, I'm here."

We sit in silence. Shadows pass over the hills. In my dream I know that we are both remembering Abraham. That's why she has come.

"I loved him."

"I know."

"He was gentle with me, but he did not love me. It was you he loved. But I loved him."

"He loved Ishmael."

"My son."

In my dream a wind now rises over the fields and hillside. It is night, and in the bright moonlight the tall grasses sway. Suddenly there is a clatter and movement, and an animal—it is a ram—bolts past the tent. To my horror I see its neck is rudely slashed. It streams blood. Its eyes are terrified and piteous. At that moment I awake.

Night Two

It seems to me that my eyes open to the darkness around me. No moon, no starlight, and it seems that someone, or something, stands beside me in my tent. I am afraid and lie very still. I want and do not want to see who or what has come into my tent. I feel it is an animal, something as august and majestic as a lion, but more sentient. Then I know that what stands above me in the dark can speak, for I feel its intelligence.

"Where is my husband?"

A voice comes to me, but not through my ears. I hear it speaking to me inside me. "He has taken your son, Isaac, on a journey."

"Where have they gone?"

"They have gone some distance from here, to the land of Moriah."

"Why?"

"I appeared again to Abraham and told him to take Isaac. It was time for us to meet."

"I don't want Isaac to know you. I want Isaac to have a different kind of life. I don't want a wanderer's life for him. His place is here."

"Abraham obeys me; Abraham is going to give his son to me."

"Isaac is my son, too. He will always be my son."

"But there is a part of him that belongs to me. It is something you cannot understand. It is not something a mother can understand."

"I understand everything. I understand this journey of Abraham's is a folly."

"Isaac wants to know what his father knows."

"No, he doesn't. The boy was terrified to leave. He clung to me. I saw his eyes. It was as if he already knew something terrible was going to happen. That's what I saw."

"That's what a mother sees."

"That's what there is to see. He's a boy."

"Only a fool would ask for me."

"Isaac is too young to be chosen."

"No, he has been chosen. He is frightened, but a part of him you can't see chooses to go with his father. His fate is with his father. He will be a man."

"What will happen to him?"

"He will die, and I will take him."

In my dream then I sit bolt upright with the single word *No!* screaming soundlessly inside of me, the cry one hears oneself utter in dreams, longer and more piercing than breath. It rises up through my bones and fills the sky. It blazes from me, rounding to a wail. I will myself in the pitch dark of my dream to see the figure that stands above me. And behold! My eyes see in that dark, rearing up above me, tall as a tree, the powerful and sinuous form of a serpent.

Night Three

I am running. With an indefatigable strength in me, I run. I seem to draw the energy of the fields into me as I run. I draw into me the energy of the animals as I run. Stream and river run through me; moon and stars course through me; the light of the sun sings in my blood as I run. I run like the wind, and as the wind I pass over the ground, stirring the undergrowth. My hair streams backward like the mane of a horse, like the foam of the waves blown back by wind, my hair flows back. My feet spark light where they touch as I run.

I am running across time to reach the man and the boy who are even now climbing the mountain. Even at this distance I can hear his voice saying, "Shema, Adonai Elohenu, Adonai Echod." The plain gathers and passes beneath me as I run toward the man and the boy, who are even now building the altar, and the voice of the man carries to me, "Shema, Adonai Elohenu, Adonai Echod." The trees of the forested hillsides part before me and make a broad path as I speed toward the man and the boy, who even now are placing the tinder on the piled-up stones. The voice of the man sounds the refrain again and again, "Shema, Adonai Elohenu, Adonai Echod." The wind lifts me above the brambles and the thickets as I race toward the man, who even now is binding the boy to lay him on the altar. The voice of the man is now joined by the voice of the boy, together saying, "Shema, Adonai Elohenu, Adonai Echod."

The stones willingly place themselves like stairs up the slope that I may fly upward toward the height, where even now the man is raising the knife above him. "Shema, Adonai Elohenu, Adonai Echod," say both voices in unison. And just as the arm begins its descent, I hurl my voice like a javelin is hurled toward the onrushing lion, like the stone is hurled from the slingshot toward the wolf: "*Abraham!*" But my voice does not interrupt the voices, which say again, "Shema, Adonai Elohenu, Adonai Echod," nor does it stop the arm as it descends. I leap toward the descending arm, my voice like the scream of the hawk that breaks the dawn, "*Abraham!*" And the knife enters my heart.

Night Four

I am dressed as a queen, and I come to a great circle of women. I recognize them all. My grandmother and mother are there. Rebecca is there, who will marry my son; Rachel is there, who will marry my grandson; and Leah, Zipporah, Bilhah, who will make sons through my grandson; the wives of Ishmael are there, and of Esau; the wives of the sons of Israel are there, and their daughters are there. Dinah is there. Tamar is there. And beyond them, circle upon circle, are the women of Egypt, mothers who have lost sons, mothers yet to be mothers yet whose stories already live in the womb of time, like embryos.

The circle of this host of women opens for me; I enter as a queen, and there at the center with their arms extended toward me are Eve and a black queen who I know is Lilith, the mother of Eve. A sound rises up in this host of women, a sound like the wind makes through the trees, a rushing whisper, and for a moment I who dream am a spectator to the dream, and I see Sarah the queen; I see her face, and just before the circle closes around her, I see that her eyes, her fading eyes, are full of tears.

10

Our Fathers' Wells

The stories of the life of the first patriarch, Abraham, fill twelve chapters of the Book of Genesis. The tales of Isaac, the second patriarch, occupy a mere four. The life of Jacob, the third patriarch and Isaac's younger son, spans another eleven chapters, and then the career of Joseph, his son, fills another thirteen chapters, bringing Genesis to a close. By this simple reckoning we can see that Isaac takes up the least narrative space of the major characters in Genesis. Moreover, the events of his life after Moriah seem relatively insignificant. He is a modest figure, an apparently unexceptional man. Or, to put in another way, where Abram became Abraham and Jacob will become Israel, Isaac is, first and last, just Isaac.

Four clusters of events mark his life. First, there is his journey to Mount Moriah with his father; second, his marriage to Rebecca; third, his experiences with the Philistines, among them the redigging of his father's wells; and finally, the almost farcical gulling he receives at the hands of his wife and his son Jacob when he is an old man. The patriarchal tradition is composed of puzzling figures, and among them Isaac is the most puzzling of all.

Yet I admit to a particular and personal attraction to him. Each time I return to read his journey to Moriah with his father I am disturbed and moved. In his act of redigging his father's wells I find an image for my work in this book and a metaphor for the tradition of patriarchy. While each of the protagonists of Genesis shows me something of myself—with Abraham a vocation, with Ishmael a divided, alienated heart, with Jacob deceitfulness, and with Joseph a link with the life of dreams and the fate of brothers—with Isaac something in his introversion and what I sense to be his lifelong engagement with his father's legacy touches some of the most vulnerable and fertile places in my soul.

I have already forged one link between Isaac and myself in my extended soliloquy. My portrait of the mystic as a young man derives from my own experience at fifteen when my religious imagination was ignited by a fly on a windowpane. The incontestable vividness and reality of that event in my youth authenticated at once and forever the language of spiritual experience. I understood that theology was not a speculative but a descriptive poetics.

From this vantage point in time, I recognize that my own mystical inclination did not develop without some preparation. Though my adolescent revelation struck me with an unheralded intensity, I can see in retrospect that a deep ground had been prepared for it in my soul, and it was my father who had, like an Abraham, dug the wells.

❀ ❀ ❀

In having had a powerful and lasting relationship with my father I am hardly unique, but the voices of sons and daughters that have been heard most in our culture recently are filled with the pain of absent or abusive fathers. Men and women justly lament their scars and feel the loss of a father's interest, companionship, guidance, or love. Too little fathering has been the plight of too many, and I feel almost guilty to remark on the excesses and perils of paternal love among those who have been deprived of it. Yet I understand patriarchy most personally because I am the son of a self-made patriarch. I have felt the burden of my father's love as an excess of interest, an intrusive, almost dependent involvement with my life, an impressing intention to direct my education and my choices for career. The ambivalences I feel about my father are based on a lifetime of vital, reciprocal engagements. I have loved him, and I have hated him; I have promised myself I would never behave like him, and I have come to see I am in fact a chip off the old block. I have resisted the influences he has had on my life, yet these influences have fed my achievements. I have wanted to make up my own mind, yet I have sought out his counsel. I can see how his will and love for me have shaped my course, and how well he has known me. His passions—whether for the old Brooklyn Dodgers or for the Sistine Chapel—permeated me. I am the son, like Isaac, of too much, not too little, fathering; and too much fathering leaves its marks in a weakened will, a passivity, an inwardness. Can such a son ever equal, to say nothing of exceed, the force of such a father?

There is a counterside of patriarchy that speaks of trespassed boundaries and of an almost incestuous intimacy of spirits. When Abraham actually circumcises his own adolescent son Ishmael, there is to my mind a sense of overstepped boundaries. When Noah's son Ham discovers his father naked in his tent and is cursed for this apparently innocent trespass, the old myth seems again to be brooding about boundaries. I have been drawn in my own study of Genesis to such moments because they resonate with my own experience as a son. For many years as an adult I worked in therapy to extricate myself from my oppressive intimacy with my father, and I was forced by truth to see that much as I sought that extrication, I also subverted it. The bond my father had developed with me as a boy and to which I responded had formed through the years a powerful psychic reality, familiar, deep-rooted, a part of my identity. The poles of repudiation *and* longing were the foci of our relationship. I tried as a man to "individuate" but not to dissolve or destroy our bond: that was the work. To gain a fuller measure of freedom from him required me to plunge into that charged place where my ambivalent desires pulled at me.

In the patriarchal tradition—biblical and historical, mythic and psychological—the impress of a father's power, so deeply and so early felt, works upon and in some way wounds the son. The effects of such fathering are complex, at least as I see those effects in my own life, in the lives of men and women I know, and as I read in the myths of patriarchy. The force of such a father instills a sense of fate in the son; it makes more real the idea of a Father God who has designs and destinies, urgent and mysterious, which the son is obliged in some way to fulfill. One feels molded by such a father, as God first molded man of clay.

It makes more real as well the dream of a patriarchal continuity, of a patriarchal project, which passes from father to son:

> *Tradition is much more than memory . . .*
> *It has a clear, a single, a solid form,*
> *That of the son who bears upon his back*
> *The father that he loves . . . The son restores*
> *The father . . .*
> *The father keeps on living in the son, the world*
> *Of the father keeps on living in the world*
> *Of the son. These survivals out of time and space*
> *Come to us every day . . . they are*
> *Merely parts of the general fiction of the mind.*
>
> WALLACE STEVENS, "RECITATION AFTER DINNER"

The love of such a son for such a father is deep; such a son feels he is in a sense made in his father's image, and though free is nonetheless implicated in a lifelong bearing of the father's work. The biblical myth expresses this in

Abraham's journey to Canaan and in Isaac's redigging of his father's wells. Such a son can always hear the voice of his father in his soul: judge, inspirer, inquisitor, and ultimate audience. My father was my first teacher, and he persists in that role to this day. He is the ultimate reader of these words.

In recent years, as I have come to a late-blooming sense of myself, a feeling for my own will and work in the world, a hard-won freedom from some of those traits my father passed on to me through our long association, I can celebrate him and love him without fearing my own loss of myself. I can appreciate his power without myself feeling powerless. At last I can look back into my boyhood and recognize that he gave me access to great sources of illumination, or, to change the metaphor, he showed me where the water was, and I saw him dig the wells.

I can remember being read to as a boy, and I can remember still my amazement at how he read and how the words seemed to light up inside him so that he shined. Often now when I read certain poems he first read to me, I hear his voice, and I can almost feel his pleasure. Whatever "meaning" these poems may have, they are first of all songs that I recognized as song because they made my father sing. He was not at all interested in an analysis of the ways poetry achieved its effects through its meter and imagery. My father did not read me poems to teach me anything about poetry. He read them because he was sharing an abundant love. He was a man enthralled; he knew the spells of language and the power of words to conjure up a reality as vivid as any objective reality or any pleasure of the sense. His trance entranced me and so made an entrance through words into the landscape of imagination. He made it possible for me to read William Wordsworth, Shakespeare, T. S. Eliot. He rode Pegasus. I saw his joy, his flight; I was enlightened by the light I saw in his eyes. I rose with him. That my father's name is Merlyn seems fitting—a magician surrounded with his books and living among their charms. And however scary he could be, I was never more safe than when he was in the presence of his God.

And what is my father's God? It is imagination. What are his relics, his sacred objects? Works of art and intellect, words, pigments, clay, bronze, the dances of Martha Graham, certain strains of music, the rose window at Chartres, the streets of Assisi, the bouquet of an old Bordeaux, the elegance of a chess gambit, the rhythms of the King James Version of the Bible. My father is a man of tastes, and he gave me the gift of a man tasting, savoring, relishing, and enjoying the pleasures of imagination. These pleasures last him into his late years even as other capacities are infirm; they are part of his legacy to me. Along with the discipline of his beatings, along with his interrogations, his prying curiosity, his searching and his cleaving, along with his expectations and standards, criticism and competitiveness, he gave me the indelible image of his transports, his enthusiasm, his response to the forces that reach the soul though the avenues of imaginative experience. He was the first person in my life who used the word *beautiful;* my father awakened and championed my aesthetic life.

My father never knew God as I was to come to know God, but he knew and he has loved Beauty both in its specific expressions of mortal genius and as a transcendent category. He sought and he celebrated Beauty. He transmitted to me the keenest respect for the arts of the word; he thrived on the passions of the intellect; he traveled in the world as if he were traveling in a storybook, and he recounted the world to me as a story. Using now the biblical term, I can see that my father was and is a patriarch of imagination, one of the father kings of that country about which I have been writing. My father and I never once went fishing, but we have had deep-sea dialogues about ideas. He never taught me how to use my hands, but we have handled together the precious ore of poetry and prose.

And there was something more.

My father marked a world for me that was not of or in this world. He read poems to a boy who would then look through them and see the world as the poet sees. He prepared me for the fly on the windowpane. He pushed out the boundaries of my boyish world, or allowed me to hold the boy's wide wonder as I became a man. I see now that in my youth he dug the wells of thought and dream and indeed of worship, and he passed on that vocation to me. In time I have made it my own.

❀   ❀   ❀

We reach the wells of Abraham and Isaac years after the journey to Moriah. Ever the patriarch, Abraham had sent his servant Eliezer back to Haran to find a wife for Isaac. Eliezer returned with Rebecca, a strong-spirited young woman, whom Isaac loved and with whom he was able to find comfort after his mother's death.

Rebecca was barren at first, but by the power of prayer Isaac was able to intercede for her, and she bore twin sons, Esau and Jacob. The story of their birth and their youth belongs to the skein of stories I will be taking up in the Tales of the Sibling Clan. Only a few other episodes of Isaac's adult life are recorded in Genesis. He comes into his own and yet in the many parallels to the life of his father, he seems the man who inherits a destiny rather than initiating his own.

We are told how Isaac sowed in Canaan and reaped a hundredfold the same year. His prosperity seemed miraculous and out of all proportion to the fortune of the other inhabitants. He acquired flocks and herds, for God blessed him, and he grew rich and richer until the residents of Canaan, the Philistines, all envied him. Spiting him, the Philistines stopped up all the wells that Abraham's servants had dug a generation earlier and that presumably marked the territory within Canaan that Abraham had used for pasturing. Abimelech, the king of that region, said to Isaac, "Go away from us, for you have become far too big for us" (26:16).

So Isaac departed and encamped in the valley of Gerar, and it is written that "Isaac dug anew the wells which had been dug in the days of his father Abraham, and which the Philistines had stopped up; and he gave them the same names his father had given them" (26:18). But when Isaac's servants, digging in the valley, found there a well of spring water, the local herdsmen quarreled with Isaac's herdsmen, saying, "The water is ours" (26:19). So he named that well Esek, which means "contention," because they contended with him.

They dug another well, and they harried him over that one also; so Isaac named it Sitnah, which means "harassment." Isaac moved from there and dug yet another well, and this time there was no quarreling over it; so he called it Rehoboth, meaning "space," saying, "Now at last the Lord has granted us ample space to increase in the land" (26:22).

This enterprise of redigging his father's wells is the sum total of the work of Isaac's maturity; yet there is something important enough in it to earn him the place as the second patriarch. In his sonship some myth is being constructed that hallows and sanctifies his labor.

Isaac is the son who returns and repairs the work of the father. In so many ways a figure akin to Jesus, Isaac could have said, as Jesus said of himself, "I am about my father's business." Our individualistic culture, our frontier mentality, which pushes always into the new, leaving old ways and old countries behind, is at a loss to know how to deal with this renovative work of Isaac. Yet in this age, which begins to respect the needs for conservation, Isaac's spirit may speak to our condition.

Whatever conservatism may mean as a political or social doctrine, it rests on a sense of the past. The will to conserve is not based on a rigid adherence to the ways of the ancestors; rather it sifts from the past what is needful for the present; it understands the necessarily integral and integrative quality of true growth; it knows that culture builds *upon* and not anew. Isaac retraces some of his father's steps; he redigs his father's wells; he gives part of his life to the past. By repeating his father's acts, he takes those one-time events and transforms them into a model or paradigm.

The prefix *re* might stand as the key motif of Isaac's life. It is not his whole story, but it is the core. *Re,* as in back or again, is the prefix of re-turn, re-collection, and re-pair. It is not that Isaac is a lesser man than his father, only that the quality of his contribution is less dramatic or innovative. Further, Abraham is great because he is fired into his destiny by a force apparently external to him. Isaac is moved from within. No one bids him undertake this work of re-pair; it is in his heart to do it. Without him the wells of Abraham would have remained stopped up. Without him the stories of Abraham, the legacy of Abraham, would have passed into oblivion. Isaac is the man who preserves the past, carries it into the present, and passes it on to a future. He is the middleman, the inheritor, whose relation to the past is full of re-spect.

But Isaac does not merely retain the past as a memory; it lives again in him. He re-animates his father's work with his own energy. Abraham's servants dug Abraham's wells, but Isaac redigs those wells with his own hands. His servants will go on to dig the wells that he will name in his time, but he alone unstops the springs that his father found. And more, he gives them the names that his father had given them. Isaac keeps the songline alive.

Songline is a word borrowed from the aboriginal culture of Australia.[1] Songlines are maps of terrain preserved in poetic and narrative chants. A place is known for the story it holds; it is found by the sequence of story-places that surround it. One travels across the continent on lines of music that mark the physical world and organize its parts into a web of images and stories.

Songlines run in two worlds. Waters and wells belong on the one hand to Mother Earth and the needs of the physical body; they are economic and political facts. Men quarrel over water rights: "The water is ours," say the herdsmen of Gerar. But on the other hand the water rises in the wells, and the wells have names. The names, old and new, belong to air, not earth. Names belong to a different dispensation. As we hear them coined by Isaac for the wells his servants dig, we realize that names are stories. Isaac the well digger conserves and extends the stories words contain. In this he serves Imagination, which is only another name for the Great Father. Isaac restores the ancient patter and pattern of the God who creates by word.

After redigging his father's wells, Isaac moves on to Beersheba. And it is written:

> *That night the Lord appeared to him and said, "I am the God of your father Abraham. Fear not, for I am with you, and I will bless you and increase your offspring for the sake of My servant Abraham." So he built an altar there and invoked the Lord by name. Isaac pitched his tent there and his servants started digging a well. (26:23–25)*

Without the drama and fanfare of the Abrahamic initiations, Isaac has his own modest epiphany. The mystery of the Father becomes present for him, and God repeats for his ears the great promise He made to Abraham. The promise is renewed for Isaac in his generation and now devolves on him. To carry this mysterious burden through time demands that it be kept vitally alive in every generation. Isaac is the true son of his father, and like his father he recognizes the significance of the apparition. Like Abraham he now builds an altar. Like Abraham he calls the Lord by a name nowhere recorded.

Then in the next narrative moment the king of the region comes to Isaac.

> *And King Abimelech came to him from Gerar with Ahuzzath his counselor and Phicol, chief of his troops. And Isaac said to them, "Why have you come to see me, seeing that you have been hostile to me and driven me away from you?" And they said, "We now see plainly that the Lord has been with you, and we thought: Let there be a sworn treaty between our two parties, between you and us."*
> *(26:26–29)*

Like his father Isaac achieves public recognition on the heels of his private revelation. Isaac steps onto the historical stage as an uncrowned king, equal to kings. He emerges in the world of his time as one whose power derives from his spiritual attainment and not from force of arms. The making of his treaty with Abimelech does not confer ownership of the land, but it secures a peaceful coexistence. Isaac makes a pact with Abimelech, whose name means literally father-king. Isaac's patriarchal status is confirmed by an equal. The two men swear peace with one another.

> *He made them a feast and they ate and drank. Early in the morning they exchanged oaths. Isaac then bade them farewell, and they departed from him in peace. (26:30–31)*

And then we read:

> *That same day Isaac's servants came and told him about the well they had dug, and said to him, "We have found water." He named it Shibah; therefore the name of the city is Beersheba to this day. (26:32–33)*

Shibah in Hebrew is the word for "oath," and *beer* the Hebrew word for "well." Isaac names this well for the treaty of peace he and Abimelech have just affirmed between them with their words. Isaac is the protagonist of oaths, the first keeper of the faith. In the making of covenants, men enact their most essential ritual of trust. God's covenant to man in the sign of the rainbow and men's covenant with God in the act of circumcision are pacts that construct a community of faith based on the mysterious power of words.

Patriarchy reminds us that as human beings engaged in the labors of vocation we place our first and final faith in words. It is not language that separates us from animals, but the agreements we make about language, the trust we place in words and the trust words make possible. The sanctifying of a language of faith and a faith in language is the deep agenda of the patriarchal tradition. In that tradition Isaac takes his place as one who keeps the words of the father alive. Isaac finds water, makes a well, and gives it the name "Oath" both to mark the place of these pacts and declarations and to hallow oath-making itself as a supreme use of language; words have the ability to bind us to our commitments, to create history.

All people of honor stand in Isaac's shadow when they participate in this commitment to the holiness of words. The idea in the ancient assertion that "a man's word is his bond" is encoded in the patriarch's loyalty to covenant and to the contract of oaths. Upon this contract the spiritual and legal traditions of the patriarchs is based. That tradition elevates language to the levels of prayer, promise, and power. Isaac alone of the patriarchs—each of whom marries a barren woman—is able by his act of prayer to intercede for his wife and bring about her fertility. Noxious as this idea might be to feminists, it is the way the biblical myth recognizes Isaac's unique relation to language. This use of language is the essence of the patriarchal sense of honor.

"What is honor?" Shakespeare's Falstaff asks rhetorically in *Henry IV, Part 1*. And then he answers himself, "A word. And what is that word, honor? Air" (v.i.131ff). But when men bind themselves to air, they create language as a code. Their words become the cornerstones of society. Such language—rightly understood as sacred—is requisite for enterprise, the essence of all acts of trust without which we would never rise above our primitive, territorial paranoia. Myth is needed to construct language to this high purpose, to raise our grunts to vows and to make a man a "man of his word."

Isaac conserves the high purpose of oath making. In his generation he preserves the words and the names and the stories of his father, salvaging them from philistinism, passing them on. But he is an originator, too. The pattern of wells, which he reestablishes and extends, transforms the landscape into a songline, and this was a work his father could not do.

No one more than Isaac appears merely to succeed a father. Yet in a subtle way Isaac exceeds him. Abraham lived in a present constantly opening into the future. Abraham was called to go where no one before him in his tribe or tradition had gone. Isaac, by contrast, remains in Canaan. Alone of the patriarchs he goes neither down to Egypt nor back to Haran. God bids him stay. However, in staying Isaac does what Abraham never does. The very act of living in his father's shadow, preserving and deepening his father's legacy, requires what we colloquially call staying power, and this power is another dimension of the father-power of patriarchy.

In his essay on Isaac in *Messengers of God,* Elie Wiesel asks: "What happened to Isaac after he left Mount Moriah? He became a poet . . . and did not break with society."[2]

Isaac a poet? What did he write? Or what did he sing? This most silent of the patriarchs is to be called a poet? Wiesel never spells out what he means by the designation, but I have my own ideas.

Isaac, who freshens his father's inspirations, restores the old names, and extends the songline, undertakes the poet's work. No one knows better than the poet the indispensable value of the past, the past as words, their associations and histories. Every poet must do as Isaac has done, redig the wells, get back into the heart of the words, where Imagination kindles meaning and inspires a world. Language itself is the poet's water; the well its forms. The poet rarely invents new words. Isaac, the poet, takes the old words and uses them afresh so that in his generation they live and flow and carry re-newed vitality. He enacts in modest ways the primal creative process of Mystery, who creates a world by words.

I know women and men who, like me, feel a vital connection to their fathers and mothers. Like me they have been troubled by a parent's powers and have lived in the shadow of greatness. We have had to come to our own sense of worth and potency through a long struggle, and we have had to see through our fathers' and mothers' greatness to their grandiosities and to find in their inflation the humanness and humanity that they hid inside. In the end we have reached our measured assessments, but we savor still the sense of having been the offspring of a special man or woman. We are rich in having had a legacy, an inheritance, a "patrimony" that connects us to the generation that preceded us and gives added meaning to our lives.

❀   ❀   ❀

The Tales of the Ancestral Family draws to a close. The stories of the brothers are already beginning; we heard hints of it in the story of Ishmael and Isaac.

That fragment will appear in retrospect as a prelude to the tales of siblings that will be the unifying theme of the remainder of Genesis. When Sarah rejects Ishmael on the grounds that he shall not "share in the inheritance," she strikes the note that will be more fully developed in the conflict over the son's birthright and the father's blessing that consumes the next generation. This same theme, branching out to a twelve-tone complexity, becomes the elaborate structure for the stories of Joseph, the final protagonist of the fourth generation. All this I shall take up in the Tales of the Sibling Clan. But first the Tales of the Ancestral Family needs its epilogue, its final image. That I find, appropriately enough, in the death of Abraham.

Immediately following the long-ago journey to Mount Moriah, we read of Sarah's death. She dies not in Beersheba but in "Kiriatharba (that is, Hebron) in the land of Canaan" (23:2).

Many readers of this story have inferred from the suddenness of Sarah's death that her loss of Isaac kills her. Others suggest that her rage at her husband for being able to undertake such a mission turns her away from him and that she dies in grief. At her death Abraham is alone in all human senses of the word: Twice forced to separate himself from his sons, he is now wifeless. The passages that tell of the aftermath of Sarah's death are taken up with an account of how Abraham procures a piece of land for her tomb, a cave in the field of Machpelah in which he lays her to rest. There at a later time he, too, is buried.

On the simplest narrative level this ending to the life of Sarah and Abraham is full of an enormous and painful irony. This man who was promised land for his descendants when he left Haran, promised it repeatedly at every phase of his faithful relation to his God, now has to haggle with the Hittites as a "stranger and sojourner" (23:4) in order to have a plot of earth for a "burying place" for his wife. The only earth he will call his own after a lifetime of migration and labor and loss is a cemetery,

> . . . *the field of Ephron the Hittite in Machpelah, which was to the east of Mamre, the field with the cave that was in it and all the trees that were in the field. (23:17)*

No word is said of his tears at Sarah's grave. No word of his reflections as he finally lays his wife to rest in the cave. No mention of Isaac. "The rest is silence," as the poet wrote, silence after so much silence, loneliness after so much loneliness, grief after so much grief. It almost seems like a punishment for a fierce old man who sacrificed too much and who, though having won the favor of his God and the awe of the generations, lost his wife, Sarah; the mother of Ishmael, Hagar; and both his sons.

But this naturalistic level, tinged with shades of human loss, yields always to the mythic, recedes into it and is swallowed up in it. The loneliness of the soul in the cave of grief is the emblem of a final loneliness, the human soul separated from nature, adrift in a mysterious universe. It underscores what we have seen from the beginning of his story, that Abraham's saga is the myth of a soul that lives alone between two worlds, fully at home in neither the world of matter nor the world of spirit. That middle world is the realm of the stranger, where both dimensions meet and mingle. For the soul that lives between the worlds there is no final human bonding, no lasting human tie. The dream of Eden that a man shall "cleave to his wife and so be one flesh"(2:24) is given the lie here. Abraham is finally alone with silence and with grief in a dark cave at the end of a field, where he, too, will be buried. He stares at his own mortality and feels what he has felt all along, that he has been alone and a wanderer, tracking the invisible and incomprehensible will of his own imaginative truth.

After Sarah's burial, he sends his servant Eliezer off to find a wife for Isaac. This mission succeeds. Then we are told in a few verses that he marries a Canaanite woman and raises another family, but that he leaves everything to Isaac. We are told that the Lord blessed him "in all things," and that he dies "in good old age, an old man and full of years, . . . gathered to his people" (25:8–9). Yet whatever the comforts of this second life, it is in Machpelah that Abraham is buried, as if this second life hardly mattered to him. Isaac and Ishmael come to mourn him there.

Who will speak a eulogy for Abraham? The participants in my psychodrama groups have had many things to say. Some spoke with the fire and ire of Ishmael, who could praise a father's devotion to a hidden God and lament his own loss of his father's love. Others spoke as Isaac, who knew more intimately than anyone what his father paid for greatness. But my own final words I borrow from the last pages of C. G. Jung's autobiography. Slightly amended I offer them here as if Jung stepped for a moment into our psychodrama group and spoke these words *as* Abraham's ghostly spirit:

> *I sense that I live in a world which in some respects is mysterious; that things happen and can be experienced which remain inexplicable; that not everything that happens can be anticipated. The unexpected and the incredible belong in this world. Only then is life whole. For me the world has from the beginning been infinite and ungraspable. . . . Loneliness does not come from having no people about*

one, but from being unable to communicate the things that seem important to one-self. . . . I am the man who has seen and experienced worth and worthlessness, and who, at the end of his life, desires to return into his own being, into the eternal un-knowable meaning. I am the old man who has seen enough. . . . I have gone alone and been my own company. I have served as my own group, consisting of a variety of opinions and tendencies—which have not necessarily marched in the same direc-tion. I have been at odds with myself and have found great difficulty in uniting my own multiplicity. . . . I have been driven by my daimon. . . . I have entered the un-trodden and untroddable regions, where there were no charted ways and no shelter spread a protecting roof over my head. . . . I am in the deepest sense the victim and the instrument of a cosmic love . . . something superior to me—a unified and un-divided whole. Being a part of it, I could never grasp the whole. I have been at its mercy. I have assented to it, or rebelled against it; but I was always caught up by it and enclosed within it. I am dependent upon it and sustained by it. Mystery has been my light and the darkness whose end I cannot see.[3]

PART III

Tales of the Sibling Clan

Behold, how good and how pleasant it is
for brothers to dwell together in concord.
It is like the precious ointment upon the head
that ran down upon the beard, even Aaron's beard,
even down the skirts of his garments.
The love of brothers is like the dew of Mount Hermon
and as the dew that descended upon the mountains of Zion,
for there God commanded the blessing
of the brothers forever.

Psalm 133

11

Jacob and Esau

The poet John Keats described the world as a "vale of soul-making"; the Bible calls this vale the "valley of the shadow." Soul is formed, like clay, in those depressions where death and suffering shade human life. Those vales of tears are places of excess and extremity, places beyond the settlements to which one is brought by a summons, by circumstance, and only in part by one's own will.

Soul, solitary and soaring, may be exhilarated on the peaks; the fly on the windowpane was the envoy of my transcendent ecstasy. But the soul does not only fly; it plods along the dark road of linear time. It struggles in its house of clay to know and to be known; it wrestles with itself. It is a stranger in the world. Much of its knowledge comes when the heart is broken. In those rending experiences we see, upon reflection, what shaped us, changed us, and opened us more deeply to the mystery of life. Those losses and self-encounters occur in the valley; those depressions test our patience. Certain experiences of soul one does not consciously design or intend; they are too painful. They erupt and intrude into our secure lives with a terrible force; they send us reeling down into the vales. Or they slowly erode the bulwarks of our certainty until we are undermined and alone again during a dark night of the soul. The vales of soul-making are those experiences that in their psychic intensity bring us a knowledge of who we really are.

The family crucible is the earliest and perhaps the deepest vale where soul is formed. Those relationships which are most proximate—father, son, mother, wife, brother, sister, spouse—by their very proximity work most formatively on our sense of identity. The complex and continuous frictions of family life shape parts of me I can never really leave behind and never fully plumb. However far I travel in flight or in pursuit, I take my family with me, internalized as voices, figures, and potencies. These collaborate in shaping the ways I relate to friends and strangers, and in the ways I form a family of my own.

In looking at some of the myths in which patriarchy imagines soul-making, we have seen the ways in which these myths were set within the crucible of family life, particularly in the relationship between the generations, between—in its masculine dress—father and son. In its latter half Genesis turns to an exploration of the sibling world, and it invites us to look at the relationship between brothers and sisters as a process of soul-making. Between the sibling polarities, at once intimate and hostile, men and women wrestle with one another and within themselves.

Brotherhood and sisterhood are images that have an external and an internal reality: Each of us has a sibling struggle within us, between aspects of our nature, and that internal struggle is played out in our relationships with our sibling kin and then by extension with our peers. The soul, in its very nature, seems a sibling thing, made up of distinct and often irreconcilable elements, an internal clan of parts that resist hierarchy, that must in the end live in community in a sibling world.

The myths of Genesis that occupy us now face into that world of brothers and sisters—brothers more than sisters, given the masculine locale of its imagination and cast. Genesis views the sibling bond as a container for the lethal *and* the loving, as a dynamic made up of extremes held in tension, the centrifugal and the centripetal forces of attraction *and* differentiation, rejection *and* longing, the desire to be dominant *and* to be atoned. The myths of Genesis remind us of the lunatic, the paradoxical, the dangerous, and the vulnerable in the sibling world of men and women. I don't know of a richer body of myths about brotherhood and sisterhood than those that follow the death of Abraham.

As we head into these myths, we do not leave the fathers and mothers altogether behind. We are still within the precincts of the ancestral narratives. Isaac is only the second of those three fathers whom tradition has called the patriarchs; his son Jacob is the third. Jacob's death is the penultimate scene of Genesis, his life having spanned the saga of his sons. But though we are by no means done with the intergenerational stories, the myths point us toward brotherhood, a gendered synonym for the generic "sibling world."

This pointing is accomplished through a compounding and echoing of incidents that elaborate brother themes and issues. To what extent the sisters are contaminated by the culturally constructed androcentrism of patriarchy I cannot say. But the sister stories, such as they are, are used to mirror the dynamics played out in the lives of the brothers. The locus of dramatic action is no longer situated in the ordeals of vocation or in a father's relationship with his son. The center of gravity has shifted to scenes of encounter, where brothers meet face-to-face to wrestle and forgive. God-talk all but disappears; spirituality is de-etherialized and grounded in the painful realities of sibling passions, needs, and wounds. Soul-making is done in the hard relational business of working out turf, inheriting the patrimony, establishing covenant not only between the self and God but between oneself and one's kin.

The shadow of Cain hangs over these myths, and Cain's question—"Am I my brother's keeper?"—seeks an answer like a ghost that will not rest. In these brother myths we find motive enough for murder, but the fraternal dramas avert it, sometimes narrowly. Instead of killing one another, brothers move toward climactic scenes of reconciliation. In such scenes the heart breaks open, tears are shed, and trust repaired. Genesis not only gives the divisive and dangerous its due, but honors as well the longing in a brother's heart for atonement. Brothers seek to be forgiven and to forgive; brothers seek some way of living in harmony, and in the end—though an end Genesis cannot realize—it is brothers who dream of the brotherhood of man.

"The brotherhood of man" is surely one of the most enduring dreams of the soul. We do not find even a hint of that dream in the myths of the Greeks or in the folk traditions of Europe, but it is one of the central conceptions of the Bible. What that book makes clear, however—especially in the myths to which we now turn—is how vexed and difficult such a brotherhood really is, what distances, differences, inequities, and fears must be overcome and accepted before men will be able to live in peace with one another.

The patriarchal imagination of Genesis sees brotherhood as the final crucible for the soul. After the elevations of the mountaintop, after the ordeals and visions through which vocation is tested, the myths of Genesis tell us that in the end brother must turn to face brother; sisters must be reconciled. In youth the brothers war and feud, fight for position, betray and bully one another; the immaturity of brotherhood is full of pettiness and is shadowed always by the mortal impulsiveness of Cain. But brotherhood is lifelong, and the possibilities for a deeper level of understanding and concord remain available to any one of us who keeps open the door to such atonements. In time a brother may learn—and such learning takes place in the vale where soul is made—that a brother's face is another aspect of one's own face, a sister's gifts may enhance our own gifts, a brother's forgiveness is indispensable to our ability to affirm ourselves, and a sister's love a necessary prerequisite for our ability to make a true fellowship with others and to call the other kin.

The complex two-sidedness of human relationships for men and women, the restless dynamic that never reaches a lasting poise, is dramatized in the give-and-take of the sibling world. Reciprocity is a universal law: What goes up must come down; what I am with my brother or sister I am with myself and with other men and women. What I cannot abide in my brother I have not found or accepted in myself; until I accept my sister I cannot live fully at peace with other women. War results from our failure as men to achieve a relationship with our brothers. It is a failure of skill, of knowledge, and of courage. If we men are ever to live in brotherhood with one another, then each man must face the brother he has and the kind of brother he has been. That facing is a confrontation, an encounter, and the myths of these encounters are told in the Tales of the Sibling Clan.

Like every relationship, the sibling bond is a two-way street. But profound differences exist between the bonds that run between us and our parents and those that run between siblings. What distinguishes the life of brothers and sisters is that in its truest form it takes place in a world of its own. While there is an aspect of the sibling relationship that parents see, supervise, and attempt to manage, there is a sibling realm that parents never know. In that realm brothers and sisters are alone with one another, alone in the bedroom or the bathroom, alone in the basement or the attic, alone in the yard or the woods or on the roof, alone in the night.

I remember how, as brothers and children, Jonathan and I veered from wrestling to gentle silences, from hilarity to tantrums, from tickling to touch and then to something that felt like a brief, even furtive, caress. With my brother I knew how near allied were my murderous rivalries and my fiercest loyalties. One day I could kill my brother, the next day kill for him. The erotic energies in brotherhood bonded us, but they endangered us; they pulled us toward fusion, and they polarized us; they sizzled in our contacts. The homoerotic and the homosexual were as yet undifferentiated.

My brother and I created a domain we could feel was ours alone. It was full of secrets, jargon, signals, codes of behavior, and unspoken truths. In that world our intense curiosities and rivalries traveled to and trespassed over the parental prohibitions. Our life as boys was a kind of Eden, and no less than the Eden of Genesis, it laid a foundation for much of what followed.

In those young days and later in puberty and adolescence, life rushed by so quickly and I had so little ability for self-reflection that I can hardly assess, even now, how soul was being made in my life with Jonathan. But I know our life together was formative. He was the first mirror into which I looked at eye level; his was the first heart I tried to win; his was the first admiration I sought; the first person over whom I exerted power. My parents were not mirrors for me; they were huge screens. But Jonathan was like me, small, subjected to the same conditions and conditionings. Two years apart in age, we were close enough to create a shared world between us. With him I began to understand myself and the other, the same and the different, the close and the faraway, the rival, the friend, the enemy, the comforter. With him, in the miniature mirror-world of our childhood, my soul made its first essays in establishing an identity. In those years I took Jonathan into my heart, quarreled with him and emulated him. And now, no matter how much distance may separate us, no matter how long it's been since I saw him last, he is still inside. He is part of my imagination of myself; he is in my dreams.

Initially I must approach the brother material in Genesis through my own life as a brother. I look to understand brotherhood in my own personal myths and history even as I ponder how cultural history and myth—among them the Genesis materials—have shaped my perception of brotherhood itself and taught me what to look for. As I reach back for my experiences, I am struck by how little time I have spent in my various therapies and even in close conversations with spouse or friend talking about the place of my siblings in my life. I realize that a veil of silence hangs over my brother world, drawn over it in part from a certain sense of shame in facing the feelings that are part of that world, in particular the feeling of inferiority.

Inferiority: the condition of being less than another. Under. Below. Beneath. The inferior is the infernal, where the dismal parts of myself lurk. I repress my sense of the inferior; it threatens me too much to admit its discomforts. It is my land of Nod. In the inferior I locate my underworld, and as underworld the inferior is the place of my crimes, where I know I am a criminal. I drive my demons down there; I seal them off so that I cannot hear their jeers. These are the fallen angels of myself. That underworld is also my place of humiliation, the hell where my ego suffers torment and dismemberment. This profound inferior is the valley of the shadow, a vale where soul is made.

Throughout most of my life my brother feelings seesawed constantly along comparative, competitive lines. The questions that resounded in my childhood mind can trouble me to this day. Who's up? Who's down? Who's better, faster, stronger, brighter, more successful, more loved, more creative, more trustworthy, clearer, calmer, cooler, handsomer, more attractive to girls, the better athlete, the better son? In all of these categories of value, while I strived to come out on top, some subtle voice whispered to me that I was second. I was inferior. And this was all the more humiliating because the person I call my brother is my stepbrother, and he is two years junior to me. Why should I care so much?

I can remember what it was like when my stepbrother Jonathan came into my life. I was eight; he was six. It was the year after my mother and father divorced. Falling into the chaos between their worlds, my attention fastened on Jonathan. I hardly noticed his smaller, frailer brother, Matthew, trailing behind him, only four.

Jonathan was my playmate and prey, my ally and my adversary. With the feral calculation of a bereft child, both threatened by and attracted to these newcomers, I maneuvered to maintain my place. Jonathan, Matthew, and I were lumped together in the lingo of my father's new household as "the three boys." I believe it was supposed to sound like the "three musketeers" and to suggest how alike we were. But our inequalities, the differences in our natures, temperaments, needs, styles, endowments, and positions in that family were strikingly evident from the beginning.

Matthew, I was immediately to learn and was never to forget, had had rheumatic fever as a small child: It had left him with a weakened heart. His mother fluttered in constant apprehension over his frailty and had schooled Jonathan to watch out for him and to pace himself in order not to tax or tire Matt. The baby in the family in more ways than simply his years, Matt struggled to join Jonathan and me, but he was met constantly by his mother's anxiety and my desire to capture Jonathan entirely for myself.

The older in his family of origin, Jonathan became the middle child in the blended family. Forced by circumstance to a precocious maturity and caretaker's competence, Jonathan was, however, an able pal when I could pry him away from Matthew. I was jealous and demanding. I had no empathy for his situation as a stranger in my father's house. What I saw most clearly was that in my father's house he had his mother with him for softness and support. But in that house I had no mother on my side. She had abandoned me to a man who had always been tyrannical in his love, punitive in his discipline, and fearsome in his expectations. When I saw Jonathon with his mother, my separation from mine made me ache. I envied him.

In those years, unable to get certain needs met, I wanted to be ruler of the brood, the heir apparent with his younger vassals. I wanted my father's exclusive love. I wanted to cut my stepmother out, but not her boys, from the little kingdom of my home. And secretly I wanted my own mother to reappear and resume her place. The divorce had broken my heart, and even before it, with my mother's drinking and my father's long hours at work, I was a needy child.

I can retrieve some fragments from the time of brotherhood's beginning.

Jonathan and I share a room at the top of my father's house in Brooklyn. Because of his delicate heart, Matthew gets my old room on the second floor from which only two years earlier I had watched the blizzard singers on Christmas eve. I am constantly taking things from Jonathan. I will put on one of his shirts rather than wear my own. He gets a box of colored pencils from his father for his birthday; I steal several. I want what he has, and when he has something too special to steal, I covet it. When he has an interest of his own, I invade it. Meanwhile I want him to want what I have, so that I can feel superior, so that I can control him.

My father taught me to play chess. I teach Jonathan. When he is stuck and doesn't know what piece to move next, I tell him. But these "good moves" always turn out badly for him. I guide him to defeat.

I take to clipping Jonathan on his arm whenever we're kidding around. The playful punch lands often on the muscle. Within a year he flinches when I raise my hand—now in jest, always in jest—when I pass him.

During the first few years I lived alone with my mother during the week and commuted to my father's house after school on Friday. I was a weekend brother, a weekday only child. Then my mother moved to California, leaving me behind. I now lived in my father's house full time. My sense of abandonment, my anger and my loneliness, intensified. I devised subtle ways of turning Jonathan against his mother. I tried to make a rebel out of him; at other times I tried, by my obstinacy, to monkey wrench the family gears. I deceived and lied and thieved. The inferior hatched its demons; I lived in fear that I would be found out for what I was, a devil disguised as a son and brother.

And during this period after my mother's flight to California, something changed. I grew wilder. With my blood heating in the first flames of puberty, I pushed limits, took chances, did things I was told expressly not to do. In all the escapades, I wanted Jonathan with me. But our parents had taken him aside. "Keep your eye on Peter," they told him; "Watch him. Watch out for him." I didn't know it, but I felt a change. Jonathan now only played at being my pawn or pal; he became my keeper and my guard. I had been betrayed.

At this stage, sexuality first intruded explicitly into the emotional mayhem of our childhood. I introduced it; it troubled our relationship, destabilized us further. I sought Jonathan out, starved for someone gentle and loving and kind. My loneliness became confused with horniness. Jonathan pulled away from me, but that early movement of desire—secret, shamed, rejected—stayed with me as a question to shadow my sense of myself as a young man. I saw it as another symptom of my lowness, of something craven and depraved.

From my current vantage point I can see that my belief in Jonathan's superiority rested in part on my own self-contempt. I was riddled with impulses I knew were destructive. I lived out the underhanded and the base. I wandered in the inferior realms of myself during the last years of my childhood. I was furtive. I stole, envied, coveted, used, and manipulated. These acts made me feel petty, small. My guilt demeaned me in my own eyes. I did things that were, I knew, beneath me—or should have been—but what was beneath me moved and motivated me. Most of all my neediness, my cravings for something I could not name, made me look up everywhere through the eyes of a hungry child.

The brother myths that dominate the last half of the book of Genesis pull up these still vexing places in my own history. My wars of competition and duplicity find their counterparts in the texts and subtexts of the myths we are about to examine. But brother stories, we might note in passing, have been part of Genesis all along.

Placed just after the fables of creation and the garden, the story of Cain and Abel opened the mythopoetical history of men's lives in mortal, linear time. The brother theme then slipped under the surface of the subsequent stories, but it never disappeared. We could have fished for it in the story of the sons of Noah; and brotherhood, as an image of a social order, was parodied in the Myth of the Tower. The story of brothers lurked in the silence of Abram's departure from Ur, his father's ancestral home, where he left behind a brother. The relationship between Abram and his nephew Lot, who accompanied him to Canaan, had the features of a sibling bond.

In the family of Abraham and Sarah the drama of the brothers moved toward the surface. Ishmael was the firstborn son of Abraham; from what we know of the customs of the time, his right to inherit his father's estate was legitimate.[1] The laws of primogeniture ensured that his father's properties would pass into his hands. Yet Sarah, Isaac's mother, insisted that Abraham send Hagar and Ishmael away so that Isaac could receive the patrimony. "Cast out Ishmael," she told Abraham, "for the son of a slave shall not share in the inheritance with my son Isaac" (21:10). "*My* son," she said, not "our son." She claimed him. Sarah will have nothing to do with their brotherhood.

With Sarah's voice a new force has entered the patriarchal narrative: the mother's will linked to the will of God as Great Father. This force brooks no disagreement; Abraham yields to it. However much Sarah may be motivated by an understandable maternal possessiveness or jealousy, she has been accorded her own annunciation. Along with Abraham, she has been made responsible for a legacy. The patriarchal imagination recognizes her role in determining the family dynamics; it portrays her as a strong matriarchal figure who bears the burden, even as Eve once did, for difficult choices and wounding acts. Sarah for a moment dominates the story with her power.

This emergence of the powerful feminine within the patriarchal narrative is continued in the next generation. It is once again the woman's part to direct the family destiny. Rebecca is entrusted with the painful task of carrying out the will of God and of arranging a reversal of the laws and customs of primogeniture. What Sarah in her time did by fiat, Rebecca must accomplish in hers with a ruse. In the end, Isaac will lose his firstborn and favorite son, Esau, just as Abraham was separated from his firstborn, Ishmael.

The presence, even the dominance, of the mother's power creates a new dynamic. Her husband's equal, the wife-mother becomes another figure whom God enlists to accomplish the promise. Rebecca, whose barrenness is brought to an end by Isaac's prayer as well as by his seed, is now called to serve the transgenerational dream. Her vocation is to ensure that God's will for inheritance and succession are realized.

Pregnant with twins, Rebecca felt them struggle in her womb, and she went "to the Lord" to understand what was happening inside her. The Lord spoke to her:

> *"Two nations are in your womb, and two separated peoples shall issue from your body. One people shall be mightier than the other; and the elder shall serve the younger." (25:23)*

In time Rebecca gave birth to twins. The firstborn emerged red-haired, and Isaac and Rebecca named him Esau, a wordplay on the Hebrew word for hair. The secondborn came out holding onto the heel of his brother, so they named him Jacob, another wordplay on the Hebrew word for heel. In this way the twins were born. Esau, we read, became a skillful hunter and a man of the wilds. Jacob, by contrast, was a mild man and stayed in camp. Isaac favored Esau, for he loved the game his son brought for him to eat, and Rebecca favored Jacob, who, she had been told, was to rule his younger brother (25:24–29).

There is no absolute truth in a family system, only the truths of the participants. These truths are often unspoken, sometimes only partially conscious, and conditioned by the perspectives and histories, the illusions and convictions, of each family member. Indeed, to be a member of a family is to live among secrets, hidden motives, suspected alliances, painful exclusions. Psychodrama, by virtue of its ability to voice the various perspectives that conspire in the family, allows us to explore the family as a system and attend at any moment to its strange polyphony. The text gives us the bare outlines for a scene:

> *Once when Jacob was cooking a stew, Esau came in from the wilds famished. And Esau said to Jacob, "Give me some of that red stuff to gulp down, for I am starved.". . . Jacob said, "First sell me your birthright." And Esau said, "I am at the point of death, so what is the use of my birthright to me?"*

> *But Jacob said, "Swear to me first." So he swore to him and sold his birthright to Jacob. Then Jacob gave Esau bread and lentil stew; and he ate and drank, and he rose and went away. Thus did Esau spurn his birthright. (25:29–34)*

The psychodrama of the brothers inevitably moves from the playing out of the biblical family story to an exploration of personal issues. On one such occasion four group members created the split symmetry of the family of Isaac and Rebecca. As we developed the character of each son, they became more and more caricatured. Jacob, captured by his mother, became fastidious and intellectual. Esau, taken by his father, was almost his father's pet, like a mastiff whose burly presence was reassuring but from whom nothing else was asked. Each son seemed to live out the repressed side of each parent.

Quiet Isaac urges his hairy son to take to the wilds, to hunt game, to roast meat; the father seems to live a surrogate life through his red-haired son. "Through him I remembered my own wild brother Ishmael," one player said, "and by favoring Esau I assuaged my guilt for displacing my half brother and inheriting his birthright."

Meanwhile Rebecca, with her fierce energy and independence, recognizes that she has married into power. God's annunciation has come, after all, to her, not to her husband. In her midrash she says, "I also have had my vision, and the burden of overturning traditions that men so blindly, so devotedly cling to falls to me." While Isaac digs wells, Rebecca dreams of kingship in Canaan; she lives, too, with the painful knowledge that one of her sons will rule the other. "I felt as if I, too, were being sacrificed, because I knew the success of one of my sons would come at the expense of the other. I could see no way for Esau to escape being hurt if God's will was to be fulfilled." Jacob becomes her instrument; she recognizes his quick-wittedness; she fills him with her dreams.

In such a way the family hardens its alliances. Esau takes to himself all the unexpressed virility of his father, Jacob the craft and ambition of his mother. The twins become extremes of the over- and undermasculinized man. Each secretly wishes for what the other has.

In our psychodrama Jacob speaks:

> *When in the beginning I saw how my father took pleasure in my brother's skills and in the food he could lay before him, I felt envy, sure, but I expressed it as scorn. I saw my brother as a brute, crude, earthy. I looked down on him, and I came also to look down on my father for favoring him. Dad was pathetic, and Esau was a peasant. My mother fed my sense of superiority; she made me feel I was better than Esau, better than my father, too, and that their closeness was almost ridiculous. Often she made me laugh at them by some way she had, in a gesture or two, of mimicking them.*
>
> *But though I came to have my airs, my snide and arrogant ways, I always felt in some strange way that I was more like my father than Esau was. It seemed crazy. I felt my father and I could have had . . . I don't know . . . something. When my father told the stories, I listened, and I remembered them; Esau only thought them strange. Or fell asleep.*
>
> *Besides, I always wanted to hunt, but my mother wouldn't let me. I wanted to be doing what Esau was doing, or at least to try it. I admired his strength and skill. I felt inept. I felt like a girl, if you want to know the truth. Sometimes my mother's chatter would drive me nuts, and then I would see my father and Esau simply sitting together without talking at all, and I would wish for this kind of silence.*

Esau, on his side, felt his mother's rejection.

> *From the first I felt there must have been something wrong with me. My hair, my hairiness, I don't know. Never did. Mom doted on her smooth little Jake, gave him the best parts, left me the scraps. Jacob learned to cook; he was very good with his hands, could do fine things with thread and clay. He could make things grow and tend sick ewes and birth the lambs. He was always a good talker, too.*
>
> *So I went off alone. Hunting is like that. I grew my beard; I found friends among the Canaanites. They liked me well enough; I liked their girls. Wild girls they were.*
>
> *I came home to Dad. I'd roast him up some game, and he'd enjoy it. Run his hand through my hair, tell me I was his hunter, and then he'd talk to me about Ishmael, told me how much I was like him, what a great hunter Ishmael had been. He would become sad and quiet. Then he would sleep. I would dream sometimes about my uncle, Ishmael. I felt he was the brother I never had.*

These soliloquies, composites of group insights, shade the characters. They are drawn not only from a reading of the myths but also from the lives of the men and women who play the roles. Lurking just behind these impersonations are the memories of sibling wounds, some long forgotten, unexplored.

Favoritism knows no winners, they tell me. "Even when you're the favorite of both your parents," one man said, "you feel the pain of your brother; you feel guilty and unworthy."

"And afraid," said a woman, "like you know that your brother is hurt and that he's mad, and you don't know how to reach out to him because there's so much resentment and jealousy."

"I was the black sheep in the family," I heard a man say in the drug program I was working in. "I felt like shit about myself. And you know, when I really look at myself, I realize I've got abilities. I'm not so bad, but I still compare myself to my brother, and every time I do I come up short."

Meanwhile, on the sidelines, Isaac and Rebecca observe this tension between the brothers. How much do they know? What secrets do the brothers keep from their parents? How much of what the brothers do serves ends they cannot comprehend? Are they merely unconscious actors in their parents' scripts? These questions are the psychological gaps in the text; the answers, our midrashim.

❀ ❀ ❀

A final scene climaxes and closes the story of the youth of the twin brothers. Jacob, having gained possession of the birthright, has yet to gain his father's blessing. This blessing, as Rebecca seems to know, is a necessary part of securing Jacob's spiritual inheritance. She also knows that, according to the laws of primogeniture and by his own predilection, Isaac should settle this favor on Esau. Having been told by God, however, that Jacob is to be heir to his father's line, Rebecca works to arrange the blessing for her favored son.

And here we witness the family conspiracy. It begins when the near-blind old Isaac calls Esau to him.

> *And it came to pass when Isaac was old and his eyesight had dimmed, he called Esau to him, his older son, and he said, "My son."*
>
> *And Esau answered, "Here I am."*
>
> *Isaac said, "Now here I have grown old, and do not know the day of my death. So now . . . go out into the field and hunt me some game, make me a dish such as I love . . . that I may give you my blessing before I die." (27:1–4)*

Overhearing this, Rebecca seems to know that these words presage an initiatory drama. This ritualized summoning of Esau and the impending blessing prompt her to spontaneous action. She improvises a skit in which Isaac is the unwitting fool, Esau the tragic sacrifice.

Telling Jacob to put on goatskins to give his arms and hands the hairy feel of Esau, she tells him what to say and how to act as he, the usurper, slips in to his father while Esau is off hunting. Meanwhile Rebecca quickly prepares a feast for Jacob to serve his father and in this way completes the subterfuge. The scene between Jacob and his father is rendered in the usual spare dramatic style of biblical narrative. Behind and between the words we are left to imagine the young man's feelings as he takes his brother's place and steals the kiss and the blessing he knows Isaac believes he is giving to the son he most loves.

Jacob went to his father and said, "Father."

And he said, "Yes, which of my sons are you?"

Jacob said, "I am Esau, your firstborn; I have done as you have told me. Pray sit and eat of my game, that you may give me your innermost blessing."

Isaac said to his son, "How did you succeed so quickly, my son?"

And he said, "Because Mystery, the One Who Provides, granted me good fortune."

Isaac said, "Come closer that I may feel you, my son—whether you are really my son Esau or not."

So Jacob drew close to his father Isaac, who felt him and wondered, "The voice is the voice of Jacob, yet the hands are the hands of Esau." So he did not recognize him, because his hands were hairy like those of his brother Esau. He asked him, "Are you really my son Esau?"

"I am."

"Serve me and let me eat of my son's game that I may give you my innermost blessing." So he served him, and he ate, and he brought him wine and he drank.

Then Isaac said to him, "Come close and kiss me, my son." Jacob went up and kissed him. And he smelled his clothes and blessed him, saying, "Ah, the smell of my son is like the smell of the fields Mystery has blessed." (27:18–27)

This scene is full of elements that remind us of earlier moments in Genesis, and it treats them almost as parody. Abel slaughters the best of his flock for offering; Cain is slighted. A goat is substituted for Isaac on his father's altar. These sacrifices are all but mocked in this farce in which a wife and a son dupe a weak-eyed old man. Isaac teeters on the brink of being a comic fool, Jacob the wily opportunist. Rebecca appears the heartless, scheming wife. We are on the outskirts of a comic folktale.

But Isaac seems not to be entirely fooled; he is weak-eyed, but not entirely blind, and some who have played his role believed that he knew what was afoot and, without being able to initiate the stratagem, consented to it. He suspects something, for he says to the disguised son, "The voice is the voice of Jacob, but the hands are the hands of Esau." And he asks again, "Are you really my son Esau?" Boldly, a second time Jacob answers, "I am." Isaac asks for a kiss, and smelling in Jacob's borrowed garb "the smell of the fields," he confers the blessing.

> *May God give you*
> *Of the dew of heaven and the fat of the earth,*
> *Abundance of new grain and wine.*
> *Let peoples serve you,*
> *And nations bow to you;*
> *Be master over your brothers,*
> *And let your mother's sons bow to you.*
> *Cursed be those who curse you,*
> *Blessed they who bless you. (27:28–29)*

We hear echoes of Elohim's very first blessing of his creature in the promise of an abundant earth. We hear, too, the echoes of the Abrahamic blessing that those who curse Jacob will themselves be cursed, and those who bless him will be blessed. Isaac is the first of the biblical fathers to speak a blessing; his words have power. Rebecca knows this because Isaac's words in prayer transformed her barrenness into fertility. Even in his dotage and at the hour of his deception, Isaac is still the poet, the man of oaths, whose words legislate the future, and he cannot take them back.

Immediately after Jacob leaves with the blessing, Esau enters with the fresh-killed game. When in a moment Isaac learns what he has done and what has been done to him, he is "seized with a very violent trembling," and Esau bursts into "wild and bitter sobbing." But it is too late. Esau can only wail his request for some remaining blessing from his father, and Isaac can only give him a partial one (27:30–39). In the face of this second betrayal Esau vows to murder Jacob after Isaac dies. The ghost of Cain chills this scene. Fearing for her boy, Rebecca sends Jacob away. He flees toward Haran, his mother's ancestral land and Abraham's, where the family plot began and where in each generation it seems another beginning must be made.

The overturning of the rule of the firstborn has been accomplished. Rebecca has set a new order in motion. The elder must serve the younger, though this is yet to be realized. The legacy will pass Esau by as it passed by Ishmael. Though we shall learn of his generations, the line of power flows through Jacob, on to his twelve sons, who will in time become the twelve tribes of mythic Israel.[2] Inferior in terms of birth order, Jacob has usurped the place of the superior.

The reversal is accomplished by doubleness and duplicity. The heel-catcher is to be the inheritor of the mantle of Abraham! Jacob *is* the inferior man in many senses of the word. Inferior in birth order, he reveals his moral inferiority first as a cold bargainer of food for birthright, then as the able trickster in his mother's play for the blessing. Jacob appears the portrait of a young man without conscience or scruple, caring about neither his brother nor his father and able, without a backward turn, to leave his mother as well. A shade of the sociopath makes him seem dangerous as well as unsavory. That such a character is the protagonist of a spiritual myth confounds our usual expectations about the alliance of God and the good. Far from being a noble exemplar, Jacob is an ironic figure, a disfigurement of the ideal.

This myth forces us against the grain of easy moral assumptions. We may even recognize something inferior about God. In taking Jacob as His protagonist, the God of Genesis seems to flaunt before us His willingness to use any available means to secure His ends. He resorts to the morally dubious in order to achieve His goals. The Mystery whom we have seen as the God of imagination, conception, creation, and plenty has His inferior side. Murky and unsettling, God's doubleness threatens to split the One into two. What is the connection between the figure and the shadow? Are they two sides of One, as the Jungians insist, or, as the Manichaeans proclaim, are they separate and two, God and the devil?

The shadow side of conception is deception. Deception draws on the energy of imagination, but works through doubleness and duplicity. Jacob is only a latest example of this tricksterish underhandedness of God. The sense of subterfuge has been part of the ways of the Father from the first. The serpent in the garden was our earliest image of the shadow. By its guile even the throne of divine intention appeared to have been tilted.

The serpent and Jacob have a kinship with each other: They are figures of the undermind of Imagination. The serpent, we remember, was cursed to strike at the heel of Eve's children. Jacob is born gripping the heel of his brother. Both the serpent and Jacob know something about the vitality of the inferior, of the infernal, and both use the shadowy powers of speech and suasion to deceive the innocent. The depraved and the deprived are also twins; Jacob knows the ways of irony.

A further irony is buried in this story. Jacob has indeed received a blessing, but it cannot fill him. He has even been kissed by his father, but the kiss was meant for Esau. How exquisite a pain for the betraying son to witness the father's immense love for his brother and to take that love into a cold heart where it cannot warm him. Father Isaac's blessing cannot animate his son with anything but shame and fear. Jacob cannot enjoy what he has gained because he has gained it through treachery; the blessing has not come to him through any merit of his own or any true love in his father's heart.

More important, Jacob cannot receive the blessing because he is unprepared for it. He has been raised by his mother; he is "the mild man who stays in the camp." What does he know of Abraham and that dangerous life of surrender he led, and which from his childhood Isaac led too? The Rebecca who takes matters into her own hands has not equipped him to receive the blessing or to shoulder the responsibility it entails. His soul is hidden in his selfishness.

This scene between father and son is a mock initiation. Jacob is still green. The Great Father, as Mystery, has not brushed him with His power. Jacob's imagination has not yet been fired by vision or dream or encounter. His real potency still sleeps, and his powers have been put to the ends not of conception but of deception. Jacob is spiritually unfathered; his initiations lie ahead of him. He must do as his fathers before him have done; he must leave his native land and his father's house and wander. He must become a stranger. God will meet him in the wilderness; the wilderness is his place of vision and adoption.

In setting out for strange lands, he leaves Esau behind. In his long exile, Jacob will sojourn in Haran. Many events will befall him, but always the memory of his treachery will remain; the shame and the fear of it will haunt him, and when the time comes for him to return to the promised land, he will meet his dreaded brother at the border.

My explorations with these twins over the years has taken me back to my own history with my brother. I have worked with men and women for whom the brother story inevitably wrings from their memories forgotten incidents, old wounds, touching losses. But I have also come to see the relationship between the twins as the relationship of two parts of myself, two aspects of my own masculinity. In some ways these two parts were conditioned by my experience in my family, but I have come to recognize that I am not alone, that others share this sense of an internal doubleness for which the image of twins is fitting.

I was, like Esau, the son who longed for a mother's love. I was, like Jacob, the son who longed for his father's blessing. Like Esau I can be trusting, innocent, and strong. Like Jacob I can be deceptive, utterly self-gratifying, and callow. Like Jacob I wish for vigor and wildness. Like Esau something in the refinement of touch, the order of things in their places, eludes me. Like Jacob I have never hunted, never killed. I am an unbloodied male, and some part of me longs for the skills and the knowledge of an Esau. Not much of an athlete, I never had a strong sense of my own physical power. Yet like Esau I hated schooling and the disciplines of the tent. I felt confined. Developmentally slow, it wasn't until the last years of high school that I got good grades, and though I stayed in school for twenty-five unbroken years, right through my Ph.D., I always suspected that my own true life, if ever I found it, would take me in a different direction. I know Jacob's shallow piety; Esau's paganism. Like Esau I do not know my parents' homeland; I have married among the Canaanite women. Like Jacob I am searching for the ancestral God.

However we experience them, Jacob and Esau seem like two sides, two extreme poles, of a single self. Intellect and instinct, spirit and body, orthodox and heretic, obedient and rebellious—these apparent oppositions jar in our internal dialogues. The persistence of this doubleness is the cause of our discontents as well, no doubt, of our growth. The dialectics of self-knowledge yield occasional moments of synthesis, only to split again into what Matthew Arnold called "the dialogue of the mind with itself." Isn't this what the poet James Stephens means in his poem "The Twins"?

> *Good and bad are in my heart,*
> *But I cannot tell to you*
> *—For they never are apart—*
> *Which is better of the two.*
> *I am this! I am the other!*
> *And the devil is my brother!*
> *But my father He is God!*
> *And my mother is the Sod!*

I am safe enough, you see,
Owing to my pedigree.
So I shelter love and hate
Like twin brothers in a nest;
Lest I find, when it's too late,
That the other was the best.[3]

The metaphor the Bible gives to this two-sided self-encounter is *wrestling.* That image and that act become the figure by which the parts are brought into strenuous relation with each other.

Like two parts of a single soul, here sundered and divided, Jacob and Esau remain apart for many years. Their reunion is prefigured, as we shall see, by Jacob's wrestling with an unseen antagonist, never named, which wounds and blesses him and frees him for his atonement with Esau. In this act of wrestling, and in the reconciliation of the brothers that follows, the patriarchal imagination speaks of its dream of the union of opposites. That union occurs, however, not as a marriage but as a fierce contest of wills between powerful masculine adversaries. This wrestling will occur at the ford of a river, in the vale of the shadow, as the dark night of the soul.

12

The Myth of
the Wrestler

A man in flight, Jacob travels to Haran. He seeks refuge in his ancestral homestead. This flight uproots him from his native land and his father's house. Though he is not "called" as Abram was called, he is nonetheless driven to exceed his father's world. He sets foot on the path of the Stranger and enters the Strange.

Strangeness begins for Jacob on his first night away from home. He finds himself at nightfall too far from habitation to find shelter. He is alone. He lies down, taking a stone for his pillow.

Jacob came upon a certain place and stopped there for the night, for the sun had set. Taking one of the stones of that place, he put it under his head and lay down in that place. He had a dream; a stairway was set on the ground and its top reached the sky, and angels of God were going up and down on it. And the Lord was standing beside him and He said, "I am the Lord, the God of your father Abraham and the God of Isaac; the ground on which you are lying I will give to you and to your offspring. Your descendants shall be as the dust of the earth; you shall spread out to the west and to the east, to the north and to the south. All families of the earth shall bless themselves by you and your descendants. Remember, I am with you: I will protect you wherever you go and will bring you back to this land. I will not leave you until I have done what I promised you."

Jacob awoke from his sleep and said, "Surely the Lord is present in this place, and I did not know it." Shaken, he said. "How awesome is this place! This is none

other than the abode of God, and that is the gateway to heaven." Early in the
morning, Jacob took the stone that he had put under his head and set it up as a
pillar and poured oil on the top of it. . . . Jacob then made a vow, saying, "If God
remains with me, if He protects me on this journey that I am making, and gives
me bread to eat and clothing to wear, and if I return safe to my father's house—
the Lord shall be my God." (28:10–21)

Here, finally, Jacob's real initiation begins. The Great Father appears to
him in a dream and imparts the promise to him. The potential effect upon
Jacob could be profound, yet he holds the experience at a distance. Something
has come in a dream to change his sense of the world, and it leaves him
shaken. ("Surely the Lord is present in this place, and I did not know it.") But
he will not engage with this reality. Instead he sanctifies the place by pouring
oil over the stone he slept on. For me there is something almost comical in the
sight of this young man setting up his little stone pillow, thinking it's a pillar,
and supposing he might propitiate or honor the Great Father by his little reverence.

He refuses to attend more fully to the reality of Imagination, but he does
make a vow:

"If God remains with me on this journey I am making, and gives me bread to eat
and clothing to wear, and if I return safe to my father's house—the Lord shall be
my God." (28:20–21)

Jacob sets up a bargain; it is his kind of covenant, self-interested, very
concrete, impervious to responsibility. He is not ready for faith or belief, but
he is ready to make a trial of God. A subtle kind of wrestling begins.

Though he is unable to yield fully to the Great Father, a seed has been
planted in a dream that lays before him in one astonishing glimpse a reality he
had never imagined. It frightens him even as it beckons. For a moment such a
dream transforms him and the world, and one might suppose that he and the
world will be forever changed. But ordinary concerns cloud the moment; the
dream recedes into the unconscious from which it came, as a wild and fabulous animal returns to its lair. Vocation passes by; he goes on about his business. Jacob will require a further and more potent experience before he will
know the Lord is God.

Jacob travels on to the east and arrives in Haran. Haran is the place where
Abraham's father, Terah, settled on his way to Canaan; here a generation later

Eliezer, Abraham's servant, came in search of a wife for Isaac and found Rebecca by a well (24:15–19). Now in the third generation Jacob returns to the ancestral home. At a well site he, too, encounters a maiden. In their first meeting "he kissed her and lifted up his voice and wept" (29:11). Is this his outpouring of love at first sight, or relief at finding safe haven, or the dawning sense that the Dream-God is actually safeguarding his life? The moment passes. Jacob learns this girl's name, Rachel; she is his cousin. Her father, Laban, welcomes his nephew Jacob. He takes him in.

In many ways Jacob is taken in. Laban takes Jacob in to his household, but takes him in in a colloquial sense: He fools him. Having fallen in love with Rachel, Jacob agrees to work for Laban for seven years to gain her hand, but on the wedding night Laban substitutes Rachel's older sister, Leah, for the bride, and in the morning Jacob wakes to find he has been deceived (29:25). Laban preserves the custom of marrying the elder sister first. Outraged but helpless, Jacob agrees to work yet another seven years for Rachel's hand, and so at last they are married. Jacob, the deceiver, is deceived.

This battle of wits between Jacob and Laban keeps the sibling theme alive. Laban is the master trickster, gaining fourteen years of free service from Jacob in exchange for marrying off his two daughters. In these years with Laban, the roles of Jacob's childhood are reversed: He is now, like Esau, the inferior; he is now the more gullible, mastered by an elder more guileful than he. Jacob is forced to give up, not his birthright or blessing, but his freedom, and he labors under Laban as an indentured servant. In those years Laban profits enormously from Jacob's industry.

Having gained the hands of two sisters, Jacob now begins to raise a family. But Rachel—as were Rebecca and Sarah before her—is barren. Though she is the one he loves, Leah, the elder sister, conceives. She gives Jacob four sons in succession, and always with the hope of gaining a place in his affection. The name of each son speaks volumes.

Leah names her first son Reuben, because "The Lord has seen my affliction and now my husband will love me" (29:32).

Her second son is Simeon, because "The Lord heard that I was unloved and has given me this one also" (29:33).

Her third son is Levi, because "This time my husband will become attached to me because I have borne him three sons" (29:34).

Her fourth son is Judah, because "This time I will praise the Lord" (29:35).

In these names, and the meanings Genesis assigns to them, is coded a chapter in the family saga. Leah's loneliness, her use of her children as a way of gaining her husband's love, her continued disappointment, and her implicit jealousy of her sister are all suggested in the names of her sons. Meanwhile Rachel, who has implored Jacob to intercede with God to end her barrenness, has been refused by her husband and his Lord. She grows desperate for motherhood, and we may imagine her eying her sister's fertility with mounting envy and alarm. The birthright will pass to Leah's line; and she has no son to receive the blessing. The elder sister appears to have it all.

Each of the wives has a serving woman, and now Rachel gives Jacob her maidservant Bilhah as a surrogate. With Bilhah Jacob has two sons.

Rachel names the first of these sons Dan, "he judged," because "God has judged me indeed; he has heard my voice and given me a son" (30:6). Bilhah's second son is named Naphtali, "I wrestled," because "With great contesting have I wrestled with my sister, and I have prevailed" (30:7).

Through these two sons, as the names suggest, Rachel attains a measure of position in the family. She has seen her relationship with her sister as a contest, as a wrestling, and in the birth of Naphtali she tells herself that she is the victress. But the contest is not over.

Leah counters with her own maidservant, Zilpah. Jacob sires two sons through her. The first of these is Gad, whose name means "luck" (30:11). In that simple word we can hear Leah rubbing her hands together in glee and triumph.

The second of the sons Jacob fathers with Zilpah is Asher, which Leah interprets to mean "What fortune! Women will deem me fortunate indeed" (30:12). And as if this weren't enough to regain her supremacy as the mother of sons, Leah resumes childbearing. She provides Jacob with two more sons. The first of these she calls Issachar, because "God has given me my reward for having given my maidservant to my husband" (30:17), lest perhaps she had some doubts about the Lord's judgment upon her for having so openly competed with her sister. The second is Zebulun, because "God has given me a choice gift; this time my husband will exalt me for I have borne him six sons" (30:20). Leah has never given up hoping that she can win her husband's heart through the gift of sons, nor has she taken her eye off her goal of being exalted over Rachel. In this cavalcade of son-bearing, the lonely Rachel can only wait.

As a kind of coup de grâce, Leah bears Jacob one child more, a daughter, Dinah, whose fate among her brothers will be told in the following chapter (30:21).

If we stop here for a moment and read back over the names of the sons, we realize something of the dynamics of this family and the relationship between the two sisters. We can also see how the sister story grotesquely mirrors some of the family and sibling themes we have already identified. The competitive nature of family life, the contest for place, position, favor, and recognition is now waged between sisters; their shared husband is loved not for who he is but for what he can do for them, while their entire interest appears to be caught up in a war of motherhood.

It is not clear how to read this story. On the one hand it seems to dramatize in the starkest possible terms the worst features of the patriarchal system. Women bear sons for men. Motherhood has been co-opted in the interests of lineage and clan; the woman's body becomes a mere reproductive engine, and her mind, her spirit, her heart weigh nothing in the economic and dynastic scales. Jacob fathers sons, and sons are the coin of the realm. Women use their sons to gain favor and place. A woman's worth, and her worth to herself, is measured in her capacities as a brood mare. The relationship between sisters has become so competitive that Rachel seizes on her son Naphtali as the emblem of some victory: "With great contesting have I wrestled with my sister, and I have prevailed." In her cry of triumph she adumbrates the central image of this chapter; she has become a wrestler. Read in this way the story of the family of Jacob gives a contemporary reader ammunition for a condemnation of the patriarchal family and its values.

On the other hand Genesis includes this story as we find it, and surely it can be read as the book's own critique of those values. Jacob is once again held up to our scrutiny and judgment: He is a callow and selfish man, the weak-willed pawn of two fierce women whose power quite eclipses his. In his family and through him we are forced to face the underside of patriarchy, the mean but intense forces unleashed in its sibling world. Between Leah and Rachel the contest rages for superiority, and each, by one criterion or another, feels herself inferior. Rachel inferior in terms of motherhood, Leah inferior in the eyes of her husband's heart. Two sisters are corrupted by a system that prizes sons.

Further, though the sisters seem victims of a world that makes their worth depend only on their fertility, they are, both of them, powerful figures. We are reminded through them of Rebecca and Sarah, mothers who, when it came to determining the family politics, took matters into their own hands. Through these strong women the will of the Great Father worked itself out in human generations. Though women are seen only as functionaries within a patriarchal agenda, their role is considerable. By comparison the men seem a little like the weak-eyed Isaac, who cannot see his sons too clearly, having been blinded by the light.

The drama of this family's saga has built but not yet peaked. The climax comes when God "remembers" Rachel.

God heeded her and opened her womb. She conceived and bore a son, and said,
"God has taken away my disgrace." So she named him Joseph, for she said, "May
the Lord add another son to me."(30:24)

In Hebrew the name Joseph may mean both "take away" and "add." How
apt; in a single stroke he has taken away her shame and added to her stature,
and he has given her reason to hope that her time of bearing other sons is at
hand. Though she delivers him into the world in a physical sense, he begins his
life by delivering her in a metaphorical sense from her disgrace. Now the
younger sister gains ascendancy; it is Joseph who will carry God's drama and
promise into the next generation. In his maturity, as we shall see, Joseph will
become the deliverer, an instrument of grace, even a kind of redeemer. All of
this is hinted here in the circumstances that make his birth, at least for his parents, miraculous. And the moment of his birth sets in motion the next movement of the story; it is now time for his father to leave Haran.

Jacob's decision to leave is prompted by a second dream in which God
teaches Jacob how to procure what is rightfully his and alerts him to the danger of remaining any longer under Laban's sway. In this dream Jacob is reminded of his first dream, and he is told:

"I have seen all that Laban is doing to you. I am the God of Beth-El, where you
anointed the pillar, where you vowed a vow to me. So now leave. Go out of this
land, return to the land of your kindred."(31:12–13)

It is time for Jacob to keep his word. The Great Father insists on the
covenant, on the bargain. Jacob must leave a land that has become his home,
but unlike his forebears, he must go on a journey of return to his father's
house, to his kindred, to Esau. Jacob prepares to set forth. He gathers his
wives and children, the profits from his long indenture to Laban, and his other
goods, servants, and household items. He sets off for Canaan.

❁   ❁   ❁

In these intervening years no word has reached him from his brother, Esau.
With a foreboding amounting to a certainty, Jacob knows his return will require him to face the brother whom he fleeced and fled.

Now Jacob sent messengers on ahead of him to Esau his brother . . . and charged
them saying: "Say this to my lord, to Esau: 'Thus says your servant Jacob, "I have
sojourned with Laban and have tarried until now. Ox and ass, sheep and servant

and maid have become mine. I have sent to tell my lord, to find favor in your eyes."' "

The messengers returned to Jacob, saying: "We came to your brother, to Esau— but he is already coming to meet you, and four hundred men are with him!"

Jacob was exceedingly afraid and was distressed. (32:4–8)

In his fear Jacob divides his retinue and chattel into two camps, thinking that if his brother strikes at one, then the other can escape. Then Jacob prays, reminding God that He promised him safe passage. He admits his fear, but he receives no reply.

Desperate now, he sends a massive bribe of she-goats, kids, ewes, rams, nursing camels and their young, thirty cows, forty bulls, and ten colts ahead to his brother. These he divides up in herds and sends in three waves, telling his servants to say to Esau, when they meet him and when he asks to whom this livestock belongs, "to your servant Jacob; it is a gift sent to my lord, to Esau, and he himself is coming behind us" (32:19). But Jacob delays, hoping these gifts will mollify his brother. Cautious and protective, he sends his wives and twelve children across the Jordan River at a fording place.

And now, the myth tells us, "Jacob was left alone" (32:24).

He was alone once before when he dreamed of the stairway to heaven and had a stone for his pillow. Alone then, alone now, the familiar world falls away from him.

This is not the first time that the imagination of Genesis has placed its protagonists in a spiritual landscape empty of companionship or community. I think of Cain alone in his wandering, of Noah alone in the madhouse of his ark, of the lonely men of Babel scattered from the valley of Shinar, of Abraham the lonely stranger, and of the isolated Isaac wandering alone in the field before the arrival of Rebecca. By its repetitions Genesis constructs the myth of the soul alone in its ultimate moments, facing the forces in itself and in the world-beyond-the-self. That loneliness, for all its nobility, is a tragic condition.

The aloneness of Jacob in this moment is a defining image in the tradition of the Western imagination. We find nothing like it in Homer and the heroic tradition. Achilles may brood alone in his tent, but he is surrounded by the fury and clamor of war and watched over constantly by a concerned and meddling pantheon. Odysseus is stripped of all he has and of all his companions, but he, too, is constantly under the protection of his patroness Athena, and if he does not know it, we, from the very outset of his saga, do. Nor does he, though often the sole actor on the epic stage, ever feel himself to be alone.

This aloneness stands as one of the earliest images in the Western imagination for a solitude mystics will later call the "dark night of the soul." It is a prophetic and spiritual loneliness for which generations have imagined Jacob in this moment as the paradigm, the ultimate image of a man lost in himself, coming to the very boundary of hope, gripped by what is called "abjection of soul." This paradigm is recalled in later sacred and secular literatures, which are conscious of their debt to the myths of Genesis. Moses ventures alone into the most distant wilderness before he sees the burning bush; he climbs Sinai alone before he receives the tables of the law. The prophet is alone in the belly of the whale before fulfilling his destiny; he is alone in the cave before he hears the "still, small voice" of God. Christ is alone in the Garden of Gethsemane while his companions sleep, alone on the cross. Lear is alone on the heath before he is illuminated by his love of Cordelia. The Ancient Mariner is "Alone, alone, all all alone / Alone on a wide, wide sea" before his redemption.

In this loneliness there is a descent and an emptiness that T. S. Eliot captured in the second of his *Four Quartets:*

> *I said to my soul, be still, and let the dark come upon you*
> *Which shall be the darkness of God . . . and wait without hope . . .*
> *And what you do not know is the only thing you know*
> *And what you own is what you do not own*
> *And where you are is where you are not.*

Thirty centuries or more after Genesis, Eliot echoes its imagery. The soul he addresses in these words is the soul that Genesis imagines in this scene of a man at night alone by the river, wife and family on one bank, he alone on the other. Divided from the world and from his worldliness, this is a man who feels at the mercy of the dark. The dialogue of the soul with itself is the struggle to be still and to be empty and to wait; it is the fiercest, even if the most silent, of all the struggles the patriarchal imagination has been able to propose. This state of soul is a kind of near-death, a waiting empty of expectation in which the mind can no longer conceive what it could be waiting for.

This is the valley of the shadow of death, the vale of soul-making in which one realizes the full mystery of the world, its otherness and strangeness, and the scale of one's own worth. In this vale the soul learns its hardest lesson: the lesson of humility. For a man like Jacob, guileful and opportunistic, the bargainer with God, the cheat and the darling, this humility is redemptive. In the vale of the shadow the soul is made a humble thing; it knows its earthliness, its vulnerability, its ultimate dependency on something beyond itself that will uphold it from madness or dissolution and death. It knows its need of a brother.

This dark night of the soul reminds me of the primal darkness before the creation of the world, a darkness that emanated from the void that preexisted creation. Into that void the soul descends before something new may be created. Here in Jacob's inner life the great macrocosmic cycle is repeated, for the actual Hebrew word *bad,* meaning "alone," occurred at the beginning of Genesis: "It is not good," ruminated Mystery, surveying Adam in Eden, "for man to be alone." This *alone* takes us back to the genesis of a man's existential condition and to the Tales of a Lonely God.

If his soul comes through this dying, Jacob may recognize in retrospect that this dark night in the vale was his turning point. Yet who turned? He did not turn himself, but something comes to turn him. Unbeknownst to him, a conversion is at hand, one so profound as to alter him physically and spiritually. In it he will be blessed and newly named, reborn. In this conversion—for it is the very nature of the process—Jacob is the object, not the initiator. In the bottom he bottoms out, and something holds him up from the abyss that he knows full well can claim him. From such a precipice he will make a new beginning. In the light that breaks in this darkness, a fresh genesis begins, a new cycle in the ancient rhythmic pattern.

And Jacob was alone. (32:24)

We can reach him in this place only through midrash. That midrash comes from whatever we may know of this state. For myself, I hear a cry in his heart, a yearning that knows it does not merit or deserve to be consoled. I have known this vale as a season in my life, long, dreary, frightening, and unmapped. If something came to wrestle with me then and to wrest me from such a place, it came as grace. Indeed, at some time in the night and somewhere in the vale, something comes to Jacob. How can he name it or know it? He cannot. How can it be figured: as an angel, a man, a god, a brother, madness? Whatever "it" is, "it" comes. It comes from somewhere that had been until the moment of its coming a nowhere, a part of the soul that the soul did not know. Or is it a touch of God from beyond the soul that the soul could not imagine for itself? Something comes to "wrestle" with Jacob, to meet him, to claim him, to wound, and to transform him.

And Jacob was alone. And a man wrestled with him until the break of dawn.
When he saw that he had not prevailed against him, he wrenched the socket of

his hip, so that the socket of his hip was strained as he wrestled with him. Then he said, "Let me go, for the dawn is breaking."

But he answered, "I will not let you go unless you bless me."

Said the Other, "What is your name?"

He replied, "Jacob."

Said he, "Your name shall no longer be Jacob, but Israel, for you have striven with beings divine and human and have prevailed."

Jacob asked, "Pray, tell me your name."

But he said, "You must not ask my name." And he took leave of him there.

So Jacob named the place Peniel, for he said, "I have seen a divine being face to face, yet my life has been preserved," and the sun rose upon him. (32:24–31)

The word translated here as "wrestle" comes from the Hebrew word *'abaq*, which means dust. Thus in a literal sense *wrestle* means something like "to turn into dust," "to be covered with dust," and "as dust to float away." It is a word associated in other contexts with dissolution, insignificance, and death. The Hebrew word *'abaq* does not so much describe an action as evoke an image. It is as if we were observers from a distant vantage point and saw a man alone, Jacob, enveloped in a cloud of dust. We cannot see what occurs within that cloud, it is so whirled up by motion. We cannot tell what he is doing; we see only the dust raised where there was no wind to raise it. Or perhaps there was a great wind.

Later Jacob will come toward us dusty in the dawn, limping; when we ask him how he came to be so dusty, he will tell us that he was wrestling. Wrestling with what? we ask. With whom? He does not know. He cannot name it. Was it a man? we ask. Yes, he says, very like a man, but it was not a man. Was it a spirit? we ask. Yes, says he, very like a spirit. Perhaps it was God Himself, we murmur. And Jacob is silent, his eyes shining with a light brighter than the morning. So might we interrogate a man who has passed through the dark night of the soul; and in such ways we might be answered. He comes out of the dust the same man and a different man. We will call him Jacob and Israel, and he has received a sacred name and wound.

The wound is delivered to that place in the body called in Hebrew *yarekh*. In other contexts *yarekh* means side or hip, the place where the sword is carried. But it is also the word for loins. Of Gideon it is written that he "begot threescore and ten sons with his *yarekh*" (his loins). Loins are the seat of masculine strength and generative power. Loins refer to a man's phallic energy, to his potency and his power to reproduce and to bear himself with a certain courage in the world.

"Gird up your loins" may once have been an injunction to put on a certain garment that swathed the hips as a girdle, but we use it to suggest a preparation of the spirit. Loins reaches our slang in the word *balls*. The loins are the hara, the whole domain of the lower chakras, the male pelvis with its armature and tenderness, its thrust and its vulnerability. This is a locus of the sacred in manhood, the seat of the "fire in the belly." Like circumcision this wound hints at some transformation of masculinity, some raising of sexuality to a new power.

Abram became Abraham when he was circumcised; Jacob becomes Israel with this wound to his virility. This event has the features of a shamanic initiation: A new name is given to a man who is now a different man. His wound marks him for life as one who has been touched by superior powers; and in the myth of his wrestling encounter, a people will take his name as theirs. Israel is not just Jacob's name but becomes the name of that people who trace their lineage back to him and to this moment. Israel is the God-wrestler, the brother-wrestler, the self-wrestler, who has known what it means to be alone and whose soul is fashioned in the vale of the shadow. Israel is the paradigm for a soul that in its aloneness grapples with the most profound issues of its existence and wins a blessing that leaves it marked, infirm with a glorious infirmity.

That blessing, which alone signals the adoption by the Great Father, is Jacob's at last. He wants it. He can claim it. He knows what it means. The blessing seals him as it sealed his father and grandfather into the covenant, into a relationship with God. As a young man he had stolen the blessing, and it had no power for him. Now he is ready for it. His long exile has seasoned something in him, though he is not yet—nor will he ever be—a man I can wholly admire. But he has kept faith with his vow, and he demands that God keep his side as well. Jacob has come back to face his brother.

❀ ❀ ❀

The most memorable biblical psychodrama I ever conducted sprang from this passage in Genesis. The group had been together for many sessions and had used biblical myths occasionally to deepen and extend our experience of the issues we struggled with in our daily lives. The prospect of wrestling with one another had required weeks of preparation. We dealt in explicit ways with our feelings about physical boundaries, sexuality, and intimacy. Wrestling, taken out of the safe context of sport or competition, was threatening *and* intriguing. We had made sure that any one of us, for whatever reason, could stand outside the match, could be a drummer, a spotter, or find any other role that at the time felt appropriate. We respected one another's *no*.

There were about twenty of us. Knowing ahead of time what we would be tackling, we had secured the use of a wrestling practice room at the university. There were mats on the floor. We began the session with a long series of physical warm-ups. Then we read the passage as a chorus but didn't comment on it in any way. Each of us had studied the passage as preparation for the session.

We lowered the lights in the room until we were almost in the dark. Three men worked up a steady rhythm on drums. In the dim light and with the backbeat of the drum, we formed a circle. I asked each person to identify who he or she wished to be in the drama. We had the whole of the Book of Genesis behind us, for we had used it as our body of myth and source for ritual.

"I am Cain."

"I am Abel."

"I am Abraham."

"I am Lot."

"I am Lot's wife."

"Call me Ishmael."

"I am Hagar."

"I am Isaac."

"I am Sarah, who watches and weeps."

"I will play the Adversary."

"I am Jacob."

"I am Esau."

"I am Rebecca."

"I am the serpent."

"I am God."

"I am an angel."

Not everyone spoke up. A few remained silent, waiting to see what role prompted them to involvement.

"What brings you here?" I asked each person, and each answered in role.

"I heard there was going to be a fight; I've got a lot to get off my chest."

"I have been wounded, too, but no one can see it. I don't limp."

"I want my father's blessing."

"I want to get to my love for my sister."

"I want to tell my brother how much I envy him."

"I want to wrestle with my brother."

"I want to see whether men can bless each other."

"I don't know why I am here."

We broke the circle at my direction, and each character spent some time alone, walking the walk of his or her character, finding the character in the body, the body in the character.

"OK," I said, "round one."

Cain came first. He asked to wrestle with God. His wrestling was passionate, fueled by his sense of injustice. The drummers supplied a heart-beat rhythm. Cain's adversary grappled with him in silence; God did not speak at first as Cain hurled his protests and grunted his curses. Then God asked, "Cain, what in you did you have to wrestle with and master in yourself? You were free; you had a chance. Wrestle with that."

Here God quit the ring, and another man came in to enable Cain to wrestle with himself. A slower and more silent struggle ensued. Various group members gave words to Cain's inner struggle. "I am fighting my pride . . . my ego . . . my grief . . . my shame . . . "

Abel stepped forward. "Now me," he said. He lunged at his brother and pinned him. Seated astride his chest, Abel screamed, "You bastard!" again and again. Cain struggled to break free, did, and once again was mastered. In the end, he let it happen, finally submitting, seeming to hear his "brother's" pain. They lay heaving against one another; wrath was replaced with sorrow. Both men were shaken. Cain asked to be forgiven. Without words Abel embraced him.

Abraham came forward. He, too, wished to wrestle with God. "I am old," he said, "but just once I would grip you and feel you as something substantial." Another man came forward and accepted Abraham's grasp. For several long moments the two stood in tableau, unmoving, God clasped in Abraham's arms, and then, as Abraham gradually let go, God's hand reached up to touch his brow in a kind of benediction, and Abraham rested his head against the chest of this blessing God.

Jacob came forward looking for a younger Abraham to match him. "I need an Abraham to fight; I want to throw off this burden of your legacy. I never asked for it. I never wanted it." An Abraham volunteered. They wrestled, and their wrestle also evolved to an embrace; they lay panting on the floor. "I never wanted it either," said Abraham, "but it was the greatest thing in my life. In the end I came to believe that I had actually desired it."

Isaac came next, the broken father, broken long before he was a father. Jacob leaped at him in a rage. "Bless me!" he screamed. "Bless *me!*"

Hagar asked to wrestle. "Who's your adversary?" I asked. She chose Sarah. The two women feinted at each other with nails, hissed and tangled in a feline fight. Each expressed jealousy, fear, abandonment, hatred; each screamed out accusations until they realized they had a common adversary and went to beat up God. Chasing the Lord around the room, we all broke up into laughter. They did not stop until they held God down and made him confess his misogyny.

"I am Ishmael, and I want to wrestle with Esau. We are both strong men, we have both been overlooked and rejected; we enjoy our roughness."

Esau came forward, and the two men leaped and whooped; they grappled, rolled, spun, used each other's force to fling and fly. Wrestling as contact dancing; the drummers beat up a storm and soon others spilled into the melee, bounding off one another, hugging, holding, pushing, twisting, leaping free. We raised the dust off the mats as we pounded and rolled. Gradually the snake-dance-free-for-all mayhem wore down until the players were strewn about, panting on the floor. The drums subsided into a simple heartbeat. There was a period of breathing and silence. Finally, at the end, I gave each person who would take one a blindfold. They put them on.

"Who in your life, or what in yourself, are you wrestling with today?" I asked them. "Wrestle toward a blessing."

In final accompaniment the drummers syncopated the rhythms and built the tempo one last time. The blind blessing-wrestle came to its various conclusions. Utterly spent, the group members now lay each in his or her separate darkness. "You can remove your blindfolds and tell the person next to you your name and who or what you have been wrestling with." In this way we moved out of the ritual drama we had created and back into ourselves.

The rest of the group was filled with stories, memories, and images that came from the enactment. We had a sense of renewed vitality. As a group we had bonded, banded, and bound ourselves in new toils with one another. We now knew this biblical passage in our muscles. We had found in the act of wrestling a form within which to experience the relation of energy to matter, imagination to action, feeling to form. Spirit had been, in some very real sense, embodied.

After the session, thinking about it, savoring it, I knew I had seen farther than I ever had before into the heart of this biblical image. It now seemed to me that *wrestling* could stand for a whole range of strenuous and contesting energies that are engaged in fashioning the self, in living the life of husband or wife, father or mother, son or daughter, or brother or sister, and in making and keeping covenant with the life of Imagination, either as our own internal gift or the surrounding mystery that enfolds us. Wrestling is a metaphor for the patriarchal sense—and my own—of the soul's existential reality. Soul is made by grappling with ultimate things: with one's own nature, with one's kin, and with God. As a poetic image and as a way of life, wrestling seemed to me the unique contribution of the patriarchal tradition, its splendid excess. Other spiritual traditions seem effete by comparison. They propose an all but genderless spirituality, purged of what is physical, immediate, primitive, and mortal.

Much of the spirituality of the East, which I had explored in my early thirties, moves away from wrestling to stillness of mind, from argument to concentration, from outcry to the lulling mantra, from the fierce grapple of the wrestler to the balance of yoga postures. The end of Eastern spirituality is an enlightenment in which the distinctness and differences of the self and the Other finally dissolve into oneness.

Christian spirituality, which I had savored since my experience with the fly, speaks of love and logos. Christ is the redeeming son and the inspiring word. He has some of the patriarchal energy, for he is in part a human being, and in his humanness we can imagine him struggling with what is asked of him. But to wrestle with God as Jacob does! Nothing so mortal or erotic is hinted at in any episode of his life. On the contrary, like the Eastern sage he will say, "I and my Father are one."

The spiritual imagination of men and women have conceived of the relationship with God in many other ways; many paths have been developed whose aim is always to open the heart and the mind to Spirit and Source. But I know of no other path that says that wrestling with God is a way to God, a wrestling in which no iota of our humanness is to be left out nor in which any particle of our free will is to be restrained.[1] We are to spare God nothing of ourselves, says the spirituality of the patriarchs, not our rage, our sexuality, our aggression, nor our fierce desire to equal, even to master, Him. Is God forever to be a distant and unapproachable Supremacy? Yes, say the patriarchs, God is Mystery, unfathomable and eternally Other. But, say these same patriarchs, who do not fear paradox or illogic, God is also something that may be wrestled with in a passionate embrace, indeed like a brother.

My own abilities as a wrestler have been strengthened by wrestling with these stories, for they are not easy tales to get a hold of. On one level that struggle has taken place between two parts of myself, one part that clings to a naive belief that the Bible is "the good book," that every word must be holy, and its God a paragon. Another part, awakening gradually through my years of reading and working with the text, is heretical: It sees the darkness in the myths, the unspeakable in the words, and evil in its God. I do not know exactly where my sense of outrage comes from, for as I said in the beginning, I was raised free of the constraints and doctrines of religion. I suspect that in part it comes from my reading of feminist criticism; in part from the operation of a midrashic imagination, which endows every character with his or her full story; and in part from an unresolved and lifelong response in myself to the storm troopers and to the reality of evil.

I am in fact immensely and continuously troubled by the stories of Genesis, and I suspect that even in my attempts to wrest them from the pulpit and Sunday school I have not gone far enough to point out in them what belongs to an imagination far bloodier, wilder, more ruthless and morbid than our own. That shadow side of God, that dark side of the patriarchal imagination, haunts the tales of Genesis in a deeper and more pervasive way than my own account suggests. The imagination that dreamed these stories knew something about its own nature that we would choose to forget, or prefer to think has been transcended or transformed through civilization. The primitive in the soul, the ecstatic and the savage—light and shadow—would seem to withstand all redemptive agendas. The world we have made should make us wonder how far we have come since Jacob, or since Cain.

I have been wrestling with these stories as narratives. They are slippery, quick, powerful, alien, intense, unremitting. They grip me, and I grapple with them. My imagination has been seized by these riddling myths. I struggle with ancient words that mean more than one thing, with characters who like Jacob refuse to be simple, and with ideas that elude me by their subtlety. The wrestler questions, and wrestles with questions, seeks answers, and is, in the end, refused. Again and again I feel the myths have mastered me.

And I am not only a reader of words but a writer of them as well. I now know better what T. S. Eliot meant when he wrote of "the intolerable wrestle/ With words and meanings."[2] Behind the facade of this printed version of my work are countless other versions in which I tried to grasp what it was I wished to say, or to get out of the way so that what needed to be said could speak through me. This wrestling with "words and meanings" has left me spent at times, at times exhilarated.

Wrestling is also a significant image for my inner life; it is a way of speaking about my heart and my mind, my relationship to my wife, my children, my parents, my attempts to make sense of the experiences of my life, my friendships, my search for career, my struggle with my own demons, my appetites, diversities, desires to excel. Some like to say that life is a dance. The heirs of Israel are more likely to say that it is a wrestle. The poet Rilke is one of these heirs when he writes "The Man Watching":

> I can tell by the way the trees beat, after
> so many dull days, on my worried windowpanes,
> that a storm is coming,
> and I hear the far-off field say things
> I can't bear without a friend,
> I can't love without a sister.
> The storm, the shifter of shapes, drives on
> across the woods and across time,
> and the world looks as if it had no age:
> the landscape, like a line in the psalm book,
> is seriousness and weight and eternity.
> What we choose to fight is so tiny!
> What fights with us is so great!
> If only we would let ourselves be dominated
> as things do by some immense storm,
> we would become strong too and not need names.
> When we win it's with small things,
> and the triumph itself makes us small.
> What is extraordinary and eternal
> does not want to be bent by us.
> I mean the angel, who appeared
> to the wrestlers of the Old Testament:
> when the wrestler's sinews
> grew long like metal strings,
> he felt them under his fingers
> like chords of deep music.
> Whoever was beaten by this Angel,
> (who often simply declined to fight),
> went away proud and strengthened
> and great from that harsh hand,
> that kneaded him as if to change his shape.
> Winning does not tempt that man.
> This is how he grows: by being defeated, decisively,
> by constantly greater things.[3]

Rilke deeply understands the necessity of wrestling; it is the process through which paradoxically we achieve a strength that can come to us only through supreme and decisive defeat. "Winning does not tempt that man." No, it is not about winning but about striving with something incommensurate, something that dignifies and deepens us by the fact of our engagement. Whatever it is that we wrestle with in *that* way Rilke calls the Angel, the emissary of God.

And lifting up his eyes Jacob saw Esau coming. (33:1)

The meeting with Esau is almost anticlimactic, for one has the sense that Jacob has met him already. Genesis is silent on the subject of Esau's wrestle with himself and the process by which he comes to set aside the forces he massed to meet his brother. The band of four hundred men certainly suggests aggressive intentions; yet Esau, with the most to forgive, appears the most forgiving. Of the two men he is the most changed, now courteous, almost courtly.

And Esau ran to meet him, and embraced him, and fell on his neck, and kissed him and they wept. (33:4)

This reconciliation of the brothers is never broken again by hostility. This scene of tears and a kiss provides balance and closure to the fugitive journey to Haran that began with a kiss and tears. The twins are at last disarmed and open, and each has in some measure integrated into himself something of the other. Esau is mild, impeccable; Jacob has a wildness in him now; he is, after all, a wrestler. Their brotherhood achieves the balance and equality of their maturity.

Courteous, perhaps even obsequious, in his gratitude and appreciation, Jacob introduces Esau to his family. Yet, dazzled by some sense of profound revelation, he cannot tear his gaze from his brother's face. He tells Esau that "looking on your face is like seeing the face of God." In this moment Jacob knows that if one sees the face of God anywhere, it will be in the face of one's brother. Esau has been his angel.

He offers Esau a gift—in Hebrew *minchah*—the very term for Cain's and Abel's offering to God. Now the offering runs between brothers who occupy the same plane of existence rather than from a man up to his God. Esau accepts it as a sign of their reconciliation. Esau invites Jacob to dwell near him and moves on ahead supposing Jacob will follow. But Jacob passes up Esau's invitation, perhaps knowing the necessity of some distance if brothers are to live in peace.

According to the story, they meet only once more, at the grave of their father in Machpelah. There they will stand in the shade of two other brothers, Isaac and Ishmael, who had come to the same place and for the same purpose, to bury a father and to face each other. Standing in the cave with its shadows and memories they offer us across the distance of myth the promise of atonement with our brothers.

I have come to that atonement in my heart with Jonathan.

Until recently I observed an exact correctness by always referring to him as my stepbrother. It was what he was, after all, not even a half brother, but kin only by the accident of a second marriage. When that marriage ended in 1975, the word *step* became obsolete. We could have gone our separate ways. Yet after 1975 Jonathan and I went on as if the divorce of his mother from my father meant nothing at all to our relationship. It changed them, but not us.

Through the years of this second phase of our relationship we chose to keep our connection alive. On my side I came to believe that the marriage of our separate parents was indeed no accident, but that Jonathan had become a kind of angel in my life. In my projective fantasies about him I came gradually to recognize parts of myself. I came also to see where his frailties and vulnerabilities lay. Some of his strengths would never be mine, and some of mine would never be his. Our differences became clearer while our connection became deeper. Time and our wills forged our bond.

When I began to wrestle with the brother myths of Genesis, trying to get a hold on the stories and their meaning for me, I had a significant dream about Jonathan. In it we were at some carnival where there was music and storytelling and dancing. Each of us was scheduled to perform at different times and places, and during this part of the dream, when I was getting ready to do my thing, I was filled with a competitive anxiety about how many people would be coming to see him, how many coming to see me. Then in the leaping illogic of dreams I found myself seated in the audience for his performance. He was playing the flute in a jazz combo. He did not see me watching, but as I listened to him I was filled with an appreciation for his skills and for him, and I leaned over and said to the person sitting next to me, "That's my brother." I was amazed in my dream to recognize that the person to whom I confided was my father.

Then the dream sequence spliced again, and I was up on stage with him. We were playing a strange musical instrument together. It was a long, hollow log, which we straddled at either end and beat upon with sticks, except the log must have been filled with something because when we beat it, it rang and chimed and boomed and clacked. We sat facing one another "playing the log." In the last image of the dream I was looking over at Jonathan, and I saw he was looking at me. His face was open, trusting, as it had been when we first met, and my eyes filled with tears.

Since that dream I speak of Jonathan as my brother.

13

Deborah:
A Midrash

Deborah, Rebecca's nurse, died and
was buried under the oak below
Bethel; so it was named Allon-bacuth,
or the oak of weeping. (35:8)

I came to understand something of Deborah during a series of training seminars I led with a group of rabbis several years ago. I was teaching them how to do this psychodramatic midrash, and we were looking at developing a life of Esau. Far more expert and educated with the text than I, these men and women wove the tiniest hints and references into a comprehensive and composite image of Esau. In the course of it, one woman gave me a glimpse into a possible connection of Deborah with Esau, and that glimpse grew slowly in my mind into this present midrash.

Deborah is an obscure figure, and the lines quoted above are the only reference to her in Genesis. They are found after the reunion of the brothers during the time when Jacob takes up residency again in Canaan, the time after Rachel's death in childbirth, when she bore him their last son. But then Deborah will tell you all that.

I died because I had nothing further to live for. I had seen the last traces of a world I loved destroyed. I had seen the works of the Father, and I would have no more to do with Him. What I knew I took with me; secrets died with me that no one would ever hear, secrets not only of the house of Jacob—and before him the house of Laban, and before even him the house of Bethuel—but secrets of the Goddess, her wonders and her ways. Of the former I shall not speak here. But some few things I must divulge, to set the record straight. Here under the shade of this great oak, it falls to me to speak of Dinah.

Of myself a few words. In the Goddess cult I was named for the queen bee, Debowrah. I am the ancient one. My grandmother Deborah served in Nahor's house. She nursed Terah, told me stories about him and his sons. She was there when Abram left. She knew how Haran died and told me, but she made me swear never to reveal the secret. This was all a long, long time ago.

My mother, Deborah, served Nahor's son, Bethuel. Bethuel married Milcah, and she bore him twins, Rebecca and Laban, he the elder by a moment, but as the man, he was doubly then her master. I, the third Deborah in the line, was Rebecca's wet nurse. Later it was my task to keep my eye on her and tell her brother, Laban, what she did. He had a power over me after his father died.

Rebecca was not attached to me, always had a mind of her own, that one. She and her brother were a pair, let me tell you. There's a twist in that family, runs like a seam from old man Terah and his wife, whom, you will notice, no one ever mentions, through all the generations. You could see it in Lot, in Laban, and Jacob; later in his boys, in Reuben, Simeon, Levi. But it showed up in Rebecca, that same twist. She and her brother! I wouldn't trust either of them out of my sight. Laban ruled over her like the petty tyrant he was. No wonder then when Eliezer came, saying he was from Abraham, Rebecca seized the chance to get away. Oh, she had her own ideas, that girl.

Laban, master Laban, sent me with his sister when she left his house. "Keep your eye on her," he said. He only half believed the emissary from Abraham, who claimed he was searching for a wife for Isaac. Too much like a Persian fairy tale, he said. She was a mere girl when we left Haran.

I served her then when she married Isaac, who was old enough to be her father. He was a quiet man, and, I will say this, he treated me well and loved my little Esau. I say "my little Esau," for it was so. When the twins were born, Rebecca doted only on her Jacob and left Esau to me. I nursed him. I taught him the ancient ways. It broke my heart to see how she and Jacob treated him. When he married among the Hittites, she wanted to disown him, made old Isaac's life miserable with her complaints. But Esau loved his father, even after Jacob had betrayed him. He came to me then, wishing only to be reconciled with Isaac, to make peace. It was Rebecca who made up the tale that Esau sought to kill Jacob, made that up to give Jacob an excuse to go to Haran and find a wife from among her kin. I tell you, she was a storyteller, that one.

I told Esau, "Go to your father's brother's house. Find Ishmael, for I believe you and he have much in common." He did, and I know he was happy there, and prospered. He was called Edom by some, but always he is Esau to me.

Later Rebecca heard Jacob was to marry Laban's daughter Rachel. She sent me back to Laban's house then; I was to be a wedding gift for her son. Nothing had changed. Laban had Jacob tied up in his web. Poor man was blind for love of Rachel. Laban got Jacob so drunk on his wedding night the fool didn't know who was in bed with him. Leah, of course, was utterly humiliated, and Rachel, I know, never forgave her father. In this way Laban sought to make Jacob a slave for life and so entangle his affairs—marrying two sisters!—that he would never leave. Too many cousins marrying too many cousins, if you ask me. Incest is only one of this family's secrets.

No need to tell you the whole story. There was never a moment's peace. Jacob loved Rachel, but when Leah gave him sons, he set her above her sister. The rivalry of Jacob and Laban was like a curse on the family; it poisoned the sisters. Jacob was unsure of himself, infatuated, easily led. He was his mother's tool, weak, but slippery, knowing how to play one against another. His sons were like hungry dogs. No one knew where they stood, and the women, even the concubines, were at one another's throats.

I watched. I schooled the serving girls. I didn't see a one among the boys who had Esau's open heart or love of the Goddess's wild world. No one among them to whom I might pass on the mysteries I had learned from my mother, and she from hers back through the generations. Only one, the girl Dinah. I was a grandmother to her, and she alone took in the tales, stored them in her heart. I told her often of Esau, of the kind of man he was, and warned her against her brothers and their kind. So I take some blame for what occurred later, after we left—I should almost say escaped—from Laban and found our way back to Canaan.

It happened later, after Jacob received the name Israel, after he and his brother Esau—my nurseling—met and wept together. They parted, though not without a lie from Jacob that he would follow upon his brother and settle near him. But no sooner was Esau out of sight than Jacob headed north and settled in the outskirts of Shechem. He even bought some land from Hamor, who was the head man of that place.

Here is the lie the scribes have written in their pernicious Book of the Father:

Now Dinah, the daughter whom Leah had borne to Jacob, went out to visit the daughters of the land. Shechem son of Hamor the Hivite, chief of the country, saw her and took her and lay with her by force. *(34:1)*

"By force" you note; they said he raped her. The story, as the brothers told it, goes on to relate how Shechem then sued for Dinah's hand, for he was in love with her, but how her brothers heard of the rape and together hatched an infernal plan. Sons of Jacob to the end, they spoke smooth words to Hamor: "We will allow your son to marry our Dinah, and we will intermarry with your daughters and your sons with our sisters on one condition, that

every male among you is circumcised. Then we will give our daughters to you and take your daughters to ourselves; and we will dwell among you and become one kindred. But if you will not listen to us and become circumcised, we will take our daughter and go."(34:16–17)

That is what they said, and their book has set it down, though why they should remember that and forget so much else is quite beyond me.

Well, these words pleased Hamor and his son, and the headman ordered all the males of Shechem to be circumcised, telling them that the sons of Jacob "are our friends." His very words. And so it was accomplished. Then this is written—and mind you, when they tell this story they laugh, these men do, they laugh at their own cleverness:

On the third day, when they were in pain, Simeon and Levi, two of Jacob's sons, brothers of Dinah, took each his sword, came upon the city unmolested, and slew all the males. . . . Then the other sons of Jacob came upon the slain and plundered the town, because [they say!] their sister had been defiled. They seized their flocks and herds and asses, all that was inside the town and outside, all their wealth, all their children, and their wives, all that was in the houses they took as captives and booty. (34:25–29)

Who will believe an old woman? If I say it was not so, only the wind will listen. Dinah *loved* Shechem. She came repeatedly to her father for permission to marry. He forbade her, ever the clan man, ever his mother's son. Yet she loved Shechem, and he loved her. No father's words have ever stopped the hearts of young lovers. She shared everything with me; she loved Shechem for his tenderness, and she loved the Hivite women, their freedom, and their keeping of the ancient ways. She, who had only rough brothers and squabbling women around her, found sisters among them. Shechem was a prince and brought her to live with him. It was his prerogative and his pleasure. This they call his rape!

The rest is as you have it, the ruse and the slaughter and the savage looting of the town. There was rape aplenty then, let me tell you. Word went out like the smoke of burning houses. It was whispered and carried along the camel-ways and into the small settlements. A scourge has come. Don't mix with the sons of Israel. There is a fierce eastern clan in the land, and they will repay kindness with unkindness, and unkindness they will repay with terror. They are a jealous people who worship a terrible and powerful god. Beware.

The Israelites moved through the land with their booty and slaves and their herds, leaving Shechem behind in ruins, its smoke hanging on the shoulder of the mountain.

I'll tell you this: It killed Dinah. By the time we reached Bethel, she had fasted to a mere wraith of herself. She had seen a people she loved destroyed, the man she loved butchered before her eyes, her sisters made whores to the Israelites. I watched her waste away; I saw the last light go from her trusting eyes. Meanwhile Rachel was again with child. I feared for her, for she was weak. Leah had Jacob's ear and bed, and her sons did as they pleased; having made a mockery of their covenant, they had become like wolves in the land.

Then, on our way to Bethel, Jacob seemed to lose his mind. Shrieking and frenzied, he railed at us: "Rid yourselves of the alien god in your midst, purify yourselves, and change your clothes!" You can read his words; they have it right. We gave up everything. Jacob himself came to my tent and took my amulets, my healing pouches, my birthing medicines, and all the sacred objects of the Mother, and he burned them.

That same night Dinah died. Leah wept, and Rachel took pity on her. Long into the night the sisters clung to one another, and I think they understood what a curse the coming of Jacob had been to them both. They asked forgiveness of each other, and both were ashamed. But I was too weak to care. I had looked into the future, and I had seen only the endless warfare of men, killing in righteousness for their God. Their power sickened me.

I went down below Bethel to a great oak that overlooked the valley to keen for the dead girl. And all the women of Shechem, now slaves, came to join me, for they knew she had been their sister. Our keening filled the valley, and it seemed that the Mother herself joined us that night. Not a man dared come near.

Dinah's death and the mourning of the night finished me. I asked Rachel and Leah to lay me to rest when I breathed my last there at the foot of the oak tree. Dig deep, I said, uncover the roots, and lay me there where the roots make a cradle in the earth. And this they swore they would do.

I shall tell you something about this god of Jacob's, who was never my god. He proves how it is possible to be his servant, to be favored by his majesty, and still to be a craven, vicious man.

Look at Jacob, and you will know this god asks no goodness of his chosen sons. The wicked trample on the innocent, and there is no outcry from their god. Their god-stories tell of atrocities committed in his name, and of worse atrocities still, committed by this god himself. And this savage god—to whom they build their altars, for whom they mutilate their flesh and the innocent flesh of sons—what care does he take of them? He is a god that cannot be pleased, who knows no beauty, no tenderness. He sends the locusts on the grain fields and brings down the deluge that destroyed the world. Look at his son Jacob, who cheated his brother and spawned a band of cohort sons, who, without exception, were each greedier, more unruly, and more selfish than the next. This is the powerful father of the clan of El! This is the tribe destined to inherit the land! You explain it to me. This same Jacob, who after the slaughter of the Hivites could only weakly rebuke his sons with the words "You've brought trouble on me," fearing for his own skin. What kind of a father is he?

And something else I know, whispered to me through the roots of the tree, for though I did not live to see it, it came to me.

This same Jacob, when his dear wife Rachel died giving him his last son and with her dying words of sorrow named him Ben-oni, renamed the child, after she died, Benjamin. They say he loved Rachel. Why then did he bury her by the road? It is Leah who lies beside him in Machpelah. She saw to that. But Rachel . . . who will weep for her? She loved him; she lived in her sister's shadow and the shadow of her sons; she had one son, Joseph, a beautiful boy, but spoiled and trouble from the first. Then, just as her time seemed to be coming, her time for motherhood and her time to be a wife, she died. She had lost everything. Jacob sniveled. He withdrew into himself; he left the household to his sons, no father anymore at all. Then Reuben, the wolf, took Rachel's concubine Bilhah, lay with her, made her his whore. Read it, read the words, and behind the words see the vileness of the children of Israel.

The examples of this crooked god and his twisted sons are countless. The tree above me has witnessed everything, and it tells me all. Many stories never found their way into their Book of Books. And besides, what do the books know? So many stories once flowed in the wind and passed up and down the camel-ways. And what remains? Only a few stories in their hard book, stories lying like bones in the wilderness, from which all the meat has been picked by vultures. The Mother never had to do with books. Who can understand this bookish god of theirs? These men go wandering off into the hills and return dazed and famished, their eyes still glowing from some vision, while they rob and cheat and abuse one another and their children and their women in the name of a god who has nothing to do with human decency. The stories they tell of El, or Adonai, or Elohim, or El Shaddai—who can keep the names straight, and is this the same god or different gods?—are frightful. Destroying the world! Would the Mother do that? I ask you. And that tale about a garden and a snake, making it all look like the first woman was the weak one, she the one who was tempted and because of her all was lost—well, that's a man's way. Blame the woman; she tempts him. They even said that of Dinah, that she tempted Shechem and brought the destruction on herself. It makes me sick.

And speaking of women. Show me a single woman in that entire book of theirs whom a woman might wish to call sister. Hagar, yes, she alone, and they banished her. Leah and Rachel loved each other until Laban used them for his own mean ends. Then Jacob's insatiable thirst for sons and yet more sons turned them against each other. They were caught up in his madness and so degraded themselves that in the end they were like the twins; their loving natures were twisted by the Father, as he twists the hearts of all those he touches, filling the mind with dreams and promises, leaving the heart empty and alone.

Why are all the mothers barren until this capricious god of theirs decides to make them fertile? Do you really suppose the blessings of fertility belong to the Father? It is preposterous. It would make me laugh were it not so terrifying. For they believe this, and with their force they can, and have, destroyed the Mother and made all women slaves. Oh, I have heard the stories. I know them well. They are there to read in their Holy Book: husbands who sell their wives, turn them into their sisters, so they can get rich off them as if they were their whores. Enough. Enough.

But let them have their god and their stories. This god and these men deserve one another. Let them rewrite history. Let them forget the small gods of the little villages; let them oppress the faiths of others. Those of us who know the Mother know she takes myriad forms and is as perennial as the spring. She is jealous of no other god or goddess, knowing herself to be the Mother of them all.

But this god of Jacob's, he is a jealous god, unpredictable, vengeful, and no respecter of justice or goodness. I pity his prophets and his priests; I fear the people who will revere him and carry his worship forward in time. When

Jacob purged us of our gods, he went too far. Too far. The Goddess will be avenged, and in time She shall return, for She will long outlive this Father, who is, in the end, only another of Her sons.

When I look back on it all, I would pity these brothers if I did not fear them. What can one expect of a being in whom no life can ever stir? The power of life growing inside you is of a different order from power over life. What man can understand the bonds that are formed when a child is at your breast? This is the wisdom of the nurse. It is my wisdom. I have no need of a god of thought, a god of the powers of the world. I understand that the destiny of woman is something bigger than her womb; we have our souls, too, and there is a part of the soul that longs for purpose and community. Long after my nursing days were done I was a teacher of my people; I led the community of women in song and dance and in the rites of birth and death. I was a healer to my people. We are not *only* mothers; our children leave us as they must, and there is life to live, an inner life, an outer life to live.

But we seem to know, as men do not, how local and mortal a thing life is. Power must begin in the heart. What is power if it is divorced from love? Men will call me a sentimental old woman, but for all their busyness, for all their dreams and covenants and enterprises, they seem to miss this simple truth. The world waits for someone to lead a people into the promised land of that simple truth.

As for me, I did not live to see the day. I was buried under the oak tree where we wept. Rachel and Leah remembered me, and when it was time to make their Holy Book, someone left these words, my epitaph:

> Deborah, Rebecca's nurse, died and was buried
> under the oak below Bethel; so it was named
> Allon-bacuth.

Now let me rest.

14

The Myth
of Power

The edge of polemic in Deborah's midrash that cuts through the pretensions of patriarchy is, of course, my own. Through her I express aspects of my own postpatriarchal perspective and confront what otherwise might be too partisan an affiliation to the patriarchal tradition. Deborah is the expression of my own wrestle with the father-powers; hers is my own opposing voice wrestling with the man in me who so deeply identifies with, and which even secretly relishes, the savage side of the brother tales. After Eve and Ishmael she is the third figure to punctuate my reading of Genesis with the excommunicant's mordant view. All three are disenfranchised; all three feel the injustice of the God who favors His chosen and ignores the unchosen.

In particular Deborah has allowed me to broach the theme that unifies the story of Joseph, the last of the patriarchal sons. That theme is power. Joseph is the eleventh son of Jacob, his first child by Rachel. Joseph's story is told in the last thirteen chapters of Genesis and occupies more than a quarter of the entire book. Like his forebears Joseph is displaced from his native land and his father's house, but unlike them he does not leave by any divine summons or lead a nomadic existence as a shepherd and clan patriarch. Though Joseph lives the life of the Stranger, he does so in the court culture of Egypt, and within that culture he gains a singular place; he is second only to the pharaoh as a man of power.

It can be argued that the entire Book of Genesis may be read as a myth-theologizing of power. After all, patriarchy means *father power*. The patriarchal narratives are justly named because of their concern with power on both a divine and a human scale. Power is the book's central preoccupation. The very idea of a masculine deity, the Great Father, into whose being is arrogated *all* power—such that this He is *omnipotent*—mirrors men's obsession with their potency. The world of men that this deity creates often appears created in His image in its concern for might and obedience, mastery and service, dominance and subjection, position and status. These are the relationships of power, and one could say that "God" is the immense projection of men's abiding preoccupations with these relationships.

According to the myth-theology of Genesis, it was He, before all, Who created the world, arranged the place of man as ruler over nature; He structured gender roles; He destroyed His creation in a flood and created it anew; He calls, promises, initiates covenants, reduces cities to ashes, and gives men new names. He is either the book's supreme creation or its supreme Creator, its conceiver or conceit, but always the Great Father dominates His world by His presence or absence. His portrait overshadows all others, and in the patriarchal narratives we are aware not primarily of His love but His power.

But if power is the central theme of Genesis, it is also its central mystery. The physical fields of power that organize matter into a universe of natural orders are only the macrocosmic expressions of fields of power felt within the soul. The patterns of affiliation and repulsion that shape human interplay, the quest for power that drives the human imagination are less apparent and less well understood than physical laws, but no less real. Joseph, like Abraham, Isaac, and Jacob before him, lives in two worlds, and like them his soul is formed in his transactions in and between the two.

Joseph is one of the few biblical figures—I would include only Moses, David, and Jesus with him—who wrestle with the ultimate seductiveness of power. In his prime Joseph is almost godlike, and the display of his power takes many forms. His is power as the energy of genius to create new structures of civilization in a political and economic sense; power as an authority that can order how and where people live, and even determine their lives and deaths; power in his passions that can twist or heal human relationships; and ultimately power as a spiritual force, a superlative charisma, by which Joseph draws people to him in love and fear. Joseph's soul is initiated in all these realms of power, and in that sense he is a complete man.

In its depiction of the last phase of Joseph's maturity, Genesis shifts its mythic meditation on power to a different level. What Joseph comes to realize about power—and through him what we are shown—forms the crux and climax of his story. In his soul's final initiation, the patriarchal imagination of Genesis reaches for a new framework within which to understand the relationship of men to power, and it will be as a brother and with his brothers that this new framework is established.

For a prelude to his saga I turn to the poet Rumi. He writes:

> *Has anyone seen the boy who used to come here?*
> *Round-faced trouble-maker, quick to find a joke,*
> *slow to be serious, red shirt,*
> *perfect co-ordination, sly, strong muscled,*
> *with things always in his pocket: reed flute,*
> *worn pick, polished and ready for his Talent*
> *you know that one.*
> *Have you heard stories about him?*
> *Pharaoh and the whole Egyptian world*
> *collapsed for such a Joseph.*
> *I'd gladly spend years getting word*
> *of him, even third or fourth hand.*[1]

Nothing is more important for us, Rumi tells us, than "word of him."

The saga of Joseph's life falls into three parts: his youth, his rise to power and manhood in Egypt, and his reunion in middle age with his brothers and father.

His biography begins abruptly in his seventeenth year. In our first view of him we see him tending sheep along with the half brothers of the serving women; we are told that he brings "a bad report" of his brothers to his father (37:2); and that because of this his brothers hate him. Perhaps they fear him, too, for Jacob favors Joseph and bestows on him a regal, ornamental cloak, the coat of many colors.

We have read enough of the earlier sibling tales to recognize how deftly the conflictual materials of the brother drama are being kindled. In Joseph the talebearer we may see a glimpse of the spoiled favorite, his father's ally—liar or spy? Jacob, the old father, blind to the obvious dangers to his son, dotes on his chosen. The second youngest of Jacob's scions seems destined to usurp the place of the eldest.

Immediately after this introduction we are told that Joseph has two dreams. Through them some energy enters his life and points him toward a distant eminence. In the first he dreams he is in the fields with his brothers binding sheaves of wheat when suddenly his sheaf rises up and the sheaves of his brothers circle round his and bow down to it. Joseph tells his brothers this dream, and from then on they hate him still more. "Would you be king and rule over us!" (37:8) they protest. In his second dream the sun, moon, and eleven stars bow down to him. This he also recounts to his brothers, and to his father as well. His brothers "envied him"; his father was troubled (37:11).

These are dreams of power, and they provide us with our first inkling of the young man's extraordinary destiny. Already the one set apart from his brothers by his father's favoring love, the dreams hint at even wider spheres of power, natural and cosmic. In his dreams Joseph is the center of a mandala, the hub around which systems revolve. His brothers say nothing about the meaning of the second dream but correctly interpret the first as a political prophecy: Joseph is going to rule them. They are unable to see that it is also a dream about being bound, all of them, on some common field and that it is also about feeding and service, reverence and circles.

These dreams of Joseph's hint at his purpose, though at the time he can have no idea of the arduous responsibility that purpose will exact from him. These dreams represent the sum total of Joseph's vocational call. They are figments of his imagination, gifts of Imagination, from which he will compose a life. These dreams contain no direct apprehension of God, as, for example, occurred for Jacob when, in his dream of angels, he saw God standing beside him. Unlike Abraham's dreams, Joseph's guarantee no future, no promised land. They hint at power, but they are after all only dreams, full of the ambiguity of dreams. It requires a certain courage to follow such dreams, to enter them, to live them out. It will be lonely.

In groups where I have worked with Joseph's dreams in psychodramatic midrash, I have heard both men and women confess that they have derived a vital sense of purpose from their own dreams or visions. "Sometimes even mission," I heard a woman say once. From such admissions and from my own life I have learned that purpose is as precious to us as love or family, perhaps even more. "I almost hate to say this," one man said, "but I need, really need, to feel my life has some purpose to it. Purpose gives meaning. Without that I can't really love fully, and even my children can't give me that sense of purpose. They can make me feel wanted in some important, emotional sense, but this is different. It feels like I have to have a purpose in life, something bigger than me that I'm involved in. It's not about feeling important, at least not in some public, egotistical sense; it's about feeling necessary."

A woman in that same group agreed. "You know," she said, "the same is true for me. I get so sick of men assuming that our biology is our destiny. Don't you think women, too, need a sense of purpose? I want to be a potter, and, damn it, that's as important to me as the master-builder with his phallic skyscrapers. And more than that, I am a soul, too; I am not only my body and my motherhood. I am not only a creature caught in the web of nature. I am deeply a part of nature, that is true; and perhaps more deeply a part of her than a man can be. I don't know. But I am part of the spirit as well. I, too, am a dream being. I, too, feel the call of God."

I remember a moment that occurred many years ago when my oldest friend, Ben, his wife, Judy, my first wife, Marilyn, and I were sitting on the grass in Boston Commons. It was a sunny afternoon in late spring. A tattered man came up to us, from out of nowhere, and asked, "What is the most important thing in life?" We took this derelict Diogenes seriously, and Judy answered first.

"Love," she said.

"Love," said Marilyn.

"Love," I concurred.

Ben answered in a single word also, but his word was "Necessity." Every now and then I think I know what he meant; some men and women seem to understand this also. Our dreams of power and the process of their fulfillment give us a path through the entanglements of opportunity and ambition. Some sense of our necessity.

For men such dreams are supremely important. I see them as our "dream babies," mysteriously seeded in the dark place we call the unconscious or the imagination, that realm of soul. These babies grow into our waking, conscious lives. Such dreams are linked to our creativity, to our fate, and ultimately to our death. "I have a dream," said Martin Luther King, Jr., and his life and his death were part of that dream story. He let himself be led by his dreams, and in his dreams he found his fate. Such dreams have the power to dream us; they are like promises, they invite us to keep some rendezvous. In our dream beginnings are our mortal ends.

As an epigraph to a book of his poems, Yeats wrote, "In dreams begins responsibility." This knowledge about the nature and importance of dreams doesn't belong only to the artist. Each of us has had such dreams, which we knew were important the instant we woke. Such dreams can be life forming. They have the power to make us aware of possible choices. As I have heard men and women acknowledge, the dreams of youth often contain deep hints for our futures, and we rightly treasure them, perilously live them out (or not, and live to regret it). Yeats suggests that our sense of responsibility grows *from* our dreams as we keep faith with their purpose for us.[2] Such dreams can set us on a journey, set in motion a pattern of choices and strange coincidences.

What is most significant about the early life of Joseph is that these dreams are all he has for an initiation. He is not visited by God as the divine and ultimate Other who shatters and shapes his life. He is not called by Mystery, confronted by the Great Father in the wilderness; he does not dream of God or wrestle with a numinous antagonist who wounds, blesses, and names him. Though God haunts and informs his life, Joseph never once has any direct knowledge or vision that God is with him. No promise sustains him. No voice beside his own guides him. In his periods of despair, Joseph leans only on his faith. He must come to his own understandings about the power his dreams hint at and the ways it will work in his life. His truths will be distillations of his own experience and beliefs.

Joseph tells both of these dreams to his brothers. It seems at first a foolish thing to do. Is he so naive as to suppose that his brothers can hear him with equanimity? Does he imagine they will appreciate his reveries? Does he tell them to gall them, incite them? Does his dreaming of their bowing come from the boyish fantasies of the underdog? Are they his boast and egotism? Quite possibly all of the above. But in my midrash of his motives I hear him tell me that he reveals these dreams because he must. They contain his necessity. They will point him to a way that will give meaning to his life. He speaks them because, though they are *his* dreams, they do not belong to him alone. Like the dream vision of Black Elk, Joseph's dreams are tribal, prophetic, and therefore political. Like Martin Luther King's dreams, they impel him toward his destiny, and the consequences of their being told are intrinsic to their realization. Joseph must surrender to his dreams; he must suffer their unfoldings.

These dreams of power precede power, and by themselves they do not empower. They initiate Joseph's movement into the world beyond his doorstep. "The way up is the way down"; Joseph's ascent to power goes through the ways of deprivation and estrangement. In three successive scenes he is stripped, cast into a pit, and abandoned.

In the episode that follows his dream telling, father Jacob summons Joseph with an echo of those words that have, all along, announced that something momentous is about to occur.

"Joseph," calls Jacob.

"Here I am," says Joseph (37:13). This "Here I am" was Abraham's response when called by God before he was sent with his son to Moriah. "Here I am," said Esau when his father summoned him for the blessing. "Here I am," said Jacob when he took his brother's place, and later "Here I am" when the angel of the Lord came to him in Haran and told Jacob it was time to return to Canaan and face his brother. Joseph's "Here I am" is the response of a man in the present, ready to accept a task whose implications cannot be foreseen. It is the *yes* of the soul's willingness to step onto the road of excess, the surreal, which leads into unknown. "Here I am" precedes the initiation.

> *"Go find your brothers, who are tending flocks at Shechem, and bring me back word of them."(37:14)*

Two things here would raise the hairs on the back of young Joseph's neck; the first, that he is being sent away from his father's protection, alone, to find his brothers, whom we know must hate and envy him; and second, that the place he is being sent is Shechem, where these same brothers killed and plundered an entire tribe "for Dinah's sake."

He goes. He does not find them where he was told they would be. A man in a field meets him. He asks Joseph, "What are you looking for?"

"I am looking for my brothers," Joseph replies, and the man points him on his way (37:15). Joseph goes north, and from afar his brothers see him approaching. Their banked rage and envy now kindle into a plot to kill him. Only the intervention of Judah and Reuben averts the murder; they convince their brothers to throw Joseph into a dry well. They strip him of his hated cloak, which they dip in the blood of a slaughtered goat, and then they sell him to a passing caravan of Ishmaelites, who bear the boy as booty to Egypt. The brothers return home with the bloodstained cloak and show it to old Jacob, who concludes that Joseph must have been killed by a wild animal. Jacob grieves inconsolably.

The Myth of the Sacrificial Son is recapitulated here with a great economy. The slaughtered goat reminds us both of the surrogate killed for Isaac and of the goatskins and meat by which Jacob symbolically supplanted his brother and gained his father's blessing. Joseph goes into servitude as a stranger, like Abraham, who went into Egypt in his exile, and like Jacob, who was indentured to Laban in a foreign land. Among the Ishmaelites he learns the bitter wisdom of the banished brother. Joseph is carried from his native land and his father's house, bound not merely into service but into slavery.

What gives this turn of events its particular edge, of course, is that it comes at the hands of his brothers. Joseph is spared death, but he is not spared a glimpse into the heart of his closest kin. From his desolation in the pit Joseph has overheard his brothers plotting against his life. He knows their hearts; he feels their sadism; their hate is naked and murderous. He is Abel to their Cain. He is stripped, not merely of his cloak of favoritism, but of all his illusions as well. This is the pit, the dry well, the depths, and this is not the last time he will know this place.

In my own life such moments have come in the vales of depression—economic and emotional—which left me stripped of my sense of dignity and hope. Having failed to receive tenure, I left university teaching to make my way by various abortive endeavors, many of which were dead ends. For two years I strayed in an occupational wilderness before I found psychodrama. Later fired from a job I had worked hard to achieve, I spent six months unemployed. The most painful of these depressions came at the end of my second marriage. In its aftermath I had to look at the most hidden truths about myself, my illusions, my blind needs, my desperation. For a time impotence was not just a figure of speech. Such sudden and frightening reversals of hope connect me with Joseph's experience here.

But his fortunes turn. Joseph the slave is elevated to the position of majordomo in the home of Potiphar, an Egyptian dignitary. He enjoys a brief period of ease, comfort, and respect. But no sooner is he "up" than he is cast down again. Hardly has he attained his position than Potiphar's wife makes a pass at him. He resists until one day, too long insulted by his rejections, she falsely accuses him of abusing his position of trust and seeking to "sport with" her (39:15). Joseph is immediately stripped of another cloak, this time his suit of office, thrown into prison, and abandoned. A second season of "ashes" begins for him.[3]

A second time we hear how he prospers. "God was with Joseph," we read, and brought him to "favor" in the eyes of the prison warden (39:21). Again Joseph rises from the depths and becomes second-in-command. "And whatever Joseph did, God made succeed" (39:23).

Then a third time this pattern of rise and fall is repeated. In prison Joseph befriends two inmates, Pharaoh's cupbearer and his baker. Both have dreams that he correctly interprets, telling the baker that Pharaoh will have him killed, and the cupbearer that he will be restored to his former position. In time Joseph is proved right. As the cupbearer leaves prison, Joseph asks him to "keep me in mind when it goes well with you; tell Pharaoh of me so that I might be set free from prison" (40:14). The cupbearer promises to do this, "but he forgot Joseph" (40:23). Two long years pass for him, further confined, further abandoned.

In psychodramas I have conducted that spring from this season in Joseph's life, men and women have presented him pondering essential questions: Who am I? Why am I here? Does my life have meaning? These are the ultimate and unanswerable riddles of the soul in its lonely cell. Time is its oppressor; time its teacher. "Doing time," "serving time," as the vernacular calls incarceration, a man may go mad or reach a hermit's wisdom. Those players have imagined Joseph as another wrestler beset by voices of self-doubt, self-pity, resentment, and resignation. In our groups we have sought to discover what story he tells himself by which to maintain his poise and spirit among his disasters. What does he do to stave off despair? No God has ever addressed him, made a direct covenant with him, or promised him a redeeming future. No revelation upholds him, nor can he summon an angel to grapple with him and give him his name. His wounds are inward and concealed; he lacks a blessing. So far his dreams have led him to a dungeon.

In the end we see him as a man who remembers his dreams and puts his trust in them. He finds some center deep within his bewilderment; there he finds a kind of peace. Like Joseph we reach for what sustains us through our various imprisonments, what restores us from our derelictions. We cannot name it precisely, but we share the experience of it in our group. We bear witness together to something intangible, sensed dimly at the time, recognized more clearly in retrospect, that we kept faith with. We acknowledge that what preserved us was a power beyond our personal will, indeed a kind of hidden, internal god.

In the next narrative moment Joseph's sense of this internal god receives an enormous confirmation. After two years Pharaoh himself is troubled with dreams. No one among his court magi can interpret them. Then and only then does the cupbearer remember Joseph and tell the king about him. Pharaoh has Joseph summoned from the pit to the palace and asks him to interpret his dreams.

Joseph speaks to Pharaoh of God, telling him, "It is not from me that you will receive an interpretation; only God can interpret Pharaoh's dreams" (41:16). By these extraordinary words Joseph delivers himself completely into the hands of a God of dreams. Clean-shaven, still gulping the air of freedom, dazzled by the most splendid court in the known world, he places himself and his faith in the crucible; his soul is in the scales. Like so many of the men before him—from Noah building his ark to Abram leaving Haran—he now must act; this is the moment when faith must be lived out as choice. While the attending courtiers gape expectantly and an Egyptian king listens,

Joseph stands in his own stillness, listening to what may be given to him from his imagination. Here is either faith or folly in the extreme; in such extremes faith and folly meet.

Pharaoh narrates his dreams. In the first dream he saw seven fat cows coming out of the Nile, but they were followed by seven lean cows, which devoured the fat cows, yet, having devoured them, they were as lean as before. Pharaoh then dreamed again. In his second dream he saw seven ears of corn on a single stalk, full and good ears, but suddenly came seven other ears, hardened and lean, which sprang up after them and swallowed up the seven good ears.

"Tell me," says Pharaoh, "what do these dreams mean?"

"The two dreams are one." Joseph tells him. "They tell Pharaoh what God is about to do" (41:25). Seven years of prodigious abundance will be followed by seven ravening years of famine, he explains. Joseph counsels Pharaoh to appoint overseers of the land to collect food from the seven years of abundance so there will be provisions for the seven years of famine.

Pharaoh is instantly struck by Joseph's acumen, and on the spot he appoints him his viceroy. His respect for Joseph goes beyond what Potiphar and the prison warden have felt about him. Almost reverently the king asks his court, "Can we find another like him, a man in whom is *the spirit of God?*" (41:37).

This phrase has been used only once before in Genesis. It was the force that "moved on the face of the waters" before the beginning of the world and that brought a world into being. For us as readers, Joseph's power is linked here to the deepest sources of human creativity; something in his soul is connected to the source of all creation. Joseph, the dreamer, is a man at home in imagination. He understands the symbolic; he mediates between a world of events and a hidden world of causes.

In recognition of his gifts, Pharaoh slips the royal signet ring onto Joseph's finger; he cloaks him in linen and hangs a gold chain around his neck. Joseph is given an Egyptian name, which translated means "God speaks and creates" (41:45). Joseph has the patriarchal power of speech. Enthroned at the right hand of the king, he receives the daughter of an Egyptian priest in marriage. At this time "Joseph's influence goes out over all the land of Egypt" (41:46). He has now entered public life and the political domain. With his new wife he has two sons. As the poet Rumi says:

> *Pharaoh and the whole Egyptian world*
> *collapsed for such a Joseph.*

This moment of Joseph's release from prison and his appearance at court is nothing short of a revelation. This revelation produces a kind of conversion experience for the temporal powers of Egypt. Through Joseph and his dreams, the sacred pours out into secular life. Joseph brings his God into Egypt, and therefore into history. The God who dwelled in the innermost region of Joseph's heart is now revealed as the same God who, through Joseph, will work in the public domain.

Joseph is revealed and recognized to be what he has been from the beginning. From his youth in his father's house, where he wore a cloak of many colors, to his tenure in the house of Potiphar, where the mistress was taken with his beauty, to his years in prison, where he distinguished himself in the eyes of the warden, Joseph has shone as a singular figure. Alone of the characters in Genesis Joseph possesses *charisma*.

Charisma is a myth word. In it we pay tribute to something alluring and dangerous about personal power that fascinates us and eludes our understanding. Though "charismatic" has traditionally modified the masculine, there is nothing gender-specific in the term. The charismatic person, demagogue or demigod, seems gifted beyond the ordinary, arousing in us the deepest ambivalence of admiration and envy, surrender and opposition. With a sexuality both potent and androgynous, such a person is often the object of both women's and men's desires. Charisma is precisely that irresistible mixture of the spiritual and the sexual that most deeply touches and at the same time confuses us. Culture forms in eddies around such men and women and turns them into leaders, national figures, superstars. Joseph's story is in part the myth of the charismatic man who is thrust into political and public life and who faces the temptations and corruptions that come with an extraordinary power.

Charisma is Greek; Hebrew has no word for it.[4] But two Hebrew words occur as leitmotifs throughout Joseph's story and convey this sense of his special grace and his power to gain favor. One of these words is *tsalach*. It means "to cause to prosper or bear fruit," "to push forward." It suggests a generative force that pushes forward and brings fertility.

The essential force of this Hebrew word *tsalach* is captured in a later biblical passage in which the young Samson is suddenly attacked by a lion.

> *Behold, a young lion roared against Samson and the spirit of the Lord favored him mightily* [tsalach], *and he was able to rend the lion as he would have rent a kid, and he had nothing in his hand. (Judges 14:5–6)*

Here *tsalach* is associated with the prowess of a Samson, his immense physical potency infused by "the spirit of the Lord."

Later in the Bible the same word is used to describe the inspiration that enables the prophets to prophesy. The spirit of the Lord "favors them"; it "comes upon them with its power" (*tsalach*). They are inflated and in this state speak words of fire; they excoriate and envision. *Tsalach* is associated, then, with Samson's splendid potency on the one hand and with prophetic language and vision on the other.

The second word used to describe Joseph is *chen,* which means "grace" as both a physical and a spiritual beauty. The fusion of these two words, *chen* and *tsalach,* in the character of Joseph defines his charisma. He articulates a certain type of masculine eros and beauty. In Joseph we find the prototype of a masculinity in which power is present as charm and can cast its spell. In a less homophobic age than ours, this loveliness was celebrated and recognized as a power. We have not met such an image of manhood in the gallery of Genesis.

If we stop his story at this point, we see in Joseph the myth of the man of power in all its glory and hollowness. On the one hand he has climbed to supreme success in the world's terms. Newly cast in the role of Pharaoh's regent, he becomes a new character, complete with new props, sets, scenes, and auxiliaries. In the eyes of the Egyptians he is, and is named, a god, having risen meteorically from obscurity on the basis of his extraordinary charisma. We see him as they see him; we, too, are dazzled by his successes.

On the other hand, we know—and the Egyptians do not—that this achievement has taken Joseph farther than ever from his own identity. He is no longer even "Joseph," but bears an exalted Egyptian name. The very trappings of his office trap him in isolation. He has lost his inferiority, and he has lost the kind of self-awareness, the wisdom, it can bring. As a prisoner Joseph was able to look past his own disappointments to notice the "dejection" of two inmates. Now he is insulated from disappointment by his supreme election.

At this season of his life Joseph represents the dangers that await the charismatic man whose life becomes so consumed with power that his inner life, his family life, his connection to his roots and sources, wither. Inflated with power, such a man acts like a god and believes that nothing can touch him. The same quality in masculine eros that can swell us can make us swells. Joseph's inflation rises toward grandiosity. He reminds me of the men of Babel, who believed they were building a tower that would reach to heaven. Joseph's imperial power and regal authority verge on idolatry. He is in danger of losing his soul.

During the years of famine he collectivizes the Egyptian economy, and by the time he is done, former landholders have become slaves. Joseph is the means for creating a centralized, totalitarian regime. Though it may be dangerous to judge him by modern democratic values, one can mark the lengths to which he goes. He beggars a people who in their hunger willingly give up what is precious to them, silver, livestock, land, and finally their own freedom in order to survive.

Genesis makes it possible for us to be critical of Joseph even as it chronicles his career. In showing us his prominence, it also shows us his emptiness. In the names of his sons we hear his pain and his denial. The first son he names Manasseh, for Joseph says, "God has made me forget completely my hardship and my parental home." The second he calls Ephraim, because "God has made me fertile in the land of my affliction" (41:51–52). He is a man who wills himself to forget his afflictions, but he cannot fail to remember his hardships each time he regards his sons. As readers we are privy to the loneliness that comes with his enormous temporal success. The seven fat years fatten him.

As the lean years begin, the Egyptians come to Joseph for rations. Having spread beyond Egypt, the famine now brings foreigners to Egypt for food. Hunger reaches all the way to Canaan and to the house of Jacob. Hunger is the hidden means by which a mysterious God, master of plots and timing, begins to move the past into the present.

❀   ❀   ❀

We have been so immersed in the saga of Joseph that we have all but forgotten the family that abandoned him and that he left behind. (Never once does he send news home to his father that he has survived.) Our saga gains new interest from the suspense of its unfinished business.

When the famine reaches the house of Jacob, it brings with it news that rations may be procured in Egypt. Thinking only of their survival, the old patriarch sends his sons "down" to Egypt for food (42:2). But he keeps Benjamin home with him, toward whom apparently he feels a special protectiveness, intensified, one may suppose, by his actual loss of Benjamin's mother, Rachel, and also by his loss of Joseph years earlier. In all innocence the brothers leave on this business trip.

In time "Joseph's brothers come and bow low to him, with their faces to the ground" (42:6). Joseph stands above them. In dress, speech, and position he has so changed that they do not recognize him. But he recognizes them. What he feels in this moment is, as usual, left up to our midrashic imaginations—a flashback to years of imprisonment perhaps, to a dry well in a wilderness, to a murderous conversation overheard, to earlier childhood wounds and ostracism, to a father's love, a colored cloak, perhaps to a dream of sheaves, to a mother's death. Joseph may have an eerie feeling of something moving from one dimension to another. The dead past comes to life in the present; old, forgotten dreams break into a settled and successful life; buried passions, deep and painful, erupt into consciousness. Ironies glint: Do the brothers come to Joseph that they might be saved, or do they come in some way to save him?

Joseph is not ready to reveal himself to them, but our anticipation of this great revelation is whetted by their arrival. He "acted like a stranger and spoke harshly to them" (42:7). The phrase "acted like a stranger" announces his assumption of a theatrical part, but the part that he plays is paradoxically the part he has been living, for he has been the "stranger" all along. The harshness he feigns is linked to a harshness he feels. In this moment he must recognize anew that he is an outsider both to the culture of his birth and to that of his assimilation. In Joseph we revisit the Myth of the Stranger, not as the God-called nomad who belongs nowhere, but as the orphan of history.[5]

Disguised, Joseph further disguises himself; he pretends ignorance, feigns a part. The suspense of the ensuing drama builds as we await the disclosure of his identity, the moment when he throws off his "acting" and lets his brothers see that he is, under the trappings, only Joseph, long lost, now found.

From this moment forward until the point when he can sustain the part no longer, Joseph is both an "actor" and an improvisational dramaturge, a psychodramatist if you will, who sets scenes, lays plots, devises ordeals for his unwitting brothers. Using his immense power, he stages their reality. Ironically, however, Joseph is unaware of a larger drama that enfolds him and within which he "acts" a part beyond the one he conceives. A greater power is moving in and through him. Though we are reading the myths of a culture with no formal theatrical conventions, we are in the presence of a profoundly theatrical imagination. There is a dizzying sense of plays within plays. As he "acts the stranger," the soundless turning of hidden gears, the *deus ex machina,* begins to act on him and moves him toward atonement.

That atonement begins as Joseph stages a theater of revenge. He accuses his brothers of being spies, and over their protestations of innocence he has them thrown into prison for three days. Then he insists that one remain behind as hostage while the other nine go and fetch Benjamin. The brothers agree to what he asks, while some sense of their ancient crime against Joseph appears to trickle into their awareness. They say to one another, "Alas, we are being punished on account of our brother, because we looked on his anguish, yet paid no heed as he pleaded with us. That is why this distress has come upon us" (42:21). Overhearing this, Joseph "turned away from them and wept" (42:24).

Two dramas are played out side by side—theirs and his. They begin to have a sense of nemesis, of something pursuing them for which a reckoning has to be made. Joseph is also pursued now by the pain of his old wounds and longings.

Simeon is selected as the hostage, perhaps because it was he who had suggested that Joseph be killed. Simeon is "bound before their eyes" in an act that replicates so many bindings (42:24). Then Joseph has the brothers' bags filled with grain and secretly has placed in them the money they had brought to pay for rations. On the way home, one of them opens a sack to feed his ass and discovers the money there; and "their hearts sank" (42:28).

The brothers return home and tell their father everything that has occurred, but so attached is the old man to his youngest son that only after all their rations are exhausted will Jacob finally part with Benjamin, and then with the greatest fear and reluctance. The brothers return with him to ransom Simeon.

As soon as he sees Benjamin, Joseph stages a feast. The brothers are understandably mystified. They fear that under their host's apparent hospitality lurks another intent; this viceroy seems to be toying with their lives. They are sure that he must think they stole back the money they had first brought for payment of the grain, but Joseph's steward reassures them.

Joseph now asks after "their" father's health and is told that he is well. He sees Benjamin, blurts out a greeting, then rushes offstage, overcome with feeling toward his brother and not ready to give himself away. He goes into a room and weeps there. Then "he washed his face and reappeared." Now in control of himself, he gives the order, "Serve the meal" (43:32).

Joseph now seats the brothers at his table, and to their immense surprise seats them in precise order, "from the oldest to the youngest" with Benjamin being served the largest share (43:33). Their feast flows with wine. But Joseph is not done with his play-making. As the brothers prepare to return to Canaan, Joseph secretly instructs his servants to fill their bags with grain, but now to put each man's money in each man's bag and to secrete in Benjamin's bag his own personal silver goblet. No sooner have the brothers departed than Joseph sends his steward after them with the accusation that one of them has stolen his drinking cup, "the very one from which my master drinks and which he uses for divination" (44:5).

The brothers are, of course, terrified at this second reversal. They protest their innocence to the steward, swearing that if the cup is found, the person who has it shall be killed for the crime. The cup is discovered in the bag of Benjamin. In despair the brothers trek back to Joseph. They prostrate themselves before him. Benjamin's life is at stake. Joseph has caught his brothers now in a net that appears fatal.

The plot is poised on the question of Cain: "Am I my brother's keeper?" It is the question that rings in Joseph's soul as he deals harshly with these brothers who once dealt so harshly with him. What obscure and conflicting motives wrestle in his heart, for justice or mercy, for retribution or forgiveness, can be fathomed only by midrash, by interpretive acts. But those motives are displayed in his uses and abuses of his power, as he jerks his brothers one way and then another. The ghost of Cain is present, as it was when the brothers symbolically murdered Joseph and ended his boyhood, his sonship, his family life. Am I my brother's keeper? is the question that sharpens in the drama's apex, and in a moment of sudden sweetness the answer is given to Joseph, modeled for him in the gesture of his brother Judah.

Judah, who had once argued the brothers out of murder, sending Joseph instead into slavery, who gave his father his life in surety for the safe return of Benjamin, now comes forward, stands before Joseph to plead their cause. His initial words work to some extent. Apparently softened, and in a "show" of mercy, Joseph appears to relent. He demands only that Benjamin remain as his "slave" rather than being killed for the "theft" of the goblet. The rest of the brothers are free to return to their father and their homes.

But Judah cannot accept this. He pleads further for Benjamin, recapitulating the entire story of his father's fear and concern for his youngest's welfare. What pours out in Judah's address to Joseph is a vein of such pure feeling—pure in its contrition, pure in its sense of filial respect and sibling responsibility, and pure in its selflessness—that it breaks Joseph's theatrical spell and precipitates his own unmasking. No sooner has Judah finished, than we read that Joseph could control himself no longer. "Have everyone withdraw from me!" he shouts to his attendants. Then "Joseph made himself *known* to his brothers" (45:1). (The same word is used when Adam and Eve, after eating the fruit of the tree of the knowledge of good and evil, first look at each other and *know* they are naked.) "I am Joseph. Is my father still well?" But his brothers cannot answer him; they are too deeply disturbed.

In the language of the stage, this moment is a *coup de théâtre;* the Greeks called it the *peripetia*. It is the moment of confession, sudden, astonishing, and cathartic; it precipitates the complete reversal of previous expectations. "I am Joseph. Is my father still well?" (45:3). The one who was dead is alive again; the past is present; the beginning is the end; the hidden is revealed; the impossible is real. Joseph, who at various crucial moments in his life is stripped and cast down, here strips himself of his own pretensions and resumes his place among his brothers. This scene has a profound impact on those who experience it. For the brothers it is as if life had a secret charge, a hidden spring, which, long unsuspected and now released, reveals the miraculous. For Joseph, who thought he knew what was going on all along, however, a mysterious knowledge now flashes upon him.

Joseph's words of self-disclosure are a prelude to a set of astonishing sentences in which he understands his life in an entirely new way. As he reveals himself to his brothers, something is revealed to him. His whole history makes a new kind of sense; he recasts it in a new arrangement. All his suffering and errancy he now sees in the light of a purpose heretofore and necessarily hidden from him. He has an epiphany:

> "*I am your brother Joseph, he whom you sold into Egypt. Now do not be distressed or reproach yourselves because you sold me hither; it was to save life that God sent me ahead of you. . . . God has sent me ahead of you to preserve your survival on earth, and to save your lives in an extraordinary deliverance. So it was not you who sent me here, but God; and He made me a father to Pharaoh, lord of all his household, and ruler over the whole land of Egypt.*"(45:4–9)

Joseph reclaims his name. He understands that he was "the one sent before to preserve." His purpose all along—it was there in his dreams!—has been to save his brothers' lives "in an extraordinary deliverance." Yet not until this moment does Joseph understand that he himself had always been—was supposed to be—the instrument of this salvation. In this moment of comprehension Joseph steps into—or is it out of?—his dreams. He knows and acknowledges in this moment who has dreamed up this complex pattern. His mind shifts from the figure to the ground; the random reconstellates as design, and "design" carries its meaning both of pattern and intention. "So it was not you who sent me here, but *God.*"

Finally Joseph knows God. This powerful prince in whose shine and intelligence everyone had always seen the halo of God is humbled for the last time, his charisma humanized by knowledge of a power infinitely beyond him. This enduring soul who stood before Pharaoh and let it be known that it was up to God to provide him an interpretation of his dreams, now knows for the first time that God is in his life and has been from the beginning. The terrible vicissitudes, his own wrestle with power and passion, his exile—all these sacrifices he now weaves into a new story. It is a story he claims as the truth of his experience. God does not come to him; he pulls God to him in the flash of his own insight, perhaps from the longing of his own belief. One can only imagine the ecstasy, release, and thanksgiving that fill the heart of this lost son who discovers in the end he has always been the Great Father's adopted child. And he knows, at last, where his power came from. For what is revealed to Joseph in this moment of his revelation to his brothers is nothing short of the providential nature of power, a sense for him that there has been a meaning in his life, a pattern in his experiences, that bespeaks a divine will. All of his personal power has flowed from a higher source.

This idea of a providential power is Joseph's legacy to us, the latest gift of the patriarchal tradition. The word *providence* is an idea, mere air, but it is an idea that provides us with a way of articulating our sense of design, not as mere scientific order, but as something at work in the apparent confusion of life, something that is repeatedly reborn as a new order out of dissolution and chaos. Providence is a way of affirming that there is a meaning in life, an emergent good from an evident evil, a possible healing from enormous wounds. This power of the present to reclaim the past lays the myth-theological groundwork for all subsequent tales of redemption. It is no coincidence that the name of the father of the messiah in the Christian dispensation is Joseph.

Joseph affirms this redemptive truth to his brothers and to himself when he tells them he was enlisted ("I was sent ahead") by a supreme Providence. He speaks of his relationship to his brothers and to the famished world as a "deliverance."

> *"God has sent me ahead of you to preserve your survival on earth, and to save your lives in an extraordinary deliverance."(45:7)*

Joseph recognizes here that his powers are dependent on a superior Power. The provider acts as an agent of Providence. What he does succeeds because it is in line with the force field of divine intention. Joseph's rise to authority had always been authorized, not self-generated. He is not powerful but empowered, and in his realization he is "delivered" from his final imprisonment, from his need to be in control. He casts off all his masks and strategies, his shows and his feigning. He stands before his brothers as who he is, delivered from his fears, from his revenge, and from his sense of personal betrayal. He accepts the suffering that yields him this current fulfillment. He pays tribute to a Power beyond him and in that tribute relinquishes the illusion of personal power. No autonomous man, he knows his inferiority and experiences it as a blessing.

According to the patriarchal imagination of Genesis, this sense of Joseph's inferiority to Power corrects the ego's drive for self-aggrandizement and autonomy. Joseph represents the soul that finds its proper relationship with the created world. With his recognition of the divinely articulated universe, and only with such a sense, Joseph can in the end truly serve. He is a co-laborer with God. Joseph has become a man of wisdom.

Such wisdom comes when we find our vocation. When we find it, we feel it is necessary for us, that it was "meant to be." Crystallizing often for us out of many trials and errors, often requiring loss, a setting forth into the unknown, a sense of soul, peril, wrestling and darkness, this quest for vocation and its gradual attainment gives us a sense of personal necessity, and of connection to the Way, the Source, the Wheel of Life, the Ground of Being. We can come in the end—so the patriarchs would have us believe—to serve, to provide, and to find our brothers. With them we can fashion a brotherhood. This is our right livelihood, our way of being in the world without destroying it, our soul's work.

It is our right livelihood to measure, save, nourish, make, and maintain covenant, but also to bear witness to a providential reality. Joseph's story affirms the esoteric truth that the flux of apparent experience is informed by hidden and benign intentions. Joseph knows that what we call reality—which once appeared governed only by Lady Luck, fickle fortune, blind chance, sheer coincidence—expresses the will of God. Joseph teaches that we are actors in a providential play; or, to use another thematic line in his myth, that we are figures in a dream.

Joseph had dreams of power, and in the end he entered them. He lived according to his dreams, even when he was unaware of the dream structure that undergirded his life. When he comes to his providential realization, it is as if he knew consciously what he had known unconsciously all along, that he had been a figure in God's dream, and that the reality he called his life was a part of a different reality altogether. Joseph understands the surreality of life, its ironies, strange connections, and odd foreshadowings.

In this sense Joseph is the one who has been "sent ahead" to provide for *us*. He has provided for us a myth that gives us a glimpse into the mysteries. His sense of providence, of life having meaning, may be ours whenever we recognize that our souls belong to a different order of reality as well as to the mundane and material. There is nothing dated about his tale or about his wisdom. Like him we can know that we live in two worlds, or that this world is shot through with glints and glimmers of mysterious connections, far-fetched coincidences that hint to us of immense designs.

In Joseph's time men called those hints the hand of God. The men of his time, who preserved these tales from some immemorial antiquity, left us this myth-theology of Providence and Power as a legacy. It is also a guidance and an affirmation: We can and do still know this experience thousands of years after them and in part because they, the old patriarchs, first constructed it. At times, with a rending force, we see momentarily through this life into another; the helter-skelter suddenly crystallizes into a design. At such moments we have entered the landscape of the ancestors, Dreamtime. For a spell the ancient wisdom of the fathers and mothers comes home to us. At such times we know that we do not know, but by some reach, some grace, we intuit the Mystery beyond and within us. Only when we accept the incomplete and partial nature of our knowledge, the provisional, may we glimpse the providential, what Wordsworth called

> *a sense sublime*
> *Of something far more deeply interfused,*
> *Whose dwelling is the light of setting suns,*
> *And the round ocean and the living air,*
> *And the blue sky, and in the mind of man:*
> *A motion and a spirit, that impels*
> *All thinking things, all objects of all thought,*
> *And rolls through all things.*

Moved by such a "sense" of the sublime, we find our place with the ancients; we stand by their wells and look into the depths. We hear their stories as our own.[6]

In the aftermath of these several revelations the last bonds of emotional control are loosed between the brothers.

> *Joseph embraced his brother Benjamin around the neck and wept, and Benjamin wept on his neck. He kissed all his brothers and wept upon them; only then were his brothers able to talk to him. (45:14–15)*

We will be reminded of an earlier moment when a brother wept on the neck of a brother, that moment after the night wrestling of Jacob, when his name was changed and he met his brother Esau in reconciliation and atonement. Joseph, too, suffers a change of name, but it is back into who he has always been. In his beginning was forecast his end.

For me the remainder of Joseph's story is denouement, a matter of gathering up many loose ends and settling his family in Egypt, receiving the blessing of his father, and then burying him in Canaan in Machpelah. Just after Jacob dies, the brothers, fearing again that Joseph will avenge himself on them, lie to him, telling him that it had been their father's dying wish that he forgive them. It is clear that the brothers still stand in awe of Joseph's powers and still live in the shadow of their own guilt. Joseph weeps and says to them:

> *"Do not be afraid. Do you think I am God? You did plot against me, but God plotted it for good so that this day might come and that many people might live. I will provide for you and your little ones." (50:19–21)*

Once again Joseph affirms providence. He seeks to reframe his brothers' guilt into a sense of faith in a plot beyond their plottings. It is written that he did in fact "comfort them and spoke to their hearts" (50:21). It is the best he can do. Their lie indicates how fragile their faith in him is. His final words reassure them, but they cannot completely dispel their fears. The tears of cathartic reconciliation do not wash away all the old paranoia. It runs so deep in men.

Everything that happens in this long finale flows within the awareness Joseph has achieved of his being an actor in a divine play. The theatrical metaphor is all but explicit in his words about plots. It is a literary as well as a providential metaphor. Joseph's story is now complete.

On his own deathbed Joseph speaks to them once more:

> *"I am dying, but God will take account of you; He will bring you up from this land to the land which he promised to Abraham, to Isaac, and to Jacob." (50:24)*

Asking them only to bring his bones with them into that land when they leave Egypt, he dies. The words of the ancient promise hang in the air after the curtain falls. Joseph links his life to the lives of his forebears and sends into the next generation the patriarchal promise: the dream of a promised land in which the fellowship of brothers will secure the peace.

At his death twelve inheritors remain.[7] When Joseph dies, they will be the progenitors of the twelve tribes of the children of Israel. This brotherhood of tribes is the Bible's way of saying that the world is made up of men living in tribes. Twelve is only a number to represent a zodiac of differences imagined in some cosmic relation to one another. The task is always the same: to find our brothers, and live with them in peace. At the bedside of Joseph the twelve stand, comforted by his words, for he had "spoken to their hearts."

In Joseph the imagination of patriarchy has constructed a new lore of power. He ultimately teaches us how we are to use power, how we are to understand it, and what relation we should have to it. He who has been possessed by power, who has had the power of a god thrust into his hands, is in the end released from its toils into a vast sense of the implicate design of a spiritual order. In the end he knows and accepts his place. He understands that a meaning beyond his full apprehension works in human life and in history, and he yields to its ends.

According to the patriarchal imagination, those ends must finally involve the creation of brotherhood: This is the ultimate work for the soul, the deepest work of provision that the Bible, and not just Genesis, proposes as our vocation. In Joseph's relationship with his brothers Genesis myth-theologizes brotherhood and brother-keeping beyond the personal. With Isaac and Ishmael, Jacob and Esau, the drama of brotherhood was still enacted between two men and played out on the domestic stage of a small family. But with the sons of Israel—twelve in number, each of whom is to become the figurehead of a tribe, the twelve tribes of Israel, and then beyond that to stand as a paradigm for the family of nations—the issues of brotherhood take on global significance. The relationship of Joseph and his brothers is a crucible for the ways men come to terms with power in order to live in peace with one another. At the crux of his story is a transition—from a sense of finite power to infinite power, from a sense of meaninglessness to meaning, from the external god to the internal god, from the parental world to the sibling world. The ends of power are newly conceived: that we might finally and freely be released from our dangerous obsession with power and transform it into something that serves a common dream.

Genesis recognizes brotherhood as the evolutionary edge of manhood, and so it has always been. Where men have failed to push to this edge, cultures and civilizations have been destroyed and lost forever. Men slaughter their brothers unless they are held by a higher purpose. Surely the poet recognizes this; that is why he says,

> *I'd gladly spend years getting word*
> *of him, even third or fourth hand.*

No Joseph—no vital cultural ideal like him—no survival. Simple as that. Unless we achieve brotherhood, we will, in the end, destroy ourselves and all human life. This is the terrible forecast of the Myth of the Murdered Brother; it is the option of Cain.

The final project of Genesis is to construct and ennoble the idea of brotherhood so that men can imagine and then can choose a life in peace with one another.

❀   ❀   ❀

I have a final midrash to offer, Joseph's own last words.

"Let me tell you a part of my story again," I say as Joseph.

> *Once upon a time I was sent by my father to look for my brothers. I set out, though my heart was full of misgivings. I knew they hated me. I had no idea how much.*
>
> *My father had said they were in Shechem. I went.*
>
> *When I came to the pastures there I found no sign of my brothers. For a moment I felt relief, thinking I could return to my father and tell him I could not find them. But I knew he would be displeased with me. Then I saw* a man standing in a field. *He saw me and approached.*
>
> "What are you looking for?" *he asked, though I am not sure how he knew I was looking for anything or anyone.*
>
> "I am looking for my brothers," *I told him, and before I could describe them, he said,* "They have gone to Dothan." *He pointed the way. I thanked him and left him standing again alone in the field.*
>
> *It took me three days to reach Dothan, but on the morning of the third day, lifting up my eyes, I saw my brothers in the distance, and . . . well, you know the rest.*
>
> *But what you do not know is how often I thought of this man in the field. In the pit, listening to my brothers slaver over me like wolves, I thought of the man in the field, and I cursed the meeting. By that small coincidence I was about to be killed.*
>
> *Yet when I went to the house of Potiphar and was given such a place of trust and eminence, I thought of that man in the field. Had it not been for the coincidence of meeting him I would still be following sheep on the hills of Canaan. Later still, when Potiphar's wife accused me, when I was thrown into another pit and saw the years of my manhood wasted in confinement, I thought ruefully of the man in the field, yet he seemed to me now a kind of presence, perhaps because I thought of him so often. There was a mystery and warmth in my memory of him, enough so that I did not freeze into despair. At times I thought I could hear his voice, but he only seemed to ask the same question: "What are you looking for?" In prison a thousand answers came.*

Then I was released, and I flew to power. Seated at the right hand of Pharaoh, I had occasion often to be asked how one so young and foreign born had come to enjoy such privilege. At such times I thought to speak of my coincidental meeting with the man in the field, but I never did. Who would understand? Also it seemed he had not finished with me, for still his question would come to me at the oddest moments, "What are you looking for?" and though it seemed I had everything a man could possibly want, in fact there was still an emptiness, a sense of deep incompletion, and I didn't know how to answer him.

Then my brothers came. Yes, I put them through an ordeal. I had my own hatred, my own rage at their betrayal, and I could see no possibility of reconciliation. My most urgent thought was how to wrest Benjamin from their grasp before they did to him what they had done to me. Yet I looked at them with such a longing in my heart, and I wept alone in longing. I thought then of the man in the field, and I knew then that what I had said to him so long ago was true: I was looking for my brothers. Through the intervening years—though blocked from me by my pain and fear—I was still looking for them. And now that they were here I felt unsure about how to meet them and how to disclose myself to them.

I don't need to belabor this. That man in the field—who was he? I never knew, of course, but in time I came to see him as a sort of angel. As the time comes for me to die and my brothers gather around me, I can still read in their faces the old traces of fear.

It seems to me now that there is another brother who stands among them, silent, watching. It is, I see, the man in the field. He has come to take my hand and lead me into the dream, more deeply into its luminous wilderness. Is he Death? I do not know, but he brings me to the edge of the farthest field. And beyond that edge I know I will meet the Dreamer. My heart leaps in a sudden ecstasy, and suddenly I seem to be running with him across that same wide field in which he first met me, except the ground is dissolving into light. We fly; under us the landscape dissolves into gold, spirals of gold, whirling back into an infinite distance. I am going home.

Tell my story. Someone must tell the children there is a dream, a Dreamer, and that this whole tangled web of living is shot through with light. Someone must tell the children to look for the man in the field, even if you will only credit him in retrospect.

Remind the brothers and the sisters that they must have an idea of a power beyond the personal in order to be released from the arid prison of personality. Tell them that power rightly understood is not self-created. Power comes to us; power comes through us. We can neither own it nor conserve it. Our powers are renewed constantly from a source. Like water in a well, we find it, we tap it, we use it, but the water, the living water—that we did not create.

I am the end of patriarchy, its flower and fruit. In me are integrated loveliness and strength, act and word. I am son and brother, husband and father, a man of the world and a man of dreams. I entered my dreams, but they were not just my dreams, they were given to me. In the season of his final blessings, my father said of me that I was the fruitful bough, even a fruitful bough by a well, whose branches run over the wall. I have known the sweet waters of my father's wells. I am part of that sweetness. Forever.

Joseph's words echo in me. Through him I tell myself something that I have always known. He is a fuller expression of a faith I, as a late twentieth-century man, wrestle to affirm. He reminds me that in my ends are my beginnings, too.

Something is circling back upon itself as I conclude these myths of the patriarchs. I have an acknowledgment of my own to make to another "brother."

This brother I refer to, whose name is in fact Joseph, has been for almost fifteen years the husband of my ex-wife and the stepfather to my children. Though our culture has no kinship term for a relationship such as ours, he and I share a number of intimate, often unspoken, connections. We meet across the lives of my two children; for them he has been a significant man for many years. He is the man who replaced me in my wife's heart and bed and about whom have raged some of the most bitter and burning emotions I have ever known. In the interest of creating the best possible family environment for my children, I have spent no small amount of time acknowledging and working with my feelings about him. I have had to wrestle with his having supplanted and in some sense defeated me; he has gained what I lost. My reptile brain has screamed, He took my woman! and has hissed in my ears its primitive fears that he would take my children, too. I have been troubled right into my dreams by this Joseph. I have faced him, and through him, my fears and losses, and I have come to embrace him in a wrestling no less fierce in its way than Jacob's with his angel.

I have come in the end to realize the truth of the law "like attracts like," for as I loved the woman who is the mother of my children so I love the one she loves. Or I can. I can appreciate the qualities in him that both my children and my ex-wife admire. I have developed my own relationship with Joseph; we share, among other things, an interest in men's issues, and our separate tasks of being fathers has the most crucial relevance to the two children we have fathered. This Joseph is now a brother, too.

The intimacy in this relationship is of a kind for which nothing has quite prepared me, unless, oddly, it is my relationship with Jonathan. Joseph and I have had to build our own boundaries; we have been thrust together by circumstance only to find deep affinities as well as differences; and our well-being in some measure depends on how well we can live with each other, if not under the same roof, as part of the same family. Our brotherhood is something made, not given, and made against considerable odds. Along with my relationship with Jonathan, it is an achievement in which I take great pride, knowing, as only I really know, how much it has cost me to sustain.

When I wrote the essay that first laid out some of my ideas about the relevance of the biblical myths to an understanding of patriarchy, I sent it to Joseph. He read it and responded with encouragement and interest. "I think you're on to something," he said.

It was at Joseph's house that one of his closest friends happened to read what I had written. "It was lying on his desk, and I picked it up and read it." This close friend turned out to be Ned Leavitt, a literary agent, and by a further coincidence a former classmate of mine at Harvard. Ned suggested that I write a book proposal; he was pretty sure he could find me a publisher. This book is the result.

In some measure, then, I owe this publication to Joseph, and I could not forget him as I worked on the mythic figure whose name he bears. This Joseph is part of a rounding pattern of events, and when I wrote to him of my appreciation for the inadvertent but essential role he played in making it possible for me to write this book and in that way live out an old dream, he sent me a letter.

Dear Peter,

Your letter moved me deeply when I read it. . . . I cried when I read it—in part from feeling more fully the complexity of emotional currents that have lived in the shadows of my heart—so much of what I hold so dear: "my family," Indira, Zak, Karali, this house and land which I love also, are so deeply connected to you. I too honor us both for keeping our hearts open to it all. . . . Tears of sorrow, too, at carrying a dream, so encrusted with history, the struggle to share my own dream. And tears of joy as I celebrate your willingness to enter the territory of an old dream.

They're the hardest, those old ones.

I wonder now whether even Joseph knew when he wrote this that his words about dreams echoed his namesake and that what he called entering "the territory of an *old* dream" would so aptly describe the struggle of the protagonist of these last chapters of Genesis. It makes me smile, this ghostly sense of odd connections, of the complex currents, as he said, that have lived in the shadows of our hearts. There is something joining parts of my life into patterns I can only sometimes see.

In My End
Is My Beginning

There are two kinds of memory. The first is the memory each person has of what happened to him or to her, what each saw personally, felt, did, or suffered in dreams and in waking life. Imperfect, edited by time and pain, of different power in different people, this is the personal memory; it is unique, and it reminds us that each of us is unique and distinct and alone. Out of the raw materials of this personal memory each of us can compose a significant part of the story of who we are.

But it is not the whole story. A second kind of memory is, paradoxically, the memory of what did not happen directly to us. Culture is the memory of what did not happen to us. This is the memory of family stories that we may have heard at our grandfather's knee, images in films, tales in books, events in history. Our memories are crammed with such materials out of which we can form a larger story about who we are. People who come out of a continuous familial or ethnic tradition possess a self that is intimately connected to other selves as part of a family tree or a tribal community. Such people are linked not only to the ancestors, they are linked to the figures of Dreamtime; such people recognize the validity and relevance for themselves of those experiences that occurred to others in a distant, even in a mythic, past. The past is "theirs" in a very real sense. For such people memory has a coherent transpersonal dimension: The pain of a distant ancestor or a wounded hero may bring tears as quickly as the pain of a remembered childhood wound.

Part of what it means to me to be a Jew is to develop this second memory and to develop it in relation to the history and the myth-theology of a Jewish tradition. The development of this Jewish memory is coming relatively late in my life. It is an acquisition, and as such it is undertaken at least in part with some intention. It is a cultivation, a choice made in terms of what I take time to learn, what I will read, where I will go, whom I will talk to and about what things, how I will think about my spiritual life, how I will pray. To me to be a Jew means to explore the tradition of Judaism not as an academic field, not as an intellectual exercise, but as a way of living, a way of life. That tradition is vast, branching out as it does over more than three thousand years of continuous history. For any one person it is inexhaustible not only in its span but in its depth. Various mystical schools of thought have given the stories and practices of the Jewish tradition a spiritual dimension as rich and complex as any mystical tradition I have ever heard of or encountered. One can practice Jewish spirituality as one can practice Buddhist meditation: for a lifetime. And during that lifetime one's awareness of God or self or soul—of Imagination—becomes increasingly profound.

Whatever else my book might be in its public persona, it has been for me the intimate act of cultivating my Jewish soul, a practice in the spiritual sense. It has involved my learning the sources and wrestling with the paradoxes of a patriarchal myth-theology. In writing this book I have been facing what is restrictive and narrow in that tradition and struggling to tolerate the strictures, to understand their hidden truths, and to connect them to my life. I have also been glorying in what is great and beautiful in this patriarchal legacy.

As a student of literature I have not come to Genesis ignorant of the values and powers of great literature, and I know Genesis to be a work of literature as great as anything I have read. One way one knows the sublime in literature is to sense the inexhaustible. I have sensed that in writing about this book. My approach, conclusions, and perspectives only remind me in the end of how much more there is to say about and to see in Genesis. It is a great and inexhaustible teacher. What I have learned I have drawn together in this book. That learning is only a beginning.

That beginning had its genesis ten years ago. It began with colleagues at Four Winds Hospital as we gathered once a week for an hour over lunch to read Genesis slowly together from start to finish. Gradually my interest in Genesis deepened and expanded beyond our group; I began to explore it psychodramatically. Then I came to this writing and this wrestling, which pushed me much further in the direction of commitment and study.

Much of what I have had to say here I discovered as I said it, and I am not the same man I was when I began. The writing itself has deepened my connection to my obscure and ancient Jewish roots. My soul has found images and figures in these tales of the fathers through which to appropriate to itself some of the wisdom the old myths contain. I have, to use my own paradigm, entered the ancestral Dreamtime, for in many senses I left my own native land and father's house to travel in the biblical landscape. I have become something of a stranger to myself in fulfilling the call to write this book.

The stories and interpretations in this book are not only my own. Though I have made no direct attributions, many of the insights and ideas in this book stem from my work with people who have played out the myths in psychodramatic form. That play, in which the authority of the pulpit or the seminary was held in abeyance, was the work of siblings. In the shared arena of our imaginative play each one of us was an equal to the other. Our groups were pluralistic and thrived on our differences. Indeed, without those differences, there would have been no diversity, none of the clash and humor of rivaling voices, none of the wrestling that exercised our souls.

When I began, I set out to think about patriarchy in ways that were both personal and mythological. I wanted to look past contemporary degradations of patriarchy and to search for the sources of soul-wisdom and spirituality I thought the old biblical myths contained. From the first my working title for this book was *Our Fathers' Wells*. Genesis is full of wells; Rebecca and Rachel are both discovered by wells and springs, and Isaac, with whom of all the figures in Genesis I identify most strongly, redug his father's wells and gave them the old paternal names. At the end of Genesis Jacob, the wrestler, evokes the image of the well when he refers to his son Joseph as a "fruitful bough by the well."

The wells of Genesis are profound. They speak to me of a fertility in the soul; they are an image for the life of the imagination. That life is mysteriously deep, sprung from hidden aquifers. Wells are essential to life; the wells of the fathers nourish us and are as essential in their way as food is for the body. Wells in the wilderness are miraculous; living water from rock slakes the greatest thirst; sweet water in the dry places is provided beyond all human provision. We are asked only to keep this water fresh; we are the stewards of the gift.

As we rush headlong into a postliterate century, we may lose the maps that guide us to the wells, the songlines that take us to the living waters, the tales that connect us to the ancestors. The Philistines have covered them—the philistinism of our appetites and idolatries. Indeed, our memory of the past is deteriorating as literacy declines. Scavenging and strip-mining the past for what serves our faddist culture, we lose an old depth and continuity. Ransacking myth and history for images and marketable ideas, we are using them up as we use up other precious resources. Important parts of our past may not survive into the future. The Bible may not live on as a rich and complex soul-poem. I fear it may become only a book of dogma for the fundamentalist or an object in the museum of the mind for scholarly analysis or a ruin of scattered stones historical sleuths will continue to dust for prints of a merely historical past. I fear that the continuous flow of biblical images and ideas that has watered the fields of literature, poetry, theology, and moral discourse for thousands of years is evaporating in the heat of our millennial ambitions. As the churches empty, as the grandparents die who heard these stories from the lips of their grandparents, the stories descend the first rung of oblivion. They will not translate to computer games; they cannot be audiovisualized. As poems they lose everything in translation to another medium.

To me the loss of the Bible as wisdom book and soul text would be tragic. For if myth is a window and mirror of the soul, then our souls require great instruments of speculation. It has been my deepest purpose to gaze into the speculative dimensions of these biblical myths. My labor has been to honor ancestral wisdom and to claim my lineage. My reading of Genesis is an act of stewardship as well as the fashioning of an identity.

NOTES

Introduction

1. Charles Olson, *Collected Poetry* (Los Angeles: Univ. of California Press, 1987).

2. Paul Cowan, *An Orphan in History: Retrieving a Jewish Legacy:* (New York: Doubleday, 1990).

3. I have often wondered what modern psychology would look like if Freud and Jung had quarried their myths and archetypes from Genesis rather than from the Greeks. Instead of Oedipus we might have had Abraham, and instead of the emphasis on the mother and child connection, a greater emphasis might have been placed on the importance of sibling bonds.

4. This is taken from Wallace Stevens's collection of aphorisms entitled *Adagia,* which can be found in *Opus Posthumous*, edited by Samuel French Morse (London: Faber and Faber, 1957).

5. Psychodrama as a clinical discipline was developed by Jacob Levy Moreno, M.D., a European psychiatrist who came to America in the mid-1920s. Moreno built a sanitarium in Beacon, New York, less than a decade later in which role-playing was a central treatment modality with a small in-patient population. In the mid-1960s the Beacon Sanitarium became the Moreno Institute, and the hospital was converted into a training mecca for action methods with applications in clinical, educational, and business fields. Psychodrama is usually practiced as a form of group psychotherapy in which patients take roles for one another in the enactment of life stories, dreams, or fantasies. For an excellent introduction to psychodrama see under Blattner and Fox in the Selected Bibliography.

6. I found this statement in Theodore Reik's book on the sacrifice of Isaac. He develops a strong thesis about the oral and dramatic origins of biblical story. See *The Temptation* (New York: George Braziller, 1961), 151–72 passim.

Chapter 1

1. Notwithstanding Harold Bloom's argument that the author of one strand of the biblical narrative was a woman. See Bloom and David Rosenberg, *The Book of J* (New York: Grove Weidenfeld, 1990).

2. I know only a little Hebrew, and my translations of Genesis into English are borrowed from a number of different versions. Principally I have made use of the King James Version of the Bible, of the translation to be found in *The Torah, A Modern Commentary*,

Gunther Plaut, editor, which contains the version published by the Jewish Publication Society: New York, 1962, 1967. I have gained insights from *Genesis and Exodus*, translated by Everett Fox, New York: Schocken Books, 1991. I have also consulted the Revised and the New Revised Standard Versions. I have studied Genesis as well through a software program produced by Parsons Technology called "Quickverse v2.0," which in addition to the King James and Revised Standard Versions comes with an accompanying transliterated Hebrew version of the Hebrew Bible and a transliterated Hebrew dictionary and concordance. I have made use of all these resources to gain access to the meaning of words.

3. For John—Greek, Christian, and mystic—the "Word" was Jesus Christ, present from the beginning ("the Word was *with* God") as the living issue of the Father. Christ, the Logos, is present in all creation, present as redeemer of man from sin; he is present, too, at the end of time to gather his chosen into a lasting peace.

4. For a close analysis of Genesis 2–3, see Phyllis Trible, *God and the Rhetoric of Sexuality* (Philadelphia: Fortress Press, 1978), 94–105.

Chapter 2

1. A few citations to suggest the range of material about midrash that I became familiar with in writing this book: a chapter on *Midrash* by Barry Holtz in *Back to the Sources* (New York: Simon and Schuster, 1986); Burton L. Visotzky, *Reading the Book: Making the Bible a Timeless Text* (New York: Doubleday, 1991); Rabbi Moshe Weissman, ed., *The Midrash Says* (New York: Benei Yakov Publications, 1980). Louis Ginzberg, *Legends of the Bible* (Philadelphia: Jewish Publications Society, 1956).

2. I know at least one teacher in a seminary—Rabbi Norman Cohen of Hebrew Union College in New York—who regularly teaches a course on modern midrash in which he invites students to create their own midrash while studying with contemporary practitioners of this old form of biblical study. A recently published book details a number of new departures in midrash under the rubric of bibliodrama. See Bjorn Krondorfer, ed., *Body and Bible: Interpreting and Experiencing Biblical Narratives* (Philadelphia: Trinity Press, 1992).

3. For a convenient review of these ideas in the context of an excellent discussion of manhood and its issues, see David Gilmore, *Manhood in the Making: Cultural Concepts of Masculinity* (New Haven, CT: Yale Univ. Press, 1990), 9–29.

Chapter 5

1. Terah's death can be calculated in the following way: He was 70 when Abram was born (11:26), and Abram left Haran at the age of 75 (12:4). That would have made Terah 145. We are told that he died at the age of 205 (11:32). However, as I learned from Nahum Sarna in his book *Understanding Genesis: The Biblical Heritage of Israel* (New York: Schocken Books, 1966), there is a Samaritan version of this story in which Terah dies at the age of 145 years, coinciding with Abram's departure (p. 108, note 12). Acts 7:4 refers to this tradition.

2. The phrase is Mircea Eliade's. See his *Myths, Dreams and Mysteries* (New York: Harper & Row, 1979). Dreamtime is the regionless region of the gods, of the archetypes, of those figures who reside in the perpetual shadowland of the psyche. We visit them in ritual or trance, and they visit us in dreams.

3. The phrase is Carlos Castaneda's from *A Separate Reality: Further Conversations with Don Juan* (New York: Simon & Schuster, 1971).

Chapter 6

1. I can cite here a few of the works that are part of a re-imagining of biblical narrative and meaning. These have influenced me by what they have shown me in the old stories, but even more their audacity has encouraged my own poetic license. See Judith Plaskow, *Standing Again at Sinai: Judaism from a Feminist Perspective* (San Francisco: Harper San Francisco, 1990); Susannah Heschel, ed., *On Being a Jewish Feminist: A Reader* (New York: Schocken Books, 1983); Carol P. Christ and Judith Plaskow, eds., *Womanspirit Rising: A Feminist Reader in Religion* (San Francisco: Harper and Row, 1979); and also Christ and Plaskow eds., *Weaving the Visions: New Patterns in Feminist Spirituality* (San Francisco: Harper San Francisco, 1989); Phyllis Trible, *Texts of Terror: Literary Feminist Readings of Biblical Narratives* (Philadelphia: Fortress Press, 1984); idem, *God and the Rhetoric of Sexuality* (Philadelphia: Fortress Press, 1978).

2. For example, there is the work of Arthur Waskow, in particular his *Godwrestling* (New York: Schocken, 1987). See also Rabbi Rami M. Shapiro's *Embracing Esau* (Miami: Light House Books, 1991).

Chapter 8

1. Alice Miller, *The Untouched Key: Tracing Childhood Trauma in Creativity and Destructiveness* (New York: Doubleday Anchor, 1990).

2. Ibid., 144.

3. Ibid., 145.

4. According to rabbinic tradition, Isaac was thirty-seven years old when the sacrifice was undertaken. They calculate his age by assuming that Sarah's death immediately follows the journey to Moriah (for it is mentioned immediately afterward in the text), and we are told in the text that she dies at the age of 127. Isaac, born to her when she was ninety, is therefore thirty-seven when she dies.

Chapter 10

1. Bruce Chatwin, *Songlines* (New York: Viking Penguin, 1988).

2. Elie Wiesel, *Messengers of God: Biblical Portraits and Legends* (New York: Summit Books, 1976), 96.

3. C. G. Jung, *Memories, Dreams, Reflections*, ed. Aniela Jaffe (New York: Pantheon, 1963), 358–59.

Chapter 11

1. Nahum Sarna discusses this point in *Understanding Genesis*, 154–57.

2. Esau becomes identified with Rome through a set of complex historical and political midrashim. Rome is the oppressor of Israel, and in the end, though it is superior to Israel in might, Rome is viewed as inferior to Israel in spirit. This reading of Esau as the force that opposes Israel utterly distorts his character as portrayed in the biblical story. As we shall see, he, more than Jacob, seems to possess an open, guileless heart and has the courage to forgive.

3. This poem can be found in *The Rag and Bone Shop of the Heart: Poems for Men,* ed. Robert Bly, James Hillman, and Michael Meade (New York: Harper Collins, 1992).

Chapter 12

1. I was delighted to find that in at least one tribe studied by anthropologists men preserve this form of exuberant play as part of their initiation rites and celebratory festivals. An account of the Mehinaku can be found in David Gilmore, *Manhood in the Making,* specifically 89–91 on wrestling.

2. T. S. Eliot, *The Four Quartets,* in *The Complete Poems* (New York: Harcourt Brace, 1952).

3. This poem is reprinted in Bly et al., *The Rag and Bone Shop of the Heart.*

Chapter 14

1. "Has Anyone Seen the Boy," a version translated by Coleman Barks and John Moyne in Bly et al., *The Rag and Bone Shop of the Heart.*

2. In his volume of poems *Responsibilities,* published in 1914, Yeats attributes this epigraph to an Old Play. In titling a group of poems, Delmore Schwartz inverted the line in his book *Dream of Knowledge* to read "The Dreams Which Begin in Responsibilities." Both ways of thinking about dreams and responsibility are linked in Joseph's story and riddle each other like the conundrum of the chicken and the egg.

3. This image is Robert Bly's. See *Iron John: A Book About Men* (Reading, MA: Addison-Wesley, 1990). He has a rich and allusive discussion of the experience of descent, dereliction, and depression. See 69–86.

4. The recently edited Stone edition of the five books of Moses—an orthodox translation—actually uses the word *charisma* to describe Joseph in 39:21. See *The Chumash* (New York: Mesorah Publications, 1993).

5. This phrase is Paul Cowan's and is the title of his book *An Orphan in History* (New York: Doubleday, 1990); see note 2 of the introduction. Paul's description of his own awakening to being a Jew resembles my own in many ways and has helped me further that progress.

6. The word *sublime* literally means something that is found or felt to be under (*sub*) the *limen,* Latin for "threshold." Though we think of the sublime as having to do with the stupendous and the awesome, it is something that does not *overcome* us but rather rises

from within us. It is a word that speaks of the inferior, the lower, the concealed. It crosses under the limits and borders of our consciousness; it was there all the time, but we didn't see it. It breaks through to us, revealing a dimension of meaning that fills us with awe precisely because it was hidden from us all along.

7. Jacob in his final blessings included Joseph's two sons Ephraim and Manasseh among the lists of his own descendants. Ephraim and Manasseh will be chieftains along with the sons of Rachel and Leah after Joseph's death.

SELECTED BIBLIOGRAPHY

Alter, Robert. *The World of Biblical Literature*. New York: Basic Books, 1992.

Blattner, Adam, M.D. *Acting In: Practical Applications of Psychodramatic Methods*. New York: Springer, 1973.

Cowan, Paul. *An Orphan in History: Retrieving a Jewish Legacy*. New York: Doubleday, 1990.

Fox, Jonathan. *The Essential Moreno*. New York: Springer, 1987.

Ginzberg, Louis. *Legends of the Bible*. Philadelphia: Jewish Publications Society, 1956.

Krondorfer, Bjorn, ed. *Body and Bible: Interpreting and Experiencing Biblical Narratives*. Philadelphia: Trinity Press, 1992.

Plaskow, Judith. *Standing Again at Sinai: Judaism from a Feminist Perspective*. San Francisco: Harper San Francisco, 1990.

Rich, Adrienne. *Of Woman Born: Motherhood as Experience and Institution*. Tenth anniversary edition. New York: W. W. Norton, 1986.

Sarna, Nahum. *Understanding Genesis: The Biblical Heritage of Israel*. New York: Schocken Books, 1966.

Shapiro, Rabbi Rami M. *Embracing Esau*. Miami, FL: Light House Books, 1991.

Steinmetz, Devora. *From Father to Son: Kinship, Conflict, and Continuity in Genesis*. Louisville, KY: Westminster/John Knox Press, 1991.

Stevens, Wallace. *Opus Posthumous*. Samuel French Morse, ed. London: Faber and Faber, 1957.

Vogt, Gregory Max. *Return to Father: Archetypal Dimensions of the Patriarch*. Dallas: Spring Publications, 1991.

Waskow, Arthur. *Godwrestling*. New York: Schocken Books, 1978.

Wiesel, Elie. *Messengers of God: Biblical Portraits and Legends*. New York: Summit Books, 1976.

ACKNOWLEDGMENTS

With relief and delight, I want to acknowledge those people who have supported this enterprise, peered over my shoulder, patted me on the back, taken red pencils to the text, or have in more subtle ways, and in some cases unknown to them, encouraged this project.

Lex Hixon, who sat in a French class with me a thousand years ago, was the first person I told of my earliest experience with God. Our friendship has been a long commentary on that experience of mine and such experiences of his.

Ben Medelsund believed I was a writer long before I did. If he were alive today, he would lovingly quarrel with every page of this book, and it would be the better for his reading.

A number of people provided intellectual stimulation and resources on the deepest levels. Benjamin Cirlin, my first Torah teacher, welcomed me when I first came to the well of my own Judaism, and over the years he has been a cherished brother. Rabbi Steve Rosman, from the first a supporter, referred me to materials that enriched my layman's grasp of traditional sources. Rabbi Elie Spitz, whose knowledge and friendship have sustained me in this work, read an early draft and stayed interested in the later ones. Professor Richard Hathaway also read an earlier version and gave me his luminous encouragement. Writer and editor Steve Lewis carefully read an earlier version of the manuscript, and his perceptive suggestions influenced the development of the book. Jim Sacks, Ph.D.—pychodramatist and teacher—read the last version of this book in installments and proved himself a canny and compassionate friend.

Many men and women—in congregations, pulpits, seminaries, and workshops—took up my offer to work psychodramatically with biblical stories; with them I discovered meanings beyond those I could have found alone. The views of the members of the Genesis Seminar at the Jewish Theological Seminary stimulated me. And at a time when I felt quite adrift, Rita Kashner in particular helped me understand a little of what it means to be a writer.

Closer to home I am thankful to Michael Westerman, who on our walks at Vassar gave me room to breathe. With Gloria Robbins, my therapist, I undertook crucial work on my relationship with my dad; she helped me gain a fuller measure of distance from, and appreciation for, him. My psychodramatic siblings, Rebecca Walters and Judy Swallow, gave me a sister's love, support, and humor.

The Torah group at Four Winds Hospital, where I studied Genesis word by word for six years and with whom I made my first pilgrimage to Israel, was the crucible that sustained my long meditation on Genesis. That group allowed me to explore my emerging views and to hear the insights of others. Particular thanks to Jeffrey, Mark, and Moira. Janet Segal, my clinical supervisor and patroness at Four Winds Hospital, helped me find ways of doing my work at the hospital and of writing as well.

Closer still I want to thank Joseph Jastrab, stepfather to my children, through whom the idea for this book reached a literary agent. Ned Leavitt is that agent. He instantly saw the possibilities and encouraged me all the way; I have been fortunate in having him in my corner. My editor at Harper San Francisco, Tom Grady, gave me all the space I needed to write and then read me better than I was able to read myself. My production editor, Luann Rouff, has given me support, latitude, and the benefit of her insights. My copyeditor, Holly Elliott, called my attention to various lapses with an unerring eye for detail.

I gratefully acknowledge Jonathan Fox, the brother from whom I learned emotionally much of what I know about brotherhood. And I salute my two mothers. The first is Brue Pitzele, who gave me a Jewish heart and so much of her love. From her I have learned and continue to learn much of what I know about endurance and the ability of the soul to grow in solitude and adversity. The second is the mother of my craft, Zerka Moreno, who has trained so many psychodramatists, myself among them.

I wish to acknowledge my children, Karali and Zak: Your love is a gift; you were happy for me, and you endured my long preoccupation with the book, knowing that I would return.

To my wife, Susan: You stayed up late many nights reading drafts; you accommodated yourself to my unavailability, and you helped me make the writing of this book a gift to myself. You are my invaluable ally.

And to the three men whose spirits, in different ways, are essential to the man I have become; without any one of you this book could never have been written: Larry Winters, my friend; Sam Klagsbrun, my mentor; and Merlyn Pitzele, my dad.

Simchas Torah, 1994

SUBJECT INDEX

wandering, xviii–xix, 78; of Abram,
87–94; Cain punished by, 54,
61–62; call to, 87–88; of Jacob,
174; in rhythmic cycle, 72, 77–78.
See also loneliness; stranger
war, 125, 129; sending sons to, 125, 129.
See also World War II
wells, 235; of Abraham and Isaac, 147,
148–53; Philistines stopping up,
149, 235
Wiesel, Elie, 153
windows, myths as, 107, 236
winning, wrestling vs., 194
women, xvi, 47–48; Bloom argument,
237n1; as central mystery, 43; created last, 17; creation of, 24, 31; in
creation psychodramas, 21; Deborah's midrash on, 203; god of, 10;
inner world separate from men,
97; and loneliness of men, 24, 31,
43–44; loneliness of, 44, 49; as
men's enemies, 43–44; and murdering brother, 54–55, 59, 63;
powerful, 167, 181; in Sarah's
dream (midrash), 142–43. *See also*
feminism; mothers

Word, Christ as, 12, 238n3
Wordsworth, William, 7–8, 224
World War II, 4, 29; holocaust, xii, xviii,
4, 29, 95
wounding, 58, 138, 186–87. *See also* circumcision
wrestling, 190–94; Cain, 58, 189; Deborah midrash, 205; as doubleness,
176; Jacob, 185–87, 194; myth,
177–96; Naphtali's name signify-
ing, 180; with power's seductiveness, 206; psychodrama, 187–91;
Rachel–Leah, 180–81; in sacrifice
myth, 127–28

yarekh, 186–87
Yeats, William Butler, 27, 209, 240n2
Yehovah, God as, 16
yetser, 68, 72, 77
yoga, xii

Zebulun, 180
Zilpah, 180.
Zion, 88

VERSE INDEX